THE INVESTMENT BROKER

Jon Climie

Cover design by First Choice Books

- Background by Creative Hat (Shutterstock: ID 596423558)
- "Gold ingots" by Ksander (Shutterstock ID: 243153334)

Back photo by Dawn Climie

ISBN - 978-0-2285-0094-0

Printed in Canada
on recycled paper

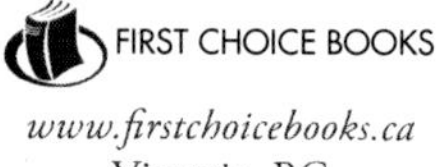

www.firstchoicebooks.ca
Victoria, BC

10 9 8 7 6 5 4 3 2 1

For Zane, Judah, and Keziah.

The world around you will urge you to pursue wealth at all costs. But the rocky shoals of the planet are littered with the rusted skeletons of once-majestic ships men sought treasure aboard. As your grandfather, I can assure you that riches beyond your wildest dreams are attainable. But you need to board the right ship. For that, there is only one investment firm I trust.

Thirteen44 Global Investments.

PROLOGUE

VANCOUVER 1995

The girl was hard to miss. A tight fitting, bright yellow dress that writhed and shifted, emphasizing every inch of her supermodel physique. She'd been chosen carefully for the assignment, as had the dress. She moved slowly through a crowd of mostly men, a sea of charcoal and black business suits, knowing every eye was upon her. Like one of the big cats at an African watering hole she wanted every person in the room to know she was there. Wanted every person in the room to feel a predator was among them. But she moved with an aloofness and raw energy that announced to each of them she wasn't there for them.

Her target wasn't a senator, though there were several of them in the room. Nothing about this assignment was as it may have seemed. She loved that part of it. Her target wasn't a celebrity or some billionaire playboy with a Forbe's magazine power ranking. Instead, her target was working as a cashier at a big-box electronics store, though few people in tonight's crowd would know that.

Clay Rawlings.

She rolled past the bar area, one of the places she knew he wasn't, ignoring the two dozen invitations extended to her to sit for a drink. And now, certain she was the subject of almost every conversation in the entire room she turned towards the far corner. Towards where she knew Clay was listening quietly to an aging civic leader drone on about gun control.

Few people had known much about Clay's startup business when he exploded onto the scene, even as it rocketed to a billion in sales. He'd been vague, almost secretive, and most people assumed he was a defense contractor. What he wasn't shy about showing off was a multimillion dollar lifestyle of yachts and personal jets that found its way into national magazines. Unfortunately it all ended as quickly as it'd begun, in a flurry of court battles and bankruptcy. The world had quickly forgotten about him. Clay was invisible in this crowd now.

Or he was until she arrived in front of him. The aging civic leader stopped talking. He and every other male within seventy feet were staring.

"Clay Rawlings?" She licked her lips seductively to make the whole thing more memorable.

"Hello?" He tried to sound casual but it was a failed attempt.

She moved in close as though she was going to shake his hand, but moved past that to embrace him while whispering into his ear. "My boss would like to meet with you. He wanted me to assure you he's not at all interested in your tech startup. He is *genuinely* interested in something you did before all of that. Show up any time to the address on the card, he'll make time for you."

Clay could feel a business card delicately pushed into the inner pocket of his suit coat.

"Thanks, Mr. Rawlings." Her lips brushed his cheek. And then she was gone, retracing her steps across the room towards the main doors, a wake of men's eyes following her.

She would have claimed her coat but she hadn't arrived with one. Instead she paused for a moment at the entrance of the banquet hall to thank several of the event hosts before continuing on towards the elaborate decor of the lobby. The Vancouver Pan Pacific was the premier hotel in the city and it wasn't a stranger to the international modeling world. The bellhop captain, seeing her approaching the lobby, was readying a large umbrella as the city streets were being washed by a downpour. She gave him a smile and then, at the last second, exited through one of the carefully camouflaged service doors to the alley.

Her last thought was that the assignment had gone really well. And then the raindrops touched her, and she vanished like sugar in the shower.

Chapter One

VANCOUVER

There was nothing memorable about the silver Porsche. Even a casual glance told you it wasn't somebody's pampered toy that rarely saw the rain. It was several years old, with the kind of mileage on it that easily identified it as a daily driver. And where it'd once been an object of envy, a bold statement about the wealth and lifestyle of its owner, its condition today allowed it to be easily lost amongst any number of far-lesser Japanese sports cars.

The young man climbing from its weathered seats had been painted with the same brush. There was something broken in him. He'd obviously once been the performance model that other men envied, that women wanted to be near, but that was a lot of miles ago. And guessing by his strained expression as he climbed from the sports car, they'd been hard miles. There was now just an emptiness he wore like a bad fitting suit.

He gave an almost imperceptible glance both ways before jay-walking across the main street of Vancouver's business district. On-coming cars hammered their brakes and gave long, angry blasts on their horns. A taxi driver screamed Punjabi vulgarities at him. He barely noticed. Arriving to the opposite sidewalk he seemed lost, momentarily swallowed up into the engineered valley of glass and steel that rose up thirty floors all around him.

With some effort he pulled the business card from a calfskin briefcase, checking the address. And then with a pained shuffle, he headed north. On the sidewalk, dozens of hard-charging executives pushed past him, all busily berating underlings on their flip-phones. Crisp white shirts and silk ties backstopping three-thousand dollar *Hugo Boss* suits and Italian loafers. The new masters of the universe. The almost god-like captains of the business world, building empires and legacies. Each of them hoping to become the rainmakers that business magazines would write lengthy articles about. The young man's steps slowed as he watched them disappear ahead of him. A sigh of envy escaped him.

Clay Rawlings had once been one of them.

The address certainly wasn't what he was expecting. It was a barber shop, one that had obviously closed. Inside was just a single chrome and red leather barber chair sitting in the center of a slim interior space. The sinks and mirrors were already gone. He checked the business card the girl had given him again. This *was* the address. The entire front of the shop was just three carefully beveled sheets of glass that continued upward for two floors, etched with swirls and shadowy designs that seemed to move as you walked past. And while he had to admit it'd probably once been a world-class-fancy barber shop, he certainly didn't need a haircut.

"Damn." He breathed out, barely able to hold himself together. He'd suffered so many disappointments lately. And now *this.* He mentally kicked himself for being so gullible.

"Oh sure, a supermodel comes onto me at a civic event and I believe her. All that stuff about her boss wanting to meet me. Admit it, Clay, nobody cares about you. You're a loser." He felt like screaming. Somebody'd obviously set him up, wanting to share a good laugh with his buddies. A perfect opportunity to spit on that arrogant fool, Clay Rawlings, now that he was nobody again. He yanked out the card again, checking the address. *Yeah, this is it.* There wasn't a contact name on the card, just a company name:

Thirteen44 Global Investments.

The card was of high quality stock. Not cheaply made. *Somebody's gone to a lot of effort for this practical joke.*

As he stood there, the swirls in the glass continued to change, flowing to form letters and numbers. The shadows that floated across the glass gained a green, and then deep emerald tone, until they settled onto the letters. And while he watched, what had been just liquid swirls hardened to jewel-like crystal. And a company name was spelled out. 'Thirteen44 Global Investments'.

Clay took a step back. *Whoa.*

And that's when the emerald lettering separated again into flowing liquid swirls. The swirls swept across the entire surface before coming together to spell out another message. And this message was certainly unexpected:

'Thank you for coming, Clay. Please step inside.'

This time his mouth fell open. *What the heck was this?* He surveyed the people passing him on the sidewalk, but nobody paid the message any attention. He scanned the front of what he'd thought was a barber shop, checking for security cameras, but none were in evidence. *Who camouflages an investment firm as a failed barber shop? Weird.* And it'd been six days since the girl at the hotel, and yet somehow they knew he'd arrive today. Or was it possible somebody was waiting for him? That was nuts! This whole thing was nuts. Why all this effort for a has-been like himself?

With a last look around, he stepped toward the solid glass door, and it opened effortlessly by itself. *Of course, why wouldn't it?* Clay shook his head and stepped inside.

The barber chair was an ancient model somebody'd spent a lot of effort to return to showroom condition. The chrome looked like it'd been polished within the hour. Butter-soft, red leather edged with silver stitching. It sat completely alone on the glossiest white floors he'd ever seen. And the three interior walls were each a single, seamless sheet of translucent glass with the same swirling and shadowy designs that changed color continuously.

"We're so glad you accepted our invitation, Clay." The voice was warm. It arrived through the walls as though from the ultimate surround sound. "If you'd be seated we can get started."

He glanced at the barber chair. "You—you don't know anything about me."

"We know *everything* about you, Clay."

He shook his head. "No, you know about the guy I used to be." He paused, forcing down his disappointment. "The guy featured in all the business magazines is gone. Stuff's happened since all of that. The money's gone." He lifted the briefcase absently. "I'm—I'm not worth anything anymore."

"You're not looking far enough back. We think you're worth plenty."

"Whatever." He shrugged. *Far enough back?* Before his tech startup he'd been in high school, broke and stupid like every other teenager. It wouldn't take more than a few seconds to convince these people they'd contacted the wrong guy.

"Please be seated."

He seated himself into the barber chair.

"Seatbelt, please."

He looked down. A thick strap was fitted into both sides of the seat, each ending at a heavy buckle crafted from what looked like a single chunk of white gold. The logo of 'Thirteen44 Global Investments' was formed as they fit together with a solid click.

"Comfy?"

"Quite." He had to smile. *This was certainly different.*

The flash of light was unexpected. But more unexpected was the instantaneous rise of almost sixty floors before he could start to scream! Long before his brain could grasp the speed, or any thought of the danger, he was jerked to a stop again. His eyes were wide, he was panting, and his fingernails were dug deep into the leather armrests, but he was stopped. Like nothing had happened.

The view had certainly changed. This building was obviously the tallest in Vancouver as he could now see as far as geography allowed in every direction. The neighborhoods of the city spider-webbing away far below him, edged by crystal waters rolling onto beaches, the green triangle of Stanley Park, and the snow tipped mountains beyond the steel curve of the Lions Gate bridge.

"The ride up is a bit rough the first time." The chair rotated around silently, and Clay faced a serious but smiling man seated behind a glossy table. He was hard to ignore, fitted out in an exquisitely tailored tuxedo. Darkly tanned, bald, with just a neatly trimmed goatee. Probably nearing retirement, but still in great shape. If he had any extra pounds the cut of the tuxedo hid them nicely.

"Welcome to Thirteen44 Global Investments, Clay."

Clay was still trying to un-pucker the exit gates of his bowel tract. The urge to throw up had set up camp in the back of his throat, but wasn't making any advances quite yet. He knew he should lean forward for a handshake, but not passing out was currently his main concern.

The room was large, with glass walls extending to somewhere far above them. It had the same glossy white flooring as the lobby. And like the lobby, except for the table and the man seated, quite empty. The only solid wall rose up behind the man across from him. But rather than displaying the company logo or some kind of promotional tagline were two large computer monitors set into the wall, each displaying a number.

"I'm Nigel Lockheed. I'm your investment broker."

"My investment broker?" Clay almost laughed. He'd mostly just done crazy stuff with the cash during the money days. He was surprised to hear that he'd hired an investment firm, though he certainly didn't remember it. "Mr. Lockheed, I'm sorry. All the money's gone. The bankruptcy completely wiped me out."

"Yes, and that's why it's the perfect time for us to meet."

Clay just stared at him. "Uh—Mr. Lockheed, I think there's been a mistake made here. You of all people should know I've got nothing left. Nothing."

"Call me Nigel. And oh, you're a lot worse off than you think you are, Clay." Another of his wide smiles. "Far, far worse." He leaned forward. "But like I said, we know *everything* about you."

"I don't even remember hiring you. How could you know—?"

Nigel held up a hand to cut him off. "Clay, we don't have time for all this. The numbers on the monitors behind me are *your* numbers."

Clay stared at the two numbers. Neither meant anything to him. The first was in the negatives. About seventeen thousand, three hundred. The second number was larger. 23,126,421. It was slowly counting down. "These are my numbers?"

"Everybody has numbers. These are yours."

"The first number is negative. Why?"

The bubbly smile disappeared for a moment, a grandfatherly concern pulling at the lines of Nigel's face. "Clay, that first number is what you're worth."

"But the first number is negative." Clay blinked his eyes.

"Yes, it is."

"Mr. Lockheed, I may not have much left, but I do have—" He struggled to get his briefcase open, and then pulled out a thick, dog-eared folder. He gently laid it on the table. "I've still got some stuff the bankruptcy wasn't able to touch. And there's some cash, too."

"Just call me Nigel, okay?" His eyes didn't even glance at the folder.

Clay nodded. "Nigel—I'm not completely broke."

"You're talking dollars and cents. And I'm talking about your actual worth."

"Look, I've lost a lot financially and I know my credit rating's tanked, but I'm not in the negatives. I'm working a real job and I've got a few bucks! Hell, I'm still driving a Porsche."

Nigel sat quietly until the room regained its silent calm. "The number isn't financial."

"You said it was my worth."

"It is. It's your actual worth as a human being."

Clay felt like he'd been punched. He leaned back slowly in the chair and stared at the number. A rapid, embarrassing montage of his life flashed across the screen in his mind. It wasn't pleasant. *Seventeen thousand in the negative. Yeah, that sounded about right.*

Nigel leaned forward. "Like I said, we needed to meet."

It took Clay a few seconds to respond. "So what's the second number?"

"It's the number of minutes left in your life."

"Twenty-three million and a bunch of little numbers. Sounds like lots of time."

"It's about two weeks shy of forty-four years."

"And so this computer somehow knows the number of minutes left for me?" Clay gave a stiff laugh. "I'm not worth anything as a person, but I've got lots of time left. Great."

Nigel leaned back again. "Actually, the display is giving the number of minutes left of what you currently *perceive to be your life*."

"What?" Clay stared across the table at him. "And why do I only *perceive it* to be my life? What the heck does that mean?"

Another long moment passed. "Clay, with a first number in the negatives, you're actually dead."

"Dead?"

"I know I'm not going to be able to convince you. So I'm sorry." Nigel lost the smile.

"You're sorry I'm dead?" Again Clay wasn't sure if he should laugh.

"No, I'm sorry we have to go to the backup plan. We don't have time for all of this." From beneath the table, Nigel pulled out a large, silver handgun and pointed it directly across the table. "Clay, it's important you're convinced that for quite some time, you've been dead. This won't leave any doubt."

He pulled the trigger.

Chapter Two

SIX YEARS EARLIER

An idea capable of changing the world will often be quite simple. Hundreds of people may have already cast aside such an idea. They'd have thought it worthless, too basic to consider valuable. But Clay Rawlings wasn't like other people. He didn't know it when he entered college, but it didn't take long to discover he had the ability to find diamonds in a mud puddle.

The idea arrived during the second semester of his freshman year. It arrived with the kind of weight that punched the air from his lungs. He knew immediately it was a game changer.

"I'm—I'm going to change an entire industry."

His coffee went cold as he found some lined paper and scrawled out a crude sketch of the entire idea. That first night the lights in his dorm room stayed lit until deep into the morning hours. His disgruntled roommate left to sleep on a sofa in the lounge. The next night his roommate kicked him from their room, and Clay trudged down to the laundry room. And there, on the flat surface of an old Westinghouse dryer, he carefully drafted out the dimensions and components of what he'd started quietly referring to as 'the money machine'.

Everything in Clay's life, except the idea, was quietly unplugged after that. His friends stopped seeing him. His college grades slipped and then went right off a cliff. He didn't care. He knew he'd never need college. This idea would be his ticket to a life most people could only dream about, the life of a multi-millionaire entrepreneur. Other people had launched billion dollar companies from college dorm rooms. He was convinced he could too. He taped a magazine cover to his wall of Michael Dell when his tech startup had passed the two-hundred million dollar mark in sales. Clay smiled whenever he looked at it. He knew that one day his 'money machine' would dwarf anything Dell had accomplished with his copy-cat computers.

And that's how it started.

He quit the liberal-arts college at the end of the semester. He rented a rundown, single-bay garage on the edge of the city. He put a mattress and a hotplate along one wall. A couple of folding tables were purchased at a garage sale and he wired in some high wattage, overhead lights to create a work space. With a stereo set up for music, he considered himself officially ready.

His first setback arrived almost immediately. He'd thought he'd be able to purchase the components for his idea 'off-the-shelf' and simply assemble them into a final package. He quickly discovered that such components didn't exist yet. The local Radio Shack wasn't ready to supply what he'd need. Instead, he'd need to design and build the electrical circuitry, and then program it himself.

Clay had none of those skills, but that didn't slow him down.

His days and evenings were soon filled with classes at a local technical college. As homework he was wiring simple circuits and calculating voltage outputs. The folding tables and every other surface in the garage were soon scattered with numerous configurations of soldering jigs, capacitors, and worn binders full of technical data. Sleep became a low priority as his soldering skills progressed. He moved on to etching copper sheets for printed circuit boards, and the staff at the electronics store introduced him to surface-mount components. Everything got smaller and his designs more complicated. The chips got more powerful. His failed early-generation prototypes, with their scorched capacitors and fried wiring were in a pile against the rollup door of the garage. There were lots of them. He'd pull another Pepsi from the fridge and keep going.

With digital search engines, like Netscape and Excite, not yet available, his research was done the old fashioned way. Each morning, after an hour or two of fitful sleep he'd find his way to the library. There, he'd disappear into a pile of engineering books and electrical schematics. He didn't have a social life. He told anybody who asked that he'd party when it was aboard his own yacht.

He was soon recognized within the college as a serious computer geek. And with that label it didn't take long for him to be welcomed into the craziness of world-class code writers. It was from them he learned to program. But while some of the people he met were intent on making it big in the burgeoning gaming industry, or in business applications, there were also the criminal hackers.

It would be the hackers who got him thinking about someone stealing his idea. He knew there was no protecting himself from the talent exhibited by his new friends, but he knew the business community was growing its own kind of pirates. In response, Clay signed up for a three-weekend seminar on applying for patents. It was during those classes he made the decision to keep his idea completely invisible. He knew everything would depend on it.

Nasty Dogs was first unveiled to a husband and wife team of angel investors in late 1990. They were absolutely stunned! Clay had enjoyed a small, groggy celebration by himself the night before after a twenty-six hour stretch of writing the final code. It was nothing like the celebration thrown for him by Dr. Ron and Mary Kealy in their Coal Harbour penthouse as they wrote him a check for seven hundred thousand dollars.

And then, at the end of the evening, Ron offered something to Clay that would singlehandedly guarantee the success of Nasty Dogs. He offered to speak with his younger brother, Michael, and without revealing any details, offer him a demonstration of 'a game-changing new product'.

Clay could hardly believe it! Michael Kealy was the tech world's latest wonder boy. He'd recently sold '1-2-3 DaVinci' and '1-2-3 Leonardo', some of the most innovative business software ever seen, to Commodore for two hundred million.

"I'll set everything up. We need to excite him about Nasty Dogs." Ron was smiling, already seeing dollar signs. "If we can get my brother's financial backing, you could dominate an industry."

Clay hadn't made it back to the garage that night. He pulled out his well-worn credit card and got a suite at the Mandarin, a thousand square foot little palace of opulence with its own lap pool. He stayed two days, sleeping for most of it.

Ron Kealy proved to be a fast worker. In three days he'd secured the use of a large, waterfront, executive home on two manicured acres. The house was situated at the end of a long driveway so it was perfectly isolated. It was the premiere place to demonstrate what Nasty Dogs could do. Later in the week,

Michael Kealy arrived to Vancouver International where Clay and Ron picked him up in a limo. The sun was sending long shadows across the grass as they approached the waterfront home. Ron had the driver stop a hundred yards from the front door. Then he invited his brother and Clay to join him on the asphalt of the long driveway. They all got out of the limo, a question chiseled into Michael's face as to why they'd stopped so far from the house.

Ron gave Clay a wink before he began. "Michael, I'd like you to consider this house carefully." He pointed down the driveway. "This is the retirement home of a Dr. Matthew Jameson and his lovely wife, Kimberley. They're not home. They're at a piano recital of their grand-daughter, Tiffany, almost an hour away. Their home is quite isolated here on the bluff, far from any of their neighbors, which is perfect—because you're going to rob it.

Michael was aghast. "I'm going to what—?"

"Oh, I'm sorry, I got that wrong. You're not going to burglarize it—" Ron laughed. "—certainly not by yourself. You *and your team* are going to burglarize it." And suddenly, six powerful men in fatigues and black face-paint arrived beside the limo. In their hands MP5 assault weapons were at the ready, forming a protective semi-circle around Michael.

"Sir, we're ready. Awaiting just your green light." The leader gave Michael a crisp nod before taking his place amongst a group who looked like they'd spent their lives in a lot of violent places.

Michael looked across at Ron who was now leaning against the limo. He shrugged and then gave the command. "Okay, uh—go."

Five members of the team immediately disappeared like smoke into the landscaping, communicating with hand signals, as they made a rapid, frontal assault on the house. The leader addressed Michael again. "Sir, you're coming with me. Please stay behind me."

And suddenly, Michael Kealy, tech-wizard, was caught up in a make-believe robbery with a team of American, retired Navy Seals. He and the team leader bobbed and weaved towards the house, staying mostly invisible in the shadows thrown by the shrubbery. Within seconds they were hunched at the front door, and while Michael caught his breath the leader went to work with a set of lock picks. In what seemed like an impossible fraction of time the leader twisted the knob of the door and yanked it open. Michael stood and hesitantly entered the house, shocked at what faced him. All five other members of the team were already standing inside!

The leader faced Michael. "Sir, it's been twenty-eight seconds since the limo. Six different access points were breached. This house is now completely, wide open. The criminal world knows in a real home invasion you'd now have six and a half minutes, regardless of what kind of alarm was blaring, to carry off whatever you wanted." He paused.

"And in some places in the world, that might include family members."

Ron and Clay had arrived to the entrance and the assault team moved back outside. Ron addressed his brother. "Michael, what I want you to do is to take a good look around this home. I'm going to give you as long as you need to convince yourself this is just a normal house, like a thousand others. You can look in the closets and under the beds, anywhere. This is just an empty house. I want you to be quite convinced of that." Ron smiled.

"But it isn't empty?" Michael glanced across the spacious entrance.

Ron and Clay shared a look. "Far from it. During the next assault, you're not going to get anywhere near where you're standing right now. Not without emptying the magazine of every weapon your team is carrying."

Michael gave the entrance a more serious look. "—Okay."

Fifteen minutes later, Michael was back at the limo. He admitted he'd seen absolutely nothing that looked unusual. He laughed, embarrassed. He'd looked in the closets of every room and dug through the garage. In his words, it was just 'a very nice, up-scale home'. Clay could barely contain his smile. A member of the assault team ran to the house and re-locked the doors. And then, the scenario was rewound to where they were all standing again at the limo. Six very serious men in camouflage and face paint with automatic weapons.

"Okay Michael, you know the house is empty. But let's pretend that Dr. Jameson's grand-daughter, Tiffany, has been left home unattended—she's nine." Ron handed his brother a little molded cube of plastic that looked like a garage door opener. "We can't leave her unprotected. So with this clicker, I want you to transform the retirement home of Dr. Matthew Jameson and his lovely wife, into a fully-protected, kill zone."

"So I just push this red button?" Michael looked skeptically at the plastic cube and pressed the button.

And like a movie that'd been rewound, all five members of the assault team disappeared again, pushing hard towards the house. The leader addressed Michael stiffly. "Sir, please stay behind me again." And with Michael in tow, the team leader was weaving towards the house. They were ninety feet from the front door when all hell broke loose.

It started with the barking of a single dog from inside the house. A big dog. Like a two-hundred pound Rottweiler somebody had kicked awake. He was immediately in a bad mood, something savage releasing within him. His barking changed, like something evil, to a low-throat howl. An ancient lust for killing that sounded primeval was filling the house. Something that made Michael's blood freeze within him. Without realizing it, he'd reached out to grip the jacket of the team leader, stopping him.

Unfortunately, the barking of the first dog awoke several other dogs. If it were possible, these ones were even bigger. And they were truly vicious. They were immediately running the length of the house in a crazed, slathering frenzy. Upstairs, downstairs. All they wanted was to escape the confines of the house and kill anybody within a thousand yards. They could smell the approaching team and wanted blood. Michael's eyes were wide, terrified of having been alone in the house just minutes earlier.

"C'mon, let's get closer, sir." The team leader pulled Michael along towards the house.

As they crept closer, Michael could hear the smashing of glass, as lamps and picture frames hit the floor. The dogs knew they were getting closer to the house, and their lust for death was ramping up. The dogs, Michael thought there must be at least five of them, were now focusing on different parts of the house. Obviously other members of the team had been blanked by their own 'welcoming committee'. He waited for automatic weapons fire but thankfully none came. The team leader had his lock picks out, but he didn't attempt it when the primitive growl of several of the dogs arrived through the steel of the front door. Michael could hear their frantic clawing at the door.

The team leader hissed to Michael. "Sir, let's move to the side of the house and hope for a better situation. We're running out of time here."

Michael wanted to just crawl back to the safety of the limo, but he nodded.

They met up with two of the other team members along the side of the house, but at least three of the dogs were waiting eagerly just inside, their frenzied barking stabbing through the frosted glass of a bathroom window. The destruction within the home continued. Several more lamps found the floor and what sounded like vases smashing. Michael was sweating. He couldn't imagine how so much savagery had been hidden within the house.

"Sir, I think we should pull back." The team leader faced Michael and jerked a thumb towards the limo. "We could do a hard breach and shoot the dogs, or use stun grenades, but we've already been out here for almost four minutes. The little girl would've already dialed 911, and we'd be facing a highly motivated platoon of cops wanting to rescue her. It's your decision."

"Yeah, let's get out of here!" Michael was already sprinting across the lawn.

The frantic pandemonium within the house continued.

"You—you let me go into that house! You let me go in *there*—!" Michael was almost screaming at his brother, punching the air towards the house.

"Dammit, you let me go in there alone! You knew those beasts were hidden somewhere in the house and yet you—" he swore again. "—and yet you let me wander around inside, completely—!"

Ron cut him off. "Michael, *you* control the dogs. You have complete control over them. You could have stopped them at *any* time, and walked right into the house."

"What—?" Michael was aghast.

"You've got the clicker. Push the button again."

Michael's shock was evident. He yanked the plastic cube from his pocket and pressed the button. The sound of the dogs quieted, and gradually their frenzy slowed. Less breaking glass and general destruction reached the limo until what had been five dogs became just a single dog. And in about two minutes even he quieted, and the landscape became still.

"Okay, how does this—" he held up the clicker. "*—do that*?"

The assault team leader stepped forward. "Sir, in a home invasion, home security alarms have become useless because everybody ignores them. Alarms can be blaring within a neighborhood, but nobody cares. So, as you've just witnessed, a vicious dog is the best protection you can get. Unfortunately, truly *dangerous* dogs, the kind fed small doses of gunpowder to build within them a hate for people; they don't make great pets."

"Gunpowder—?" Michael grimaced.

"Mr. Kealy—" Clay tried to sound confident as he faced Michael. "The dogs within this home are an integral part of what will soon be marketed as the greatest home security system ever created. What I've done is designed a way to control vicious dogs through the clicker you're holding. One dog, a dozen dogs, all perfectly controlled by that clicker."

Michael looked down at the little cube of plastic. "So the dogs in the house are— *safe* now?"

"Absolutely safe." Clay smiled. "And I'd like you to come into the house with me to see them. I think you'll like them."

Michael stayed behind the team leader, and his assault rifle, as he unlocked the front door. And then very hesitantly he peeked past the leader's wide shoulders to look into the house. No dogs arrived. He, Ron, and Clay moved into the house, across a tiled entrance into a formal living room. The first thing he noticed was none of the lamps were broken. The house wasn't completely trashed as he'd imagined. In fact, it felt completely empty. There wasn't any evidence of five dogs having just faced off against an assault team.

"Where are they?" Michael was now quite confused. "Where are the dogs?"

"Right here." Clay pulled back the drapes to reveal a narrow plastic box. He lifted the shoe-box sized container from the floor, its power-cord still connected to a wall outlet.

"What's in there?"

"The future of home security." Clay pulled back the plastic lid to expose the circuitry and cooling fans of a tightly packaged, electronic device. "Mr. Kealy, I'd like to introduce you to Nasty Dogs."

Michael Kealy, the newest wonder boy of high tech, was completely floored. The dogs had been recorded at several junk yards and then digitally altered to deliver the levels of savagery Clay wanted. Their anger was then sent to more than a dozen speakers throughout the house. But the recording also included lamps smashing across the floor and crystal being demolished as the imaginary dogs ripped apart the home. The sounds of a vicious dog clawing at the steel of the front door were actually of an Alaskan grizzly bear trying to get into a gas station. It and the frenzied running had been digitally mixed at a sound studio. Being a tech junkie, Michael wanted to know how the entire thing worked, and so Clay began with the sensors located across the property. The entire yard was divided into protective zones. Human movement turned it on. As soon as Nasty Dogs sensed movement in any of its outside zones, it sent a higher concentration of dog sounds to those speakers in the house.

"Our imagination works against us when we're scared, as you probably discovered." Clay shrugged. "There's something primitive and wild about Nasty Dogs. You truly believe they're bent on killing you."

"You do. You believe."

That first night, at a Denny's restaurant, Michael, Ron, and Clay sat and discussed the huge implications of what Clay had created. The residential security market would be just a start. Michael could already see commercial applications, with the thousands of warehouses across the nation. And soon they were discussing the possibilities of getting it into other countries. Ron was convinced that it'd easily do five or six hundred million in sales overseas. Trainloads more at home.

Near midnight, after some brief negotiations, Ron and Michael Kealy were each granted a twenty percent equity stake in Nasty Dogs. That left Clay Rawlings, a twenty-two year old, sixty percent of everything his 'money machine' earned. He was already calculating what sixty percent of three hundred million would look like. Or what if it did five hundred million? The numbers were staggering. He was already spending the money.

With Michael's investment of fourteen million dollars and his contacts within the tech industry, Nasty Dogs hit the security market like a tsunami. It went from prototype to production in six weeks. With that kind of speed none of the conventional home security companies could respond in time. Nasty Dogs catapulted to forty-one percent of market-share in the residential security world. Other companies tried to retool their systems and bring out their own versions, but by then Nasty Dogs was the gold standard in security.

Clay was suddenly busy across the globe. With dozens of suppliers and several manufacturing plants in Asia, and a sales force across America and Europe, he was rarely on the ground. He abandoned commercial flights almost immediately, instead pulling together the financing for a Gulfstream 320, a very nice corporate jet. But boxcars of cash continued to flood into the main offices of Nasty Dogs in Vancouver.

During this time Clay was being introduced to other tech wizards who were making billions as personal computers went mainstream. With one voice they all declared there wouldn't be time to spend all the money they were going to make, no matter how fast they spent it. Clay embraced that maxim with gusto. He flew to Orlando where he purchased *Bravado*, a hundred and sixty foot mega-yacht. It fulfilled his personal promise he wouldn't party until it was aboard his own yacht. And it was quite a party. It wouldn't end until it had gobbled up a billion dollars and Clay was a broken man.

Chapter Three

Nigel was pointing the handgun directly at Clay! Somehow it looked so out of place amongst the glossy white and glass of the office. The entire space was an architectural study in quietness and calm, the weapon arriving like a splash of blunt trauma. Clay remained seated, his mouth falling open but no sound arriving. The barrel of the handgun was aimed three inches above his sternum.

"I'm sorry, Clay. You're dead. You have been for a while. And *this* won't leave any doubt."

Maybe he should have scrambled for cover or tried to wrestle the gun from Nigel's grip, but he would never know.

Nigel pulled the trigger.

Clay's entire body was punched back into the chair like a travel-trailer hit by an eighteen wheeler.

His mouth fell open and his eyes fluttered twice, but everything within him immediately shut down like a main power cord had been yanked out.

Everything around Clay was just blackness, a deep void of emptiness reaching out forever in every direction. No heat. No light. No movement. Nothing except a crushing loneliness that gripped him like a vise. He'd never felt so alone, so completely isolated, but somehow knew he was a thousand miles from anybody who'd care. Or a hundred thousand miles. Distance wasn't measured here in miles but in eternities, like entire universes separated him from another person. He'd already screamed for hours. Or was it days? Weeks? Months? His voice never tired of screaming as it required no effort. It didn't wind him or raise his heart rate. Like screaming was the native language of such a place. And fear the only emotion. There was never a moment he wasn't afraid. He'd been completely forgotten and it terrified him. There was no escape, no hope of rescue. Every minute was just like the last minute. Were decades passing, or had it been longer? He had no way of knowing. But somehow he knew it would never end. Not ever. He'd be imprisoned here forever.

He'd tried at first to lose himself within the confines of his own mind, thinking he could escape into his own thoughts. But that proved to be the worst trap of all. Anything of beauty had been stripped from his thoughts. Anything calming or restful had been erased. Instead, his mind was filled with only the worst moments of his life. Stuff he'd stolen as a kid on a dare, his buddies waiting outside to declare him a hero. The girls he'd lied to, and exploited, as the never-ending pursuit of satisfying himself now openly roamed the stage of his mind like some kind of hideous cabaret act. Those people throughout his life, often those who'd considered him a friend, whom he'd cheated and taken advantage of, now seemed legion in numbers.

He tried to think about good things, those happy moments when he'd enjoyed himself, but they were gone. Erased. Like an eight-track tape scratched beyond repair, playing only the worst song. His mind now only played the moments in his life when he was ashamed of himself. When he saw how mean-spirited and selfish he'd been.

There was no escape route within his own mind. Those waters had been poisoned.

He tried to blank out everything within his mind, to shut off thinking altogether, but that forced him to the most hard-edged madness. For there, he was left with nothing except the next minute of being completely, and absolutely, alone.

But even there, fighting to keep his mind blank, a shard of memory was forced upon him. Like being roughly strapped to a table and having his eyes peeled open, he wasn't able to stop it. An image of such horror and magnitude that it was worse than the darkness, or the loneliness. It was of a teen girl, her tattered clothes covered in dust. She was bleeding badly from a head wound, her legs crushed beneath a concrete pillar. Her hand extended in a pitiful gesture of desperation. She was dying. And still, in what were obviously her last moments of life, she cried out in a fading voice, "Help me. Please, help me. Help me. Oh please—"

It was the worst shard of memory because Clay knew he'd done this to her. She'd died because of him. He started screaming again.

Decades passed in the moldy darkness, every minute the exact same as the last. No hunger or thirst was available to distract his tortured mind. He'd stopped a long time ago wishing to go crazy, realizing he'd forever be in his right mind, fully experiencing the endlessness of having been forgotten.

He tried to steel himself, squeezing his eyes shut against thinking, but he couldn't shut out the teenage girl's pleading for rescue. Her pitiful cries entered through his skin, and bombarded his mind.

Clay's screaming was soon constant.

His sufferings continued without relief. He'd already concluded that time, with its cycle of minutes and hours had been abandoned here, that even decades and centuries had been deemed far too short for such a place. There was only the constant and forever *now*. He somehow knew none of it would ever end; all of recorded history barely filling the time it took him to blink. Entire civilizations had risen up, dominated the earth, and disappeared again since he'd arrived here. He didn't care. His mind was again being shredded by the pitiful cries of the girl. He screamed louder in another futile effort to drown her out.

And then it all changed.

A dot of bright light, a vision of absolute purity, was suddenly rushing towards him, swallowing up the darkness as it came. It arrived with brutal force, wrenching Clay forward. He was being yanked along like a child's toy chained to a locomotive. And then he was crashing through barriers he couldn't see, like a pile-driver through plate glass. He was twisting, screaming, flailing; desperate to escape the brightness and warmth and goodness of the dot.

Right onto the gloss white of Nigel's office floor!

Clay was swinging his fists, trying to protect himself, as he collided with the hardness of the flooring. Deep, gasping breaths exploded from him, his eyes wide, terrified. His legs were sprawling, kicking, trying to push away from whatever pursued him.

"Hello, Clay." Nigel's voice arrived with the same warmth it'd had before. He was still seated, no evidence of the handgun.

Clay didn't respond in words. Instead a high pitched scream escaped him as he scrambled in panicked movements to the farthest edge of the room. He balled himself into a protective crouch, his legs trying to push him through the glass. Trying to escape the confines of the room, even from sixty floors up. His eyes flashed back and forth, desperate to wrench himself from the grip of whatever had followed him, something unseen, something horrible.

"Clay—?" Nigel rose from his chair and moved slowly towards him.

Clay's breath escaped in deep, gasping volleys, like a buffalo downed by an under-powered rifle. His movements were spastic, clawing at the air.

"Clay, it's okay." Nigel was kneeling now. He moved until he could touch Clay's fingers. Then he gently gripped his hand. "It's me, Nigel."

The wide-eyed terror etched into Clay's face didn't leave. Instead, like a child bolting from a house he feared was haunted, he scrambled away from the glass to throw himself into Nigel's embrace, a hard-edged wail of emotion escaping him.

"It's okay, son. It's all gonna be okay." Nigel placed his hand gently on Clay's shoulder. He could feel the rigidity of Clay's body slowly melt away, and then the tears arrived. The kind that emanate from deep within.

The two of them stayed that way for a long time.

"*What was all of that—?!*" Clay was seated again in the leather and chrome of the barber chair. He was wiping away tears of thankfulness. He knew maybe he should've been angry, but there wasn't room for it. Instead, an emotional gratitude flooded through him. A deep thankfulness for having escaped. He was still struggling to speak, his words unsure. "Where was I—where was I for all that time?"

An extended silence settled onto the room, as though Nigel was considering his answer carefully. "Clay, you were gone about four and a half minutes."

"What—?"

Nigel stared at him. "It may have seemed longer." He shrugged. "But it was four and a half minutes."

The number plowed right through Clay. He'd just suffered for a thousand years, he was convinced of it. *Four and a half minutes?*

"Like I said—you're dead." Nigel pointed towards the number displayed on the monitor behind him. It was still in the negative. The same seventeen thousand and change.

Clay stared at the monitor. What had Nigel said earlier? The number was his worth as a human being. And then he looked at the second number displayed. The minutes left in his life. *Or what he perceived to be his life.* Clay swallowed, his throat instantly dry. *No. No!* He didn't want to put this together. The obvious conclusion of where he'd been couldn't be true!

It just couldn't be.

Nigel leaned forward. "I need you to be convinced you're dead." He shrugged. "Everything depends on it. Everything."

"No! —I can't do this!" Clay violently shook his head, as though trying to escape a nightmare. "I don't know what all of this is, but I don't want any part of it!"

Nigel nodded as though he'd known this would happen.

"I just—I just want to get out of here!" Clay was fighting with the straps of the seatbelt, struggling to clasp together the heavy, white gold buckle. "Please, just—just send me back down to the lobby. All I want is my normal life back!"

Nigel didn't respond. As soon as the two clasps of the buckle touched together, the barber chair rocketed down the sixty floors to the lobby again. Clay barely noticed or cared about the speed. He wrestled the seatbelt from himself, fell ungracefully onto the floor, picked himself up, and in four anguished strides burst through the glass doors onto the streets of Vancouver. He didn't stop running for eleven blocks.

Chapter Four

It was a mostly empty café. Clay was seated near the back, a few weak bulbs barely providing enough light to see his coffee mug. Behind him the snap and sizzle of frying was emanating from the kitchen. It was a warm day, but he was shivering. He kept his eyes glued on the entrance, not entirely sure who he was worrying would've chased after him. *Nigel, maybe?* He'd spent the last hour trying to scrub the entire experience from his tortured mind.

Four and a half minutes. The evidence that it'd only been four and a half minutes was all around him. He couldn't have explained how so much raw fear, and a hundred lifetimes of loneliness could've been stuffed into four and a half minutes. He just knew it had been. He sat there, alone, his eyes barely blinking, listening to the chatter of the cook staff. The minutes ticked by.

He could feel the first tear find his cheek. He didn't wipe it away.

Seventeen thousand in the negative. What had Nigel said? It's your worth as a human being. He hadn't argued the number the first time he'd heard it. And he certainly didn't argue it now.

You're dead. Why had Nigel chosen *those* words? It sounded so mercenary, so harsh. And yet, Clay knew he was right. In a dozen ways he *was* dead. And had been for a long time. The second tear splashed lightly on his cheek.

He sat there shivering in the half-dark of the narrow café, staring at the entrance door. He knew this was nuts. He'd somehow survived a thousand years of pitch-black isolation where the only thought within him had been a longing for the sound of another human voice, or the touch of someone's hand. And now, returned home, he wasn't celebrating his escape. He wasn't running towards people—he was hiding.

Hiding. Clay gave a stiff little smile even as he looked around. Hiding out in a ninety-cent café made no sense. He hadn't been discovered—he was sure of it. Nobody knew about the girl. Nobody knew he'd killed her. Nobody knew it. And so the posse chasing him was actually himself. And how could he hide from the judge and jury of his own mind?

He didn't know, but he stayed until the place closed anyway.

Clay didn't return home, instead walking the streets all night. *Who the heck was this guy Nigel?* He wasn't an investment broker; that was obvious. And what about the tallest office building in Vancouver having an entrance that looked like a defunct barber shop—what was that all about? Clay had no answers, but around two a.m. he formed a plan to discover some.

He knew whoever was doing this had been three steps ahead of him from the beginning. That had to stop. So as a first step he moved his Porsche almost twenty blocks in the wrong direction in case they were tracking him through some kind of GPS device. And then he chose a coffee shop for some covert surveillance. It wasn't directly across the street from Thirteen44 Global Investments, but it was close enough. And it was open all night. *Perfect.* Clay approached it in a zig-zagging sprint, a few minutes after four in the morning. He chose an obscure direction and a route that Nigel's staff couldn't possibly observe, regardless of their vigilance. His plan was simple. He'd settle in, have a couple of coffees, and observe everything that went on from the minute the place opened.

He pushed through the doors of the coffee shop a bit too abruptly, and every eye in the place looked in his direction. *Smooth move, Clay.* Actually, the entire clientele was just three construction workers in a booth, and a middle-aged Chinese guy in a suit at the counter. Clay gave them a narrow smile and they all promptly forgot about him. The front booth had a better view than he'd hoped, and so removing his jacket, he settled in. A tired girl approached him with a menu, but he waved her away with a request for coffee and a cinnamon bun. She retraced her steps to the kitchen.

And now I just wait for the place to open. Clay smiled. The lobby of Thirteen44 Global Investments remained empty. He stretched out his legs under the table, realizing most offices didn't open until at least five or six. *I'm in no hurry.*

"Your coffee and cinnamon bun, Mr. Rawlings."

Clay turned to greet the young girl serving him. But it wasn't the girl—!

Nigel Lockheed, dressed in a black button-down shirt and jeans, set two coffees and a pair of cinnamon buns onto the table. He slid in across from Clay. "Proper surveillance is difficult, so don't be hard on yourself. That stealth approach through the alley off Thurlow Street was a masterful stroke, but—" He shrugged as though the rest were self-explanatory.

Clay leaned back against the bench, unsure of what to say. "Nigel, I just wanted to know who you are, and—"

"I'm your investment broker."

"Okay, let's just pretend that's true. So why are you tracking me to an all-night coffee shop?"

"I think I've told you several times we're in a hurry." The smile disappeared. "You're running out of time."

"I've got forty-four more years—your computer system told me that." Clay tried to keep the edge from his voice.

"And we could accomplish so much together in those few years." Nigel leaned forward. "Clay, this firm invests in places where others don't. We find gold where others see only sand. And I'll admit to you most of the places where we invest aren't very nice. Some of them are in this country, but most of them aren't. They're in the hard places of the world. But we've found the harshest situations often deliver the greatest returns on our investments. Clay, I'm offering you riches—*true riches*—real wealth beyond your imagination. It's within your grasp. I want you to experience *everything* this firm can do for you."

Clay could easily remember the opulence and premier location of Nigel's office. His firm had obviously been built with obscene amounts of money. He nodded. "Okay. Obviously, I'd like that."

"Excellent." Another flash of the smile. "But I need to tell you, if you sign on with us, it's not going to be easy. We're not like other investment firms. Our strategies are radically different. I'll be suggesting opportunities to you that will seem the complete opposite to everything you've always thought about building wealth. You'll need to learn to trust me, and not be swayed by other people's opinions. Can you do that?"

Clay nodded.

"No, you'll need to trust me—*and only me*—because you're going to be making decisions people won't understand. And you can try to explain it to them, but that'll only offend them. So you'll often feel alone. My only assurance to you—" He paused, studying Clay. The grandfatherly concern was back. "—is it'll be worth it."

"I can handle a bit of criticism. No problem."

"Good. So there's just one rather large obstacle left." Nigel locked eyes with him. "You still need to be convinced you're dead."

What this had to do with building an investment portfolio Clay couldn't imagine, but he quietly replied, "I am. I'm dead in a dozen ways."

"No, you're not really convinced yet." Nigel reached out to grip Clay's shoulder. "Don't worry, I'll know when you are. And we'll start then." He stood and looked like he was about to leave.

Clay was completely lost. "Nigel, I have no idea what you're looking for from me."

"That's because in your mind your history always starts with the creation of Nasty Dogs. What you don't realize is that was actually *the end* of your life." Nigel laid a twenty on the table to pay for their coffees. "You need to look at what happened before that, and rediscover *true* living. You found it once, and I'm confident you can find it again."

"I was a greasy-headed high school student before Nasty Dogs."

Nigel sat back down. He reached into his pocket and pulled out what looked like an expensive diver's watch. Thick silver wrist links gripped onto a stainless cover. He set it on the table in front of Clay. "I don't usually lend these out. But I *really* want to work with you."

Clay picked up the watch. Or what he'd thought was a watch. It most assuredly wasn't! It had a face plate and digital numbers, but it wasn't displaying the time. Instead, staring back at Clay were the two numbers from Nigel's office. The negative seventeen thousand indicating his worth and the twenty-three million minutes left of his life.

"If you're good at math, you'll see you're down almost a thousand minutes." Nigel frowned. "A thousand minutes and you're not even out of the gate yet. Your worth is still in the negatives."

Clay exploded. "I don't know how to change that!"

"We don't make mistakes. We chose you because you did it once." Nigel stood. "We're confident you can do it again. The firm is betting on it."

Clay reached out and scooped up the watch. He slipped it onto his wrist. *Perfectly sized for me, of course. Damn.*

Nigel was already at the door. "Oh, by the way, your Porsche is sitting next door. And we don't use GPS for tracking you. Nice try, though."

Clay sat in the coffee shop for another hour, just staring at the watch. Every minute the number on the right lost a single digit, but the seventeen thousand remained constant. The little negative sign was in red, and it certainly didn't change.

He glanced towards the clock on the wall. It was almost six in the morning. *I gotta get to work.* He knew he'd be early, but anything was better than just sitting here. Nigel's words made no sense. Why would an investment firm—especially one of this caliber—care about anything Clay had done back in high school? He'd been a gangly kid with average grades and a weird bent towards creative ideas. His life *had* started with the creation of Nasty Dogs. He breathed out in frustration and went to find his car.

Circuits Circus advertised itself as the largest electronics warehouse in the city. And in 1995, with the popularity of computers on a meteoric rise, the section of the store devoted to computers and software was far larger than it would have been even three years earlier, but the greater proportion of their sales were still coming from televisions and stereo equipment. And so it wasn't computers that made Circuits Circus the 'geek mecca' of western Canada. That moniker had been earned because of an area on the second floor. There on the second floor were the specialized parts and components needed for even a backyard hobbyist to build their own military-grade communications satellite. Or a particle accelerator, if you had need of such a thing. At least that's what their nerdy clientele claimed.

At the register, Clay was wrestling a customer's new Power Macintosh across the checkout counter when he saw her. He swallowed; his throat instantly dry. She was Asian, the same age and petite build as the girl crushed under the pillar! This girl wasn't even looking in his direction, but Clay was immediately cold. Shivering. He tried to push aside his worries of being discovered, but they clung fast. *What would people think if they knew? What would he do? Would he have to run? And if he ran, where would he go?* His worries arrived with the same weight as always.

The new owner of the Power Macintosh handed over a credit card and Clay fumbled to slide it through the machine. He handed the customer a receipt and tried to not look past him at the girl.

But she moved forward, plunked down an answering machine, and peeled off eighty dollars cash, her round little face so alive and full of life. She smiled and rambled on about how this machine was exactly like one her sister had purchased the day before, and the funny messages they'd put on the playback. Clay counted out her change quickly, several coins spilling onto the counter, and thanked her for shopping at Circuit Circus, but inside he was dying. His afternoon dragged badly until five when he clocked out and stumbled home.

His condo was a single bedroom chaotic mess, which he figured was usual for bachelors. Rent of almost seven hundred a month got him a third floor walkup four blocks from Jericho Beach, a single parking space, and coin laundry. He'd once had a seven-thousand square foot luxury home in British Properties, the exclusive haven for Vancouver's professional hockey players and hedge fund managers. Clay kicked off his sneakers, placed a Subway sandwich onto the scarred kitchen counter and poured himself a Pepsi. *The down-graded life.*

After a few bites of the sandwich he went into the bathroom. He faced the mirror and slowly removed his shirt. *Whoa.* Almost dead center in the middle of his chest was the puckered flesh and whitish indentation of a gunshot wound! It looked several years old already. He twisted so he could see his back in the mirror and what stared at him wasn't pleasant. Exit wounds are always bigger and this one was almost an inch across. Clay leaned against the cool of the mirror and tried to slow his breathing. *Okay Nigel, how are you able to do stuff like this?*

He pulled his shirt back on, laced his sneakers again, and headed out. He wandered the neighborhood until he found himself at the beach where a stiff wind was foaming the waves as they crashed onto the shore. The beached logs were too wet for sitting, so he kept walking. And then, unwittingly, he looked at the watch.

The same maddening seventeen thousand, still in the negatives, stared back at him. But even as he walked, there was something different about the sound of the water. He was drawn to the rhythm of it. Absently, Clay lifted his wrist up until he could see both the numbers of the watch and the waves that were crashing onto the shoreline.

And immediately something crazy happened—the minutes left in his life started scrolling downward! It only took a fraction of a moment, but before the digital numbers settled again he figured he'd lost almost two hundred thousand minutes! He'd earlier calculated a week at ten thousand minutes, so he'd somehow hastened his death by five months! *Oh crap.*

Clay staggered away from the water and sat on one of the beached logs, his mind overwhelmed. He couldn't look at the watch. *What the heck was this?* After a long time, he glanced down at the watch again. The minutes were disappearing roughly sixty seconds apart again. He hesitantly looked out towards the water again. *Were the two related?* He held his breath as he aimed the watch towards the water. This time he lost a full year, the digits flashing downward in a blur.

But this time he understood.

The sound of the waves carried him back. He'd have been about fourteen at the time, he and a buddy sitting on the bow deck, leaning against the windshield of the *M/V Bruce Mclean* as she plowed through the six foot waves. The Bruce Mclean was a wooden boat, a thirty-nine footer, and plenty seaworthy for such weather. Clay and his buddy, completely soaked by now, had been taunting the captain, a good-hearted old guy with a heart for kids, to find bigger waves. This was always the highlight of the summer. Crossing the wild, open water on the outside of Vancouver Island on their way to summer camp. There were other kids aboard, but they were all inside, safe from the weather. *Cowards.*

Clay smiled. Esperanza Camp. Even all these years later he still remembered it as the best week of his young life. A week of campfires and capture the flag games, hotdogs and running across empty beaches. But something had happened on that very last night. Something he hadn't thought about for a long time.

On the last night, he and a girl had sat out on the dock and talked. And what she'd told him was important to her. *Really important.* And suddenly, Clay Rawlings knew what he had to do.

Chapter Five

The Porsche had been washed and waxed, its aluminum wheels buffed to a brilliant shine. It was rolling along looking every inch the exotic it'd been six years earlier in the showroom. Clay roared off the freeway, maneuvered down several tree-lined streets, and pulled into the expansive campus of what could have been an upscale business park. It wasn't. Instead, *South Wind Community* was one of the fastest growing churches in the city. Clay found parking near the entrance doors, noting the number of BMW and Mercedes sports cars parked near him.

He sat there amidst the leather and familiarity of the Porsche for an extra second. He didn't look at the watch. It'd been three days since the beach. If this wasn't the place, if he was wrong, then the numbers would remain the same. His worth as a human being would stay in the negatives and the minutes of his life would continue slipping away at the usual pace.

No, this is the right place.

Esperanza had been a *Christian* summer camp. A Bible camp. On the last night of camp, Clay had sat on the dock with a girl, but it hadn't been a romantic fling. Instead, the girl was one of the camp counselors. And on that dock she'd poured out her desperate hope that Clay might understand the message of the Gospel. That he could understand the meaning of the cross. They'd stayed on the dock until almost two-thirty, her explaining the message. Clay had asked questions. She'd flipped back and forth through her weathered Bible, him asking more questions, her listening and then flipping more pages. Clay *had* been convinced. He was convinced he was a sinner and his actions were deserving of death. But then God himself, in the person of Jesus, had wrapped himself in human robes so He could walk amongst us, before sacrificing himself for our salvation on a brutal Roman cross.

And so that night, on an island dock, Clay had become a Christian. He'd left camp aboard the Bruce Mclean the next morning thinking his life would *forever* be different.

It had lasted less than three years.

Nothing good in my life ever sticks around. Clay sighed. He'd been a different person for those three years, a better version of himself. They'd been good years. He'd made some friends—*great friends, actually.* He shrugged off the pain of that thought, exited the Porsche, and was soon pushing through the entrance doors of South Wind Community Church.

Clay hustled through the lobby, stepping past women hugging and groups of people laughing and talking. He slowed at what looked like a self-serve coffee bar, but then remembering that he had far more urgent business within the sanctuary he continued forward.

Inside the sanctuary, he settled into a padded theatre-style seat identical to the seven hundred others that fanned out from the stage. Sitting there, he fidgeted with the bulletin to stop himself from looking at the watch. It was a failed attempt. Since the beach he'd stared at the numbers a lot, but his worth as a human being had only plunged further into the negatives.

He breathed out, trying to calm his mind. *This is the right place. Isn't a church the place where people come to make themselves better people? Of course it is!* Clay knew he'd found religion once, and he'd been a better person during that time. He smiled. He'd simply do it again, Nigel would take him on as a client, and the serious money could start rolling again! *Yeah.*

The worship band opened with a high energy tune and Clay stood to sing with six hundred others.

The senior pastor was deep into the windblown pages of Hebrews when Clay's mind first started to wander.

Hannah Taylor. Clay sighed. She'd definitely been one of the greatest discoveries during his religious days. Long, dark hair and a trim little physique highlighted by the most beautiful green eyes. She was a member of a local youth group Clay had discovered after his return from Esperanza Camp. She'd never dated, supposedly having promised her parents and God that she'd wait for the 'Billy Graham of the teen world' to appear. But something about Clay's testimony of what happened on the dock vaporized those promises. They'd gone together for their sophomore and junior years of highschool.

Clay swallowed. Hannah had been happy at first, just being with him. In those early days, he hadn't known anything about the Bible. If handed one he couldn't have found the New Testament, but she'd helped him and answered his questions. He'd started to study the Bible on his own. At some point she'd introduced him to the elementary-aged kids she was mentoring as a volunteer with *Urban Possibilities*, an inner city after-school ministry. Soon he and Hannah were one of those high school couples who seem inseparable.

Until the day she'd decided they weren't.

Clay grimaced, the loss of Hannah still hard to face. He'd dated after that, but nobody was her. Nobody again would *ever* be Hannah.

He shook off the memory. The pastor was finishing, his voice serious, as he made an invitation for "anyone who wanted to begin a new life in Jesus" to come forward. Clay was the first one to the stage.

Clay stumbled back through the emptying sanctuary, across the lobby, and out into the parking lot unable to believe it. He'd been wrong! *Damn.* The numbers on the watch hadn't budged. His worth remained solidly locked in the basement of the negatives, the same seventeen thousand, three hundred. He leaned against the Porsche and stared at the watch. As though to emphasize the futility of his efforts, the left hand number pushed three digits further into the negatives!

What was this?! I'm standing in the parking lot of a church! And my worth as a human being just went down! Clay wanted to scream. None of this was right. He'd arrived to a church, listened carefully to the pastor, and then in a surprise move he hadn't considered until he was halfway to the stage, had gone forward to dedicate his life to God! He glanced around the parking lot where happy couples and families were getting into their vehicles and others were arriving for the next service. What the heck was going on here?

He looked down at the watch, which chose that moment to lose another digit in his worth. *No!* Hadn't Nigel insisted he'd found real life as a highschool student? Clay looked across the church campus. This was what he'd discovered, so why wasn't it working?

There was no one to ask; no one to confide his questions to. *Oh sure. How do I tell someone this little silver and glass instrument is displaying my worth as a human being, and it's sliding deeper into the negatives even as I stand in the parking lot of a church?*

Clay had no answers, and so he fired up his car and accelerated away.

Little changed in the following weeks. The watch had directed him towards the church, but it wasn't working. But he remained convinced the answer to everything that had happened since he'd met Nigel was somewhere here, so he continued. He changed churches several times hoping for better numbers. Nope, that didn't help. He started attending on Wednesday nights as well as Sunday morning, and then in a desperation move, he joined a Bible study on Thursdays. His numbers continued to plummet.

And worse yet, dark thoughts of the girl being crushed by the pillar were back, dominating his mind, destroying even the few enjoyable moments he did find. Her fragile little voice pleading for rescue had now become like acid in his eyes.

So with his worth plunging to almost eighteen thousand in the negatives, and the fear of the worst secret of his life being discovered, he was going out of his mind. He rarely slept now. He struggled through his shifts at work mindlessly, no longer caring. At night, when he did sleep, he was returned again in fractured dreams to the crushing loneliness and isolation of the blackness he'd suffered for what had seemed like centuries. He'd wake up screaming, his body bathed in sweat.

He was beyond the point of desperation when a speaker at a church talked about opportunities at a homeless shelter in Vancouver's Downtown Eastside. The mention of the roughest area of Vancouver reminded Clay again of Hannah Taylor. The kids she'd mentored with Urban Possibilities had lived on the edges of the Downtown Eastside. Poor kids living on the edges of the skid row area.

He smiled. Maybe *this* was what the watch was directing him towards. Hannah had been a mentor to those kids, and she certainly wasn't dead. Nobody—*nobody* was more alive than Hannah! If anybody had huge numbers solidly in the positives, it'd be Hannah. And if he wanted to be more like her, and match her worth as a human being, then maybe he'd have to start *acting* like her. Serving among the poor and disadvantaged might be the road to better numbers.

At least he hoped so.

He arranged to visit the shelter after work. But then, not wanting to take his car anywhere near the skids, he rode the bus to the shelter being operated from the basement of a crumbling

Lutheran church. He stepped off the bus at Powell Street, barely avoiding two grunting and wheezing, unshaven guys lurching at each other in an angry, drunken brawl. A wine bottle found the concrete at Clay's feet showering his sneakers in foam and glass. His assailant was a black woman high above him on the fifth floor. A volley of profanity arrived from her, mostly directed at the men fighting. Clay backed away from the fight, stunned by such an open display of raw violence. Nobody else seemed to notice or care, even as the men rolled around on the sidewalk pummeling each other with their fists.

The director of the shelter, Molly, wasted no time in recruiting Clay into the kitchen. "Ya ever peeled a potato, son?" Her question arrived with a huge matronly smile. She was pasty white, nearing sixty, and quite overweight.

"Uh, not many."

Molly grabbed Clay's hand and pulled it up closer to her eyes. "Ya got no callouses, so I'm guessing ya didn't grow up on a farm." A laughing snort escaped her, and then she let go of his hand and waddled across the ragged linoleum of the kitchen. "We're gonna git along just fine, son. I'm gonna turn you into a true servant of the Lord Jesus Christ, right here in this kitchen." Another snort arrived, her eyes twinkling.

"Excellent." Clay was ready.

Molly tapped a huge sack of potatoes with her foot. "We gits the potatoes for free, so we serves lots of them. Mashed mostly. They stick to the ribs when you're out there suffering in the cold and rain, know what I mean?"

Clay certainly didn't know, but he nodded his agreement.

She continued. "We'll be serving about ninety meals tonight, so you'd best git busy." She handed Clay a potato peeler and pointed towards a heavily scarred wooden counter.

Clay didn't look at the watch. He peeled a mountain of potatoes and then two bags of carrots appeared. He peeled those, too. He still didn't glance down to check his numbers. And then, with another of her famous snorts, Molly arrived to the kitchen.

"Ya gonna stick around long enough to help us on the serving line?"

Clay smiled. "Of course." And so, with as much enthusiasm and friendliness as he could muster, he was soon greeting each of the mission's ragged clients and offering them a big helping of the stew that was tonight's meal. Molly hovered as he served the first few of the homeless, admonishing him to not dig so deep into the pot where the few pieces of beef were hiding, but also to not give *just* vegetables. It was a delicate art, and he heard several disgruntled comments as he perfected his technique.

After dinner, with the kitchen area of the shelter returned to a level of quiet, Clay washed dishes and wiped tables with several other volunteers. It was nearing eight-thirty when Molly appeared again. She leaned her considerable girth against a counter and faced Clay. Another of those matronly smiles arrived. "So, did ya want me to add yer name to the volunteer schedule?"

"Yeah, that'd be great." Clay smiled. "You can pencil me in for every evening this week."

Clay was on the stained sidewalk outside the shelter when he first allowed himself to look at the watch. *This is it! My worth will be higher now, it has to be!* He couldn't remember much of the Bible, but he was quite sure Jesus had spent a lot of his time with folks like the homeless crowd he'd served tonight. So, if ever he'd behaved like the Jesus of the Bible, he certainly had tonight. He'd been celebrating the hope of higher numbers since he'd peeled that first potato.

He scrunched up his courage and glanced at the watch.

He stood there and stared, incredulous. *Damn. The number was the same.* The bright little red negative symbol lit up the octagonal case, as though mocking him. He wanted to just smash the watch on the sidewalk and walk away. Instead, he sank to the steps of the shelter and watched the street population of the Downtown Eastside shuffle past.

Clay returned to the shelter the next night and the next. His number was still taking steps in the wrong direction, spiraling deeper into the basement. He was past eighteen and a half thousand in the negatives now. He soldiered on, peeling more potatoes and washing more dishes. His mind argued it was a doomed effort, but some part of him held onto the fading hope his worth might be somehow tied to faithfulness. And if so, he had to keep going. He had to keep putting in the effort. That was all that kept him climbing onto the bus after work.

He returned *every* night.

Unfortunately, on his second Friday, his arrival to the shelter held an unpleasant surprise. He got off the bus, walked the usual two blocks through the filth and anger of the Downtown Eastside, and pushed through the steel doors of the kitchen. But someone was there ahead of him! She had her back to him when he first entered, but in Clay's usual spot was an attractive, dark haired girl already peeling the potatoes.

It was Hannah Taylor.

Any opportunity for it to become a joyous reunion between two highschool sweethearts disappeared immediately.

"What are you doing *here*, Clay?!" Hannah exploded, her eyes aflame.

Clay wasn't prepared and so his response wobbled out like a badly thrown grounder. "I'm, uh—I'm the guy who sometimes peels the potatoes."

"Not here you're not!" Hannah's venom roared out of her. The other volunteers were staring now. "Why don't you go back to your mega yacht and all those shallow bimbos that followed you around when you had mountains of cash?! Where are all your groupies now, Clay?!" Her finger punched the air inches from his nose. "Where are they—?!"

"Hannah—" The oxygen was being sucked from the room for Clay.

"Don't you dare come in here like some shade of prodigal son, trying to crawl back after the stuff you've done! You were pretty vocal about my not being good enough for you back in your so-called glory days, or don't you remember that?"

Clay wanted to respond, but his tongue was cardboard.

She stepped towards him until they were almost touching. "If you think peeling a few potatoes is going to impress me, you're even stupider than I thought." With that, she threw down her apron and stomped loudly from the kitchen.

Clay didn't make it to the bus. Instead, he staggered from the shelter, a jagged hole blown through his heart. He made it across the street to a soaked bench in Oppenheimer Park. He slouched down, barely able to breathe. The park was dark, but he could see the shadowy lumps of fallen humanity all around him. Derelict winos were sprawled face-down in every direction, hidden under scraps of plastic and torn blanket. Clay knew most of them were barely conscious, and right now he envied them.

"Hannah—oh man, Hannah." He felt like crying. His mind wasn't attempting a defense, there was no point. Her anger had been completely justified.

Clay grimaced. During the money days he'd once pulled up at her parent's home in a Maserati convertible with a half-naked supermodel in the passenger seat. He'd buzzed the doorbell, and when Hannah opened the door he wasn't entirely sure what happened. Best guess was a bad combination of his gloating loudly about his new-found status with women *better than her*, and a groveling attempt to reclaim her as a girlfriend. He'd been drinking and somewhere during the rather hideous performance he'd fallen from the porch. *Oh yeah. How classy.*

Clay leaned back against the soggy wood of the bench. He'd been an arrogant ass, there was no defense. There'd been three separate incidents at her parent's house. The most notable had been him being removed forcibly by police. He couldn't remember much about it except that he'd slept the night with his head in the toilet of the Burnaby drunk tank.

The last incident was especially memorable because it'd gone public. Canada's national news magazine, *MacLean's,* had declared him to be

Vancouver's most eligible bachelor when his net worth eclipsed two hundred million. During the celebration party aboard his yacht he'd been interviewed by several local television stations. Again, he'd been drinking and his rather sudsy comments wavered between a marriage proposal for Hannah and how he was dating *far better girls* now. That clip had been picked up by the national networks and broadcast repeatedly across both Canada and the States.

He'd stopped drinking after that. He'd tried phoning her dozens of times with apologizes, sent entire nurseries of flowers, and written her long, pleading letters. Tonight was the first time they'd faced each other in several years, but there hadn't been a day since highschool that wasn't filled with his hope they might someday be together again. He was pretty sure her response tonight had driven a hefty tent peg through those hopes.

He cursed himself. *It was over. Everything* was over. His life had truly collapsed!

And that's about when one of the comatose winos directly in front of Clay stirred. Like on oiled hinges, a shadowy collection of ripped blankets and plastic were thrown back in a single, fluid move and a man sat up. There was no hesitancy or drunkenness in his movements as he stood, and then headed towards the bench. Without invitation, he sat down beside Clay.

Clay's mouth hung open. He stared at the pile of torn blankets and then back at the man sitting casually in a thick sweatshirt and weathered jeans beside him. "Nigel—?"

Chapter Six

Clay stared at Nigel in the darkness of the park. "It *is* you."

"I thought you might need my help tonight." He turned to look at Clay. "Hannah beat you up pretty good in the kitchen there. You all right?"

Clay couldn't form words at first, desperate for an explanation. "How could you—" he pointed towards the ragged blankets and plastic. "How could you possibly have been wrapped into that pile of blankets before I got here, and still know what Hannah did—?" His words trailed off.

"I'm your investment broker." Nigel gave a shrug.

"*That's* your explanation for how you could know—" Clay was breathing hard now. "—how you could know, first of all, that Hannah, whom I haven't seen in several years, would be *here* tonight. Second, that we'd have a major brawl where I'd flee from a homeless shelter. And third, that I'd only make it to *this exact bench*—a bench in a park that scares me."

"Are you done?" Nigel sounded exasperated.

"No—wait." Clay leaned back as though something far bigger had occurred to him. "How do you even know about Hannah?"

Nigel reached over and pushed up Clay's sleeve, exposing the silver case of the watch. "You're wasting precious minutes here. We both know you have more important questions to ask me. So ask them."

That stopped Clay. He pulled his knees to his chest and wrapped his arms around them. He stared out across the shadowy park for several seconds trying to formulate his questions. "Okay—I lost almost seventeen months of my life because I looked at the waves at Jericho beach. That's all I did. I simply looked at the waves, and the watch eliminated seventeen months from my life. What's that all about?"

Nigel smiled. "Don't be too careful with your life. Don't count your minutes as though they're precious. The minutes of your life only have value when your worth numbers are in the positive. Right now, in your current state, the minutes of your life are worthless. But when you get your numbers into the positives remember that your minutes and your worth are closely linked. For you, because of who you are, you'll have to sacrifice some minutes—*years of them*—to get your worth as high as possible."

"Wait. I have to die early—?" Clay stopped.

Nigel gave him a look. "Remember what I said. Don't be too careful with your life. Don't pull back when the watch indicates you're losing minutes. Don't regard those disappearing minutes as too precious. Some of your greatest investments will subtract minutes from your life."

"Subtract minutes—?" Clay sat bolt upright. "No—! No, I don't want to invest in stuff that'll shorten my life. That's not part of this!"

It was quiet between them for a long moment. "Clay, I'm your investment broker, and I want the best for you. I've promised you wealth beyond measure, but yes—it'll come at a cost. The huge number of minutes eliminated on the watch at Jericho Beach should be evidence of that. I can promise you everything you can imagine, but yes, it's going to shorten your life. It'll shorten it a lot."

"Oh—great." Clay sagged down onto the bench and stared up at the night sky. It was quiet for a few long minutes between them. "But I've got nothing left anyway. What difference does any of it make? My life isn't worth anything anymore, so yeah, we may as well keep going." A deflated sigh escaped him.

"Okay. But you've got another question you want to ask me." Nigel looked down at him.

"I do." Clay sat up, again puzzled how Nigel could know it. "I—I became a Christian as a kid at a summer camp on an island. For three years after that I was a good person, or at least a *better* person. It was the waves at Jericho Beach that reminded me of that experience."

Nigel nodded.

"So I've been trying to recreate that experience. The whole church-thing." Clay lost his smile. "But I've been at it for weeks now, and my numbers do nothing but go down. Nigel, I've actually seen my worth fall by several digits while singing hymns. You hear me? My worth went down while singing in a church!"

"Okay. But what's your question?"

"Nigel, don't you get it? I was in a church! *A church.* Isn't a church the place to reverse everything that's happening? Shouldn't my numbers have gone up?"

The quiet of the area was suddenly broken as a shouting match between two of its drunken residents spilled out. There was a blast of profanity and accusations of some rather nasty indiscretions. It lasted only a few seconds before being buried again into the usual sounds of this part of the city. Nigel had leaned back against the bench during those moments. As the shouting subsided he faced Clay again.

"Do you see that pile of canvas over there?" He pointed towards where a bearded man was barely visible under the torn canvas of an old army tent. He was facedown into the soggy grass.

Clay nodded.

"His name's Geoff." Nigel waited until Clay looked over at the man again. "Geoff's minute count is down to nine and half days. He's an alcoholic, and his life hasn't been especially pleasant."

Clay turned to stare at Nigel. "How could you *possibly* know any of —?"

"Do you want to know *his* worth number?"

Clay stopped. "Okay, uh, yeah. What's—what's his worth number?"

Nigel's words slowed. He continued to look towards Geoff. "It's in the negatives. Eleven thousand and forty-one."

It wasn't easy for Clay to hear that a wino passed out in a park had better numbers than him, but he pushed past it. "Why are you telling me this?"

"You asked about your numbers going down while sitting in church."

"But how does that relate to *this* guy—?" Clay pointed towards Geoff.

"The church you visited four days ago is evangelical." Nigel had turned again to face Clay. "It's one of the most respected, Bible believing churches in the city. And yet more than half of its current attenders have worth numbers that are worse than Geoff's."

"What—? *Half* of them?" Clay glanced towards where Geoff was sprawled into the wet grass. "How is it possible that half of the people in that church—?"

Nigel was silent for another few long seconds. The wail of a police car in high speed pursuit could easily be heard several blocks away. "Clay, don't be fooled by a rather elaborate masquerade. You see nice clothes, fancy cars, and a North American, middle-class lifestyle. Nice people with nice manners and a well-practiced church etiquette. And they do a great job of hiding it, but for half of them, there's not a lot of substance to what they claim. Their numbers are in the negatives."

It got silent again as Nigel seemed completely deflated by his own words. His smile returned as he continued. "But there was a time—*and it was an incredible time*—in each of those people's lives. And for some of them it was twenty or thirty years ago, but their numbers were enormous! Every day their numbers were climbing up, climbing higher, scrambling upward. Their worth was rocketing upward!" Nigel's words were tripping over each other now, like an eager grandfather describing a favored grandchild being drafted into the major leagues. "Their numbers were doubling and tripling almost hourly!"

"What happened to stop it?"

Nigel didn't answer for a long time. And when he did his tone was flat, like he'd lost a friend. "The same thing that happened to you in highschool."

Clay didn't want to respond to that, so he kept quiet.

"I know you're wondering why any of this stuff matters. Your number is spiraling deeper into the negatives and you're not sure why I care. You're partially convinced the watch directed you to return to church, but you don't know why. But more importantly, you're trying to figure out what any of this has to do with investment returns, right?"

Clay nodded.

Nigel stared off into the darkness. "Clay, Thirteen44 Global Investments is different than other investment firms. We're not one of those clean-energy, tree-hugging environmentalist firms. We're involved in some of the most racially-charged, and dirty places on the planet. We've got huge investments in places where despot dictators rule through fear and an iron glove, military presence. And places where human trafficking and prostitution enslave thousands. Places where children starve and assault rifle shell-casings cover the ground. I'll be counselling you to invest buckets of cash in places where violence and savagery are what drives the entire economy. And yes, your returns will be wildly beyond what you can even imagine, but there's a delicate balance to making it all work." Nigel paused as though considering how to explain.

"To keep your moral compass when investing in such places you need a new set of values. A set of values far higher than the people around you. But that's a big problem. Because adopting a higher set of values isn't possible with who you are today."

"It's not possible for me?"

"No. No, it's not. Not even close. Clay, you need a new heart."

"A new heart—?"

"Sorry, the one you're currently running thinks like everyone else. Its tastes and desires have been too badly influenced by the society around you. To invest in the places I'll be offering to you, you'll need a different heart, one that understands what's truly valuable." Nigel looked over and locked eyes with Clay. "*That*—is what the watch is working on right now!"

Clay nodded, though he had no idea what Nigel was talking about.

Nigel continued. "You need a heart that blanks out what everybody's doing around you. A heart that will literally dance as you shovel more and more of your cash into a project while everyone around you is screaming you're being stupid. It's kind of sad, but those same people will be investing in shredded paper while you're piling up gold bars."

Nigel paused for a second. "What I'm offering you is rather simple. There are some horrible situations in the world today. I'll be directing the best opportunities for investment in such places, towards you. And I always have an eye for the highest returns. And so yes, you'll be introduced to the worst evil on the planet, and it'll be in those places I'll be encouraging you to invest every dime you've got. Make no mistake about it, for *that* kind of investing—you need a new heart."

Clay nodded slowly, trying to process what he was hearing. "Okay, but I'm still confused. The watch directed me to return to church, but it's not working. My numbers are in free-fall, which I guess means I'm a bad person who's only getting worse."

Nigel smiled. "And that's why it isn't working. You're following the usual, flawed thinking of our society, because the church has never been about making bad people *good.*"

"No—?"

"No. The message of the Gospel of Christ is about making dead people *live.*"

Clay glanced down at the watch. The little red negative symbol was bright in the darkness. "Dead people. You mean me?"

Nigel didn't answer right away. "You've forgotten what happened on that dock at summer camp all those years ago, and everything depends on it. It's the only heart surgery that's going to open the door for our journey to begin." He stood up, preparing to leave.

"So what do I do?"

Nigel pulled out a card and handed it to him. "Be at this address on Thursday night by seven-thirty. There'll be three men speaking. You want to focus on the second man. He'll talk for less than thirty seconds, so pay close attention."

Clay looked down at the card which was blank except for an address. He looked back up to ask about the man, but Nigel wasn't there. Clay took a long look around, but he was definitely gone.

Clay shook his head. "Oh sure, and I'm supposed to believe he's an investment broker."

Thursday night traffic was light as Clay accelerated the Porsche onto the freeway and headed towards Surrey, a suburb of the city. His mind had been scattered since he'd spoken with Nigel on the bench. And now, with some empty miles before him, he had time to think. *Could Nigel be serious about investing in war-torn countries and pulling investment returns from places where children were suffering, or even starving?* Clay shuddered. This was all so messed up! Wasn't Nigel directing him in two different directions at once, trying to pile up the greatest amount of wealth while also trying to improve his worth as a human being? Weren't those goals rigidly opposed to each other—a lust for cash facing off against becoming a good person?

Clay ran his fingers stiffly through his hair. He knew he'd never been a goody-two-shoes with a flawless record. Maybe he'd never been good at all. The screams of the girl being crushed by the pillar remained a constant raping of his mind now, and wasn't that part of the hideous fall-out of his pursuing money at any cost? *Damn. What am I doing?*

He exited the freeway, checked the address again, and continued towards his destination. The neighborhoods got decidedly worse, with many of the storefronts boarded over. Broken glass littered the parking lots and most of the neon signs were dark. *Whoa. Should I have brought the Porsche into this neighborhood? What could somebody possibly say in thirty seconds that was worth risking it for?* He was already imagining car thieves stripping his car when the address appeared.

It was a weathered community hall. A tilted, hand-painted sign on a rusted pole advertised ballroom dancing and a swap meet. Of course, anybody who'd attended either of those events was probably now in a rest home. The sign was ancient.

What weren't ancient were two dozen Harley Davidson motorcycles that sat outside in a tight semi-circle. Most of them were hand crafted customs, their polished chrome glistening in the limited light of the parking lot. Their burly owners, and their girlfriends, stood around them all draped in black leather. Across the back of every jacket was an unidentifiable logo, declaring what Clay concluded was probably their allegiance to Satan.

He parked in the farthest corner of the parking lot, as far from the bikers as possible, again questioning his sanity in trusting Nigel. *Of all places, why would he send me here?* He pushed open the door of his car, hoping for a casual entrance. He looked up in time to see a rather formidable group of six or seven of the roughest men heading towards him. *Oh, crap.* He had no idea what he was going to say to them. The thought of trying to explain that he wanted to sit in on their meeting seemed like insanity.

The leader of the group approaching him was a giant. Older, but still in formidable shape. He was dressed in a black, oilskin, knee-length duster coat with the Harley logo emblazoned down the sleeve. A salt and pepper goatee, with the same grey streaked through thick hair pulled into a long pony tail. He arrived to Clay and stuck out a hand. "Hey, I'm Tonk. You gonna be joining us tonight?"

Clay was stunned. "Uh, yeah. Is that okay?"

"Brother, that's fantastic!" His weathered face lit up as he clapped a meaty hand onto Clay's narrow shoulder and led him across the parking lot towards the entrance. The others were soon introducing themselves and shaking Clay's hand. It was hard to ignore the tattoos that covered their hands and wrists. Several more motorcycles arrived and they all waved as they roared past Clay. His entourage escorted him past the ring of motorcycles and into the entrance where he was surrounded by more bikers who seemed eager to meet and welcome him.

Someone offered him a drink and he was going to decline, thinking it'd be a beer or maybe even whisky. Instead, they were holding out a coffee.

"Thanks." Clay looked over at the girl offering him the coffee. She was Asian, wrapped into a black, leather fringe jacket. She had the same tattoos and piercings that decorated most of the girls, but that wasn't what halted Clay. She was an older twin of the girl crying out for rescue beneath the concrete pillar! Clay's mind was immediately paralyzed, his insides tightening into a knot.

He hurriedly took the coffee, spilling some of it onto the floor, and pushed towards the meeting room of the ancient hall. His thoughts were no longer focused on the hardened crowd that surrounded him. Instead, he focused his efforts on continuing to breathe.

The hall was quite large, with a stage and nine or ten rows of folding chairs. But it was what hung above the stage that suddenly made the mystery of his enthusiastic welcome clear. A huge banner announced this to be the meeting place of '*The Disciple Riders*' of Surrey. Clay looked back to where dozens of tough men in black leather and tattoos were laughing and talking. *It was a Christian biker club!* He smiled. How recently had it been since these men had been out there flying the colors of the Hell's Angels or The Rock Machine? These had once been the bad boys of society, and Nigel had purposely sent him here. He found a seat and sat down.

Okay Nigel, what do you want to show me?

It was a prayer meeting. Somehow that impacted Clay mightily as he watched men and women who'd probably once torn apart entire towns, still dressed in the black leather of their culture, now kneeling on the floor, pleading with God to rescue other bikers. Clay just listened silently, but what he heard fascinated him. Everyone around him had once been bent on violence and hatred. And now here they were, so dramatically changed that they were sprawled across the floor unashamedly crying out for others caught up into a lifestyle they themselves had once celebrated.

About fifteen minutes into the meeting, a twenty-something young man stood up. He faced the group and announced that on the Tuesday of that week he'd celebrated nine months clean of cocaine. He gave a brief description of his current struggles, but mostly his words were of thankfulness to Jesus Christ. There was a huge round of applause and then he was mobbed by the guys around him.

Clay silently made note. *That was the first man to speak.*

The prayer meeting continued with more thankfulness to God for individuals who'd been radically changed. And a pleading with God to bring the day when thousands of other outlaw, motorcycle gang members would surrender their lives to Jesus.

And then an older man, highly scarred and tattooed, stood. Clay saw him rise and exhaled slowly. *Was this the second man?* He wasn't particularly tall, but heavily muscled and solid, his shirt pulled taut across a barrel chest. He stood there for a second, wavering slightly in weathered leathers, his eyes closed tightly, arms raised towards the heavens, the shine of tears across his cheeks.

"Father God, you were with me through the brutality of prison. For fourteen years you carried me, though there weren't nuthin' of value in me. Oh Lord, you know me. I wasn't worth your effort, but you continued to pursue me. You were there when I was dealing weapons in Miami—" His words arrived with a thick accent, made harder to understand as he choked back emotion. "And you know the lives I destroyed as the Gypsy Jokers stamped their brand of hatred across the Southwest." He paused to wipe his face.

"Father, I stand before you in thankfulness tonight, not by my own strength, but because of what your Son did at the cross. You took all of my sin and gave me, in exchange, your righteousness. And so Lord, I thank you for prison, for it was there I learned of repentance, the most necessary step towards forgiveness. For as I fell onto my knees in repentance, you met me, and I found the only freedom that matters." He continued for several more seconds in a language Clay guessed might be Russian, finally finishing with a quiet amen.

It was quiet across the entire hall for several long seconds after that. And then other men moved to embrace him. Clay found himself fighting back emotion.

The prayer meeting had finished, and Clay could hear the squeal of spinning tires as bikers accelerated away from the parking lot outside. Others milled about inside, still laughing, talking, and drinking coffee. The second speaker's name was Tagger and Clay was waiting, hoping to speak with him. He stood hesitantly outside the circle where five guys and several of the girls surrounded him. Until the circle opened and they all looked towards Clay.

"You're waiting to speak to me." Tagger stated it firmly. It wasn't a question.

Clay swallowed. "Yes sir, if you've got a minute."

"The fact that you came in here tonight—and *then stayed*, tells me I should make time for you. We got all night, son." He smiled, forcing the series of scars that crisscrossed across his face to wrinkle upwards.

Clay looked around the circle, unsure of how much he wanted to say with an audience. He began quietly. "Tonight in your prayer, you used the word repentance. I think I know what you meant. But what if you've done stuff there's not—?" Clay couldn't continue, his shame already pulling him under.

"You're asking if repentance works if we've done sumpthin' truly horrible." Tagger's smile disappeared, replaced with concern. He stepped closer and reached out a hand to place it on Clay's shoulder. "I think we need to pray before I answer this." A chorus of quiet 'amens' arrived from the circle, and then Clay felt them press in to lay their hands on him.

"Father God, you've sent this man here tonight, I'm convinced of it. Lord, I'm asking that my answer to him would be filled with your love, that he would know I'm but your servant, and that as we talk, you'd give me the words to describe your incredible grace and what you've done for all of us here."

Tagger finished with a quiet amen and then retrieved a weathered Bible from a nearby chair. Someone organized the chairs into a circle and they all sat down.

"Let's take a look at the worst religious terrorist of the entire New Testament—" Tagger winked at Clay. "The apostle Paul." And with that, the pages of Tagger's Bible were flipping back and forth as he painted for Clay a rather grim picture of the man Paul was before his conversion on the Damascus Road. It wasn't a flattering picture of a man who'd hunted and captured the early followers of Christ. And then, without any kind of trial, had left them to rot amidst the brutality of first century prisons, where most of them died.

Tagger stopped and locked eyes with Clay. "My young friend, I was an enforcer for the Russian mafia. I've killed and mutilated people. I was Sergeant-at-arms of a gang in prison, responsible for two riots, one where six guards died. And yet, there on the cold concrete of solitary, I cried out to the Lord Jesus Christ and He rescued me. And in that moment, I found out everything the Apostle Paul taught is true. No matter what we've done, or what we think we've become, the Lord Jesus Christ eagerly waits for us to approach Him in repentance, and find a completely different life. A life of freedom and forgiveness. A life of beauty."

Clay looked around the circle. Every person was nodding in agreement, none of them seeming to be horrified by what Tagger had shared about himself. And right then, he was taken back to that dock at summer camp. For it was with that counselor he'd shared the ugliest secrets of his teenaged years.

He knew this would be far worse.

Clay started slowly, trying to avoid anybody's eyes. "Six years ago I was the creator of a tech product for the home security market called Nasty Dogs. It—it did well financially..." He shook his head. *Was he really going to tell them this?* "We had sales of hundreds of millions… trainloads of cash… more than you can imagine… but it was never enough. It was *never* enough for me! I had—I had a jet and a gated home in the Bahamas. Cash was piling up around me, but it wasn't enough." Clay was gritting his teeth now. He forced the words to continue.

"We had suppliers all over Asia… they were in horrible places. Places nobody … nobody should have to—" Clay stopped. *This was a mistake. He shouldn't tell them this! He shouldn't ever tell anybody this.* "Those places kept our… they kept our costs down." He swallowed. "We were assembling audio components in a warehouse… it wasn't more than a patchwork of discarded tin in the center of Dharavi, the largest slum in Mumbai." Clay's eyes jammed shut as he remembered it. "It's the most inhumane place in all of India... open canals of human crap, right outside our windowless facility... often pushing a hundred degrees inside." He paused again, his eyes now staring blankly away. "I visited the place... maybe twice. The stench made me puke." Clay wiped his forehead.

"Many of our workers... were children." Clay's words stopped again, like he couldn't breathe. "We gave them uniforms... probably to make ourselves feel better... the rest of the time they were dressed in castoff rags. What option did they have—?" *Damn. How could I have done this?* He tried to swallow, but his throat felt like it'd been lined in sand. "We paid them... a dollar seventy-five a day... *a dollar seventy-five... for thirteen hours work.*

"Dammit, I'm cruising the skies in a Gulfstream 320... and three hundred of my workers are eating a single bowl of rice a day! *A single bowl!*" Clay stared at his hands, which had started to tremble.

"I had—backers... they'd helped me... helped me build... whatever the hell this was..." Clay rubbed his temples. "They begged me... *begged me! Do something about the working conditions and the wages—!*" He shook his head. "My own backers were begging me, but I craved the money! *I craved it.*" Clay stopped. "They wanted to help the workers... all *I wanted* was the money." He stared blankly at the floor. "Behind my back, they removed the kids... paid for them to go to school and raised the wages... across the board." There was a long, empty pause. "The cost so small one of my partners paid it himself."

Another long, fragile pause.

"I discovered what he'd done... and I closed the place—I just closed it!" Clay covered his face with his hands, reliving that decision. His voice now barely audible as he continued. "In my insanity I canned all our workers...moved our audio assembly to a worse slum in the north... up near the border between India and Bangladesh. A horrible place. My partners both quit..." Another empty silence arrived.

"They just... walked away... didn't want another cent from what they declared to be 'the killer of my humanity.'" A tear was working its way down Clay's cheek.

"It was. I wasn't human anymore."

There was a long pause. "I moved it. I moved the audio assembly..." *Don't go on. Don't tell them any of this.* Clay could barely breathe now. "I moved it. The new place was a death trap... four stories tall, built into the side of a mountain. Construction was never completed..." Clay blew out several ragged breaths, willing himself to continue. "Was supposed to be all concrete, but many of the support columns were still just rusty, tied re-bar... none of the concrete for those supporting columns had been poured. The walls just a loose collection of tin and faded plywood. It was… a death trap… and I didn't… care."

A small puddle had formed on the floor beneath Clay as his tears, one by one, fell from his cheeks. "*Our advisors warned me*—they warned me the place was… unstable." Clay cast a brief glance up at the small group surrounding him, his eyes pleading. "*They warned me!* I wouldn't listen." He breathed out. His eyes returned to the floor.

"The place swayed when it was windy… *the whole place swayed.* And I—I didn't care. We'd gotten the place for a song and I'd just… bought a yacht. I was on the cover of magazines, like some kind of scumbag rock star of the business world…" Clay stopped. *I can't do this.*

"While ragged children…and teenagers… worked at unheated benches… completely exposed to the frigid winds rushing down out of the Himalayans…" He wiped his face with his arm, his nose leaving a trail. His words slowed even more. "I was paying them each a dollar forty a day… a savings of thirty-five cents, which I actually *celebrated*."

A tissue arrived from somewhere in the group. Clay blew his nose loudly.

He wasn't sure he could force out the last words of the story. He was openly weeping now, his shame spilling onto the floor. "I was on a tour of our places in Bangladesh… when I got a call." Another long pause as he relived the moment.

"There was a work stoppage at the audio facility." Clay's words staggered to a stop. "Something about a supporting pillar having collapsed in high winds." A pause. "I was gonna head there immediately… but what I'll never forget… was yelling into the phone, swearing at the management of the facility…" Clay swallowed. "To get those workers… *back to their benches!*"

"I was on the far edge of the slum when it went down…the entire building collapsed…" A huge sob fell from Clay. "Even at that distance… I could see a dust cloud billowing into the sky as four stories of half-finished concrete and plywood plowed into the ground…" He gave another huge sob. *"And I did that to… them. I did."* A long pause.

"Thirty-eight people died… almost a hundred and seventy others were injured… many of them mutilated, having lost arms and legs." Clay stared blankly at the floor, reliving the moment. He blew his nose again.

It was silent for a long time.

"I arrived on site… I didn't know what to do… dust in the air so thick I couldn't breathe—"

Clay stopped. He could feel the hands of every person in the circle reaching out, now resting lightly on his shoulders. He looked down to see the scarred and tattooed hands of the Disciple Riders gently gripping him. Another huge sob poured out of him. He took a ragged breath and continued.

"Death was everywhere… but one girl I remember well." He tried to swallow but his throat was dry. "I can't forget her... probably sixteen or seventeen. A fractured support column had ripped loose…" His words got quieter if that was possible. "She'd been crushed by it. Still alive… but dying, blood flowing down her forehead… her legs mangled, bent at a horrible angle." Clay slowed as a shiver rippled through him. "Her final words were hollow… and faint. 'Help me. Please—please help me.'"

The room was silent, like all of creation held its breath.

"I didn't—I didn't help her. I… didn't… help any of them. I was back into my Mercedes…" Clay was reliving it again. "...and far from the wreckage before she died. She'd looked into my eyes…" A ragged pause. "…the eyes of her killer, and in my cowardice… I abandoned her, to die alone." Clay stared at his feet, now openly bawling.

He could feel it, but could hardly believe it, as every person in the group moved to surround him, to hold him. They stayed that way for some long minutes. Nobody spoke.

Clay continued, still afraid to look at anybody. "I couldn't deal with what I'd done." A pause. "I still can't. Most days I think I'm going insane." Another sob.

"For the first year I considered suicide every day, but again, I was too much a coward." He raked his hand roughly through his hair. "Instead, I ran Nasty Dogs into the ground. My accountants went berserk as I went on a blitz, buying up lousy companies already in foreclosure… piling up debt and destroying our credibility as a company…" Clay exhaled slowly as he finished. "In our final months, I sat in court as bankruptcy lawyers killed off Nasty Dogs, secretly rejoicing… to have it all end. Just to have it end."

There was a long silence in the ancient hall.

Clay lifted his head to face Tagger, who now sat just inches from him.

Tagger remained expressionless. "So your question was: Does repentance work if you've done stuff that's truly—*truly* evil?"

Clay swallowed. "Yeah."

Tagger's gaze never shifted from Clay. "Have you ever told anybody what you just told us?"

Clay thought back to his recent visits to three different churches where he'd been encouraged, rather flippantly, to just admit to God that he'd missed the mark in life, and to ask God to forgive him. He most assuredly hadn't breathed a word of this. "—No."

Tagger reached out and laid his hand onto the pile of hands that were still holding Clay. "Son, there is rescue available. Even as you drove away from that young girl, abandoning her, a rescuer was already running down the road. He was pursuing you, hoping with every ounce of love imaginable that you'd turn to Him to find forgiveness. That in Him you'd find a completely different life. And *in Him,* you'd become a completely different person."

Clay gave a tiny nod, wanting to believe it, but quite sure such a thing wasn't true.

Tagger reached back to retrieve his Bible. Flipping forward several hundred pages, he turned it around so Clay could read it. "Son, we're not that different, you and I. We've both destroyed people and ruined lives. We both see ourselves as monsters. But right here, right now, in the eyes of the One who matters the most, your past can be erased. Tonight, you can know the righteousness of God. The blood of those people that covers your hands can be washed away, making you completely clean."

Clay looked down at his trembling hands.

Tagger pointed to a line in the book of Romans and asked Clay to read it aloud.

Clay hesitated. He wiped his face, and then read slowly, "This—this righteousness from God comes through faith in Jesus Christ to all who believe. There is no difference, for all have sinned and fallen short of the glory of God, and are justified freely by His grace through the redemption that came by Christ Jesus."

Tagger stared at Clay. "So according to this, *who* is able to become a new person, completely drenched in the righteousness of God? What kind of person?"

"Those—uh, those who've sinned." Clay choked out the words.

Tagger allowed a thin smile. "I think you and I qualify, son."

Clay nodded slowly, still looking at the words.

Tagger flipped several more pages, ran his finger along and then pointed. And again, Clay slowly read it aloud.

"If we confess our sins, he is faithful and just and will forgive us our sins and purify us from all unrighteousness."

"So what do you need to do to know God's righteousness in your life?"

"I need—I need to confess to God that I—" Clay's voice stuttered. Tears were coursing down his cheeks. "That I killed those people." He sat there for several seconds awash in his own shame. "That my greed—my desperate lust to become somebody— sentenced hundreds of people to a ruined life as disabled amputees." His words weren't more than a squeak now. "And that I killed that girl. And then allowed her to die alone. Completely alone."

"And what's God's promise if you do that?"

Clay looked again at the text. "It—it says He'll forgive me."

"Son, there are lots of people who'll tell you what you're about to trust in here is a cheap version of forgiveness. I can assure you it wasn't cheap to the One who's offering it. It cost the Judge of all the earth, God the Father, having to watch His precious Son flogged with a whip until he was unrecognizable, and then be nailed to a rough chunk of timber."

Clay nodded.

"Son, it was your sins and mine that put Him on that cross—"

The words were barely off Tagger's lips and another voice from the circle arrived. "—And mine."

Another voice. "And mine."

And another. "And mine."

"And mine."

"And mine."

Clay looked around the circle of black leather, scars and tattoos, and listened as nine people who'd once known only violence and chaos, one after another, echoed the same words.

Tagger gave a small smile, the scars across his face wrinkling upward. "As you do this, remember you're not talking to us. You're not confessing to us. You're meeting face to face with Almighty God. We consider it a privilege to be here with you, but only as those who've faced our own desperate need of the grace of the Lord Jesus Christ."

Clay slid from his chair onto his knees, and the entire circle did the same. And then, for eight minutes, as a hundred million angels in heaven held their breath in wonder, the Lord of the Universe sat on His throne and listened.

Clay and Tagger embraced outside the community hall. Tagger pulled out a card with the Disciple Riders logo emblazoned across the top. In smaller script below it was a title, *'International President'*. He wrote a phone number on the card. "Call me anytime. I'm just up here from Amarillo visiting a friend, so yeah, it's long distance. Call anyway. And yer gonna need somebody in yer life who really knows the Lord, son. Somebody who can encourage you when it gets difficult. Got anybody like that?"

Clay smiled. Nigel's face raced into the view-finder of his mind. "Yeah. I think I do."

Tagger leaned over to embrace him again. And then the entire group moved past Clay, each with a rough embrace and words of encouragement. The last person in the line was the Asian girl who'd offered him the coffee. That seemed like a decade ago. She was tiny, probably less than five feet, her fringed jacket tight to her petite figure.

"You looked at me when I handed you that coffee in a way I couldn't translate. Hearing your story, I now understand. Thank you that you would trust us with your story. Hearing it, I didn't want to leave until I could share with you the assurance that as of tonight, *as of twenty minutes ago*, the old is gone—and the new has come!

"I want you to have this." She held out a Bible. "For only within *this* book will you find everything you need to make sense of what's happened here tonight. For you, Clay Rawlings, are now a child of God, clothed in His righteousness, and living for His purposes." She reached up and hugged him, and then stepped towards her motorcycle, a gleaming chopper bathed in airbrushed pink flames.

She was about to strap on her helmet, when she stopped and looked back towards him. "What are you going to do now, Clay? You've got your whole life ahead of you, a brand new, empty slate of possibilities. Remember your incredible thankfulness of this night. Remember it for the rest of your life—and live out every minute, proclaiming your thankfulness by what you do. Okay?"

She pressed the starter and the big v-twin exploded to life, its deep rumble vibrating the ground. She gave a final nod to Clay and then, with a twist of the throttle she was rocketing across the parking lot, leading the entire group out into the night.

Clay sagged to the asphalt in the shadowy light, completely overwhelmed.

Chapter Seven

Clay lay on the asphalt of the parking lot for a long time. His heart was doing cartwheels as his mind replayed Tagger and Eve's words, 'You are now a child of God, clothed in His righteousness. As of tonight, you've been forgiven. You're a new person, with a clean slate and a brand new life, set free from the need for self-hatred.'

And *nine* other people had echoed their words!

Really—? He stared up into the dark, cloudless sky. *Was any of this possible?*

He lay in the darkness, reliving the electric feeling of the Disciple Riders gripping his shoulder as he'd walked them through the most foul, shameful actions of his life. He was a killer. He'd destroyed lives, and yet they hadn't pulled back from him in horror or condemnation! Instead, they'd reached out to touch him, to connect with him, while listening to his hideous example of cowardice and greed.

Part of him wanted to leap up and dance. Another part wanted to fall down and weep in sheer thankfulness. It was the most exhilarating moment of his life! But also the most conflicted. The main stage of his mind was filled with the brilliance of a fourth of July celebration, a thousand trumpets filling the air with joy. But along the edges, shrouded in darkness, were his doubts, eager to re-capture the stage and blow flaming holes through his confidence and drag him back into the swamps of self-hatred. *What Tagger claimed is impossible for someone like you!* The God of the universe hadn't met with him on the weathered floor of a dilapidated community hall. Clay was a fool to believe such a thing!

His doubts could've easily recaptured the main stage, except for the peace. Since he'd gotten off that floor surrounded by the Disciple Riders, his mind had been clear. Clear and pure like a windblown, prairie field. For the first time since abandoning that girl to die, his thoughts of self-harm, *of suicide,* were gone. And that alone made him want to dance. And to cry.

But his doubts weren't going peaceably into the night. Instead they were scratching and clawing to reclaim his mind. They were throwing up graphic reminders of his mutilated workers, their bodies being pulled from the wreckage—all because of Clay's greed. *'How dare you seek forgiveness—!'*

That thought ended abruptly. It was vaporized as a gentle voice touched down lightly onto his mind, arriving and then departing in a fraction of second, leaving just the feathery imprint of a spoken message. *Look at what my Word says about you.*

"What—?" Clay sat up, expecting to see someone standing there. He looked across the parking lot. It remained quite empty. And so, considering the words, he picked up the Bible that Eve, the Asian girl, had given him. He stared at it but kept it closed. *What had God said about him? And where, among so many pages, would he look to find such a thing?*

He was in an empty parking lot approaching midnight. There was nobody to ask. He felt foolish. Not knowing what else to do, he allowed the Bible to fall open at random. And these were the first words he read:

'Therefore, there is now no condemnation for those who are in Christ Jesus, because through Christ Jesus the law of the Spirit of life has set me free from the law of sin and death.'

Clay was stunned. What were the chances that a random flip of pages would arrive him to—? He read it twice. And then he read it a third time, this time declaring it aloud, his words echoing across the parking lot.

"Through Christ Jesus, the Spirit of life has *set me free.*"

"He has set *me* free! God himself—has set me free!" *That was His message to me!* He sagged to his knees, his thankfulness desperate to take voice.

And so there, in the midnight shadows of a hand-painted sign on a rusted pole advertising a swap meet, Clay Rawlings worshipped the Lord of all the earth.

Clay pulled the Porsche into its numbered stall outside his condo and sat there for a moment. Okay, it was almost three-thirty in the morning and yes, he was supposed to be at work in less than four hours. But who could sleep on such a night? He pulled himself from the seat, grabbed the Bible, kicked off his shoes, and sprinted towards the beach.

Three blocks through vacant streets were covered quickly. There was a light wind and the waves were slapping against the shore, the lights of the city reflected in the water. At first, Clay just stared out across the waters, a concert of celebrations exploding across his mind. And then he was running, dancing, spinning, his bare feet punching divots in sand painted wet with early morning mist.

He ran until his ankles were buried into the frothy water's edge. And then he was kicking and splashing, his toes slapping across the shallow water, his jeans quickly soaked in the bursts of spray. On he ran, arms waving like a crazy person, along the shore. And with each footprint carved into the sand as he raced along, his mind was proclaiming the wonders of his new-found freedom!

The length of two beaches later, his heart beating like it'd rip from his chest, Clay allowed himself to slow his pace. And then, finding a drift log to sit on, he leaned back to watch the sun come up. Today was a new day!

He was a new person.

His slate was clean.

The Spirit of life had set him free.

It was all too much for him, too overwhelming. *Who am I that the Lord of the universe should care what happens to me, a heartless killer of my own penniless workers?*

He sagged from the log onto his knees and wept. "Thank you. Lord. Oh—thank you, thank you." And again, he worshipped. What he couldn't have known was that his words weren't being lost into the breeze. Surrounding the crystal throne, standing shoulder to shoulder, as far as anyone could see in every direction across heaven, the entire angelic host now sank to their knees in worship of what Jesus Christ had accomplished.

It was almost an hour later that Clay got up from his knees. He sat on the drift log and stared out at the water. The waves continued to splash against the shore in a gentle rhythm. He didn't want to ever leave this moment. So much had happened. So much had changed! He'd been given his life back.

Somehow Nigel had known that Tagger would be there. He leaned back and smiled. How Nigel could've been so certain that Tagger would be the second man, or predict he'd speak for less than thirty seconds, he couldn't imagine. The details didn't matter. Clay's life had been repainted in a hundred colors of hope since meeting Nigel!

Nigel.

The thought of Nigel forced something else to his mind. The watch!

He hadn't looked at the watch since before the community hall. He jerked his wrist up, a thousand hopes and possibilities colliding together.

And there it was!

Just a single digit, displayed in electrical brilliance. The red negative sign had been extinguished. A bold, unwavering, '1' stared back at him.

Clay whispered it aloud. "One. The negative sign is gone. I'm alive!"

There was something about seeing it displayed on the watch, something that made it undeniable. He broke into a smile and sank back to his knees.

He was late for work that morning.

Chapter Eight

Circuits Circus was in the midst of one of those gimmicky, slash and burn sales where radio ads declare "Our boss has gone crazy and everything must go!" Bright, yellow banners announcing 'insane' price reductions were plastered across every surface of the place, and the atmosphere was frantic. The lineup at every register was out into the aisles, impatient customers bumping and jostling trying to maneuver bulky, rear-projection TVs past each other. Clay smiled at each customer as they laid down their purchases, many of them now angrily grousing about the wait. Ironically, the loudest complainers were often those who couldn't find a credit card that wasn't maxed out until their third or fourth try. And so as they fished through their purses or wallets, the mood of customers behind them only grew worse. It was a zoo.

Clay barely noticed any of it.

On his way home he picked up a meat-lovers pizza and two cans of Pepsi. He stopped by his condo just long enough to change his clothes and get rid of his shoes. And then he headed to the beach where dozens of people were enjoying the last few minutes of a disappearing sun. The happy bark of several dogs could be heard at the water's edge as they chased sticks into the waves.

He sat down against a drift log, and stared out towards the water, ignoring the pizza. And then he did again what he'd done a dozen times throughout the day. He examined the watch. And yes, that glorious number '1' was still there. His worth as a human being was still holding firm in the positives! Everything the Disciple Riders had told him was true, and again he celebrated.

Clay pulled a slice of pizza from the box and then opened the Bible. He knew the difference between the New and Old Testaments, and so he flipped to where he knew he'd find the Gospels. And within a few paragraphs he was transported back to the first century, journeying on foot along dusty roads and enduring blistering storms in very small boats.

An hour later the pizza was gone and Jesus had become a real person for Clay. *A Savior with skin on,* as he'd once heard someone say. Darkness had settled and the dogs were gone from the waterfront. Clay moved to a bench beneath a streetlight and kept reading.

And that's how Clay spent the next week. Going to work. Eating meals. And reading his Bible. And for page after page he celebrated what God had done in the lives of others, especially the messed up people like himself who'd found freedom in Jesus Christ. And the New Testament seemed full of them.

It was enough. *It truly was enough.* He was happier than he'd ever been. And so every time he looked at the watch, he was conflicted. That single digit—that glorious '1' represented everything he now wanted for *other* people. He wanted it for others! He wanted those who carried numbers deep into the negatives to know the incredible joy of being alive. And he wanted people like himself who'd destroyed lives and lived within a prison of regret, their thinking reduced to the long frigid tunnel of suicide, that *those* people could discover what he'd found. He knew there must be others out there.

He wanted to find them!

What had Eve, the Asian girl, said before pulling away on her motorcycle? "Remember your incredible thankfulness of this night—*remember it for the rest of your life*—and live out every minute, proclaiming your thankfulness by what you do."

That's what Clay wanted.

And so the conflict in his mind was about Nigel. Yes, he knew that Nigel had been the one who'd aimed Clay in this direction. There certainly wasn't any argument about that. It was Nigel who'd arrived him here, dancing and spinning in thankfulness, completely set free of self-hatred and a hollow desire to kill himself.

But Clay wasn't the same person he'd been even a week earlier. And suddenly Nigel's offer of incredible wealth didn't sound nearly as attractive. Clay had been there once, with more money than he could spend, and he knew how it'd ended.

Far worse for him was the idea that Nigel and Thirteen44 Global Investments were investing huge amounts of cash in places where children were being exploited. Clay shuddered. He'd ruined the lives of kids and had no plans on ever returning to such activities. And what about investing in places where human trafficking was rampant? *No! No! No!* He'd visited the slums in Asia where ragged children spent their days begging in the streets without any hope of an education, or a future. He knew it was often their desperate parents who were unwittingly duped into giving them up, to be sold into prostitution across the planet! He certainly didn't want to be party to anything like that.

Clay wasn't sure how he'd explain his change of mind to Nigel. There were still moments when Clay could easily imagine leaving behind his lowly status as a clerk at Circuits Circus and jetting away again in the twenty million dollars' worth of leather and aeronautics of a Gulfstream. But those moments were rare, and becoming rarer.

And the more of the Bible he read, the more convinced he became that God's greatest desire for Clay was he'd help people with negative numbers find Jesus. That maybe he could become like Tagger and the Disciple Riders. That thought made him smile. Because, of course, he'd have to do it without a Harley. And— without the tattoos.

It was a Monday night, the Porsche was splashing north along the main street of the Vancouver business district. It'd been raining most of the day. Clay had spent the afternoon wrestling with his decision, but he now felt convinced he should return the watch to Nigel. He'd been incredibly thankful for what it'd been able to show him, but with the '1' permanently staring back at him now, and his resolution to not invest with Thirteen44 Global, it was time to hand it back.

He looked at the number on the watch as traffic slowed. Nine days before it'd been eighteen thousand in the negatives! Now, like some kind of spiritual Super Bowl ring, Clay wore a '1' that reminded him of the victory that had been accomplished for him. He knew he'd spend the rest of his life thankful for what *that* number had cost God.

He parked in an underground lot, exited the Porsche, and was walking in the direction of Thirteen44 Global Investments when something stopped him. Sitting near the stairs along the concrete wall of the second-level parking garage was a young boy pulled tightly into a ragged blanket. His head was down, but Clay could see a nasty shiner already camouflaging his left eye in mottled purple. Clay certainly wasn't sure what he was going to say, but he approached the kid anyway. Thin, boney fingers moved the blanket upward like a shield as he got closer.

"Hey, you okay?"

A stiff nod was all the response he got, a pair of frightened, wary eyes staring out from within the blanket.

"Have you eaten today?"

It took longer for a response to exit the blanket. A quick shake of the head. *No.*

"C'mon, I know of a diner just around the corner that makes a great steak sandwich." Clay didn't actually know what the diner served, but he thought the sound of a steak sandwich would be irresistible to a runaway. The eyes in the blanket were undecided for only a moment, and then he was trailing along a step behind Clay, still wrapped in his blanket, to the diner.

His name was Jeremy. The details of what he was doing in Vancouver were sketchy, and he got really vague whenever the topic was breached. Something that shamed him. Something ugly, that much was obvious. The shiner had arrived recently.

The *Electric Hazel Diner* had a steak sandwich on the menu. Clay ordered two of them and two Pepsis. The place wasn't busy and their meals arrived quickly. Jeremy ate like he'd never seen food before. His sandwich disappeared in seconds. Clay ordered him another and this one seemed to make a dent in his hunger. It was wolfed down *a bit* slower. But it wasn't until the third one he probably tasted any of it.

It was over strawberry pie and milkshakes that Clay told the kid about Jesus. And what it'd felt like to start a new life. A life of freedom. Clay tried to hold his voice steady, but it was a failed effort. He chastised himself for his emotions, telling himself to get a grip, but his concern for Jeremy kept him talking. Jeremy remained expressionless, but his eyes never left Clay's as he spoke.

Clay had come to a rambling finish, not sure what else to say, when the kid spoke.

"I'm from Calgary. And my name's actually Brent—not Jeremy." He looked away for a second. "I was afraid you were another person trying to hurt me."

Clay nodded, not sure of the proper response to such a thing.

"My parents don't want me." That was delivered with the first evidence of tears.

A long silence descended upon the table.

"Is there anybody else who you could—?" Clay stopped, knowing he was out of his league here.

Another long silence.

"I got an uncle and aunt in Lethbridge who wanted me there when I first ran. That was almost a year ago."

Clay didn't hesitate. "So if we could get you on a bus, you could go *there*?"

"Yeah, but Mister, I got nothing."

"C'mon—!" There wasn't a decision in Clay's mind. A wad of bills were thrown at the waitress as Brent and Clay ran from the diner. The Porsche laid down three thicknesses of rubber leaving the underground parking and Clay was in third gear, already pushing seventy, as he rocketed through sparse traffic heading for the main bus station of the city!

It was almost nine-thirty when the kid pulled away on a Greyhound, a fully paid ticket to Lethbridge and sixty dollars cash in his jeans. Clay watched him leave, his face pressed to the glass and his hand waving. Clay stood there until the tail-lights of the bus turned the corner and disappeared into the night. And finally a whisper escaped him. "Goodbye, Brent."

He went back inside the bus station and slumped onto one of the mahogany benches. He wasn't ready to return home yet. So much had happened, and he just wasn't ready for it to be over. Clay smiled. He'd phoned Brent's uncle and aunt, explained who he was, and they were overjoyed their nephew was coming to live with them in Lethbridge. Their relief and worry, after him being on the streets for a year, was raw. His aunt had cried for most of the call.

Clay leaned back and grinned. It was like the whole thing had been orchestrated! If he'd parked on any other floor of the parking garage Brent would still be huddled in his blanket leaning against the concrete. Or if Clay had picked any other day to go and see Nigel he'd never have met Brent.

Nigel.

One more time, Nigel had played a huge role in accomplishing something incredible in Clay's life. *If I hadn't been heading towards him to give back the watch—*

Clay never finished that thought. He'd glanced at the watch and everything in his mind fell apart. A very bold, digital '2' was now lit up in the display!

Clay sat there on the bench and stared at the watch. His mind was a whirl, a huge celebration again filling the main stage. If there'd been less people in the bus station, he was sure he'd have been dancing again. There was only one conclusion of why the new digit had appeared and it wasn't hard to formulate. Somehow the watch was responding to what he'd done for Brent!

That was the easy explanation, but it certainly wasn't easy to accept. Clay was overwhelmed by a sense of unworthiness. He was humbled at the thought of there being a visible record of what he'd done. And of course his doubts told him such a thing wasn't possible, but the evidence of it being *quite* possible was displayed on a shiny, silver device on his wrist.

He wasn't sure what he should do now, but somehow thanking God seemed appropriate. And so there on a mahogany bench in a bus station, he bowed his head and silently praised the Lord of the universe for allowing him to play a role in getting Brent off the streets and home to Lethbridge. He fought back emotion as he told God he was unworthy of such an honor.

"Father God, who am I that you should care about me? And how limitless is your grace that you're willing to use *me*, a murderer of penniless child laborers, to help Brent get home?"

Clay then prayed for Brent to be able to sleep on the twenty-hour bus trip, and that he'd enjoy an incredible 'welcome home' celebration with his uncle and aunt.

He'd had his head down for about eight or nine minutes when he could hear the rubbery skitter of wheeled luggage approaching across waxed floors. Just before he looked up, a person sat down lightly on the bench and crossed their legs. Clay opened his eyes and looked to his left, ready to introduce himself.

There was no point. It was Nigel!

"Evening, Clay."

"Nigel." Clay resisted the urge to ask how he'd arrived here.

"So how's the kid?"

"Good. He'll be in Lethbridge by about five-thirty tomorrow night."

"Excellent. His uncle and aunt are good people."

"They sounded real nice on the phone." Again, Clay resisted the urge to ask how Nigel knew them.

"So how much did all of that cost you? Dinner, the cash you gave him, and the bus ticket, what'd it cost you?"

The question caught Clay completely off guard. It seemed so abrupt. *What did it matter what it cost? A kid from the streets was on a bus heading towards a new and better life!* "I don't—I don't know, maybe a hundred bucks."

Nigel smiled. "You over-tipped the waitress with a twenty, which brought dinner to $61.50. You gave Brent 60 dollars cash. And the bus ticket was $67.50. That brings the total, if we include the $6.27 worth of premium gas your Porsche burned up leaving that parking garage, to $195.27. *That's* what it cost you."

Clay was stunned. The numbers rolled off Nigel's tongue like he'd known them forever. "Uh, yeah. I guess it was about that, give or take."

Nigel locked eyes with Clay. "You'll find I take the numbers incredibly seriously. You just rescued a thirteen-year old boy from ever taking his clothes off for another porno film. It cost you—"

"What—?!" Clay cut him off, horrified. "What do you mean—? *Brent?*"

Nigel nodded. Clay had never seen him so serious.

"It cost you $195.27. And you didn't flinch once forking over that cash. You did exceptionally well." Nigel smiled as he said it. "We at Thirteen44 Global Investments are incredibly proud of you, and yes, this entry will be logged into your account."

"My account—?"

"Of course. Your financing the return of Brent to Lethbridge is your first investment with Thirteen44 Global. It's now locked into your account."

"Nigel, I don't have an account with you." Nigel allowed a thin smile. "What does your watch say?"

Clay didn't have to look. "It's a '2'."

"You might want to check it again."

Clay knew it was a '2'. So he lifted his wrist with an elaborate twist, to present it before Nigel. And there, in full digital glory was a '3' shining back at him!

"I don't understand." He stared at the new number.

Nigel allowed a quiet to settle between them before answering. "Brent is telling somebody on the bus right now what you told him. About the freedom you found—in Jesus Christ."

Clay leaned back against the wood of the bench, unable to speak. His thankfulness was spiking to levels he hadn't known existed! Wasn't this *everything* he'd wanted since he'd gotten off the floor of that community hall—everything he'd hoped for?

"Your investment portfolio is already showing some rather dramatic returns. Good job. Those are nice gains." Nigel was serious again. He stood up. "I don't think you're going to want to return the watch to me now, and I've got a bus to catch."

"What—? Where are you going?" Clay motioned towards Nigel's suitcase, which somehow seemed out of character for Nigel. He again resisted asking how he'd known about handing the watch back.

"I have a client in Atlanta who's struggling." No details followed. Nigel had turned away from him, and then hesitated. He turned back. "Clay, tomorrow at about dinner time, the number on your watch is going to increase by two more. That'll be the kid telling his uncle and aunt *what you told him* about the new life available in Jesus."

Clay just shook his head. No response seemed sufficient. And Nigel was already heading towards where an eastbound bus was loading.

Clay didn't move to a window to watch Nigel pull away. He *knew*, or he was pretty sure he knew, Nigel wouldn't actually be riding on that bus. Even as he saw him exiting the station, in that fractional moment immediately after he disappeared from view, he was quite sure Nigel was probably *already now in Atlanta!*

"He's my investment broker." Clay shook his head and headed towards his car. He had a huge praise and worship celebration planned at the beach! Arriving to work on time tomorrow wasn't looking at all promising.

He laughed and broke into a sprint.

Chapter Nine

Nobody could escape unscathed from something that left thirty-eight people dead and crippled almost two hundred others, but Clay had come close four years earlier. The factory having collapsed in an isolated state in northern India, far from a major city, helped. The fact nobody in North America could have pronounced the name of the slum greatly reduced its attractiveness with CNN or any of the other networks. But the sheer number of multi-national corporations with crumbling factories and exploited child labor already destroying lives with complete impunity across Asia played the biggest role.

He'd had the driver of the Mercedes pull from the road twice that afternoon. He'd vomited both times into the bushes, his shame already gutting his mind. He'd struggled onto his Gulfstream on rubbery legs and sobbed for the entire nineteen hour flight home. He knew he'd just fled the scene of the biggest wreck in his life, and knew he was in serious trouble. His mind was already contemplating jail time, so he headed directly to the headquarters of Nasty Dogs. He could barely talk by the time he got there.

The legal arm of the company was headed up by a shriveled prune named Eustace Green. A man who'd probably never smiled, ever. He'd been with Shriver, Gatling, & Webster, the most raw-knuckle legal brawlers in Toronto, before being hired away by Nasty Dogs. By the time Clay pushed through the doors in Vancouver, the legal team already had the long knives out and were ready to battle. Eustace listened to Clay's description of the carnage for about ten minutes, took a few notes, and sent him home.

Two days later, a note arrived to Clay's desk. *'It's done. We're clean. You're in the clear. Remember me when you're signing the bonus checks.'* It wasn't signed, but it'd been Eustace. Clay never asked how it was accomplished, but he assumed a lot of Nasty Dogs' cash had oiled the rails for what he could only consider the cover-up of the murder of thirty-eight people.

Eustace was wrong. It never went away. When you hurt people, it never goes away. You carry it forever, like a knife left in after surgery.

Clay now carried a secret and it wasn't carried lightly. It was like dragging an engine block. He was ashamed of his running, of abandoning those people, of caring only about himself. But there was a worse bone in the pile. Now that the whole thing had been covered up, and he'd been kept from facing charges, he worried somehow his friends would discover what he'd done.

And that never went away.

The thought of his friends finding out a murderer sat among them. Clay was guilty and knew it. But the thought of relatives and those who'd known him, even those from high school, discovering what he'd done, never left his thinking. So when he wasn't mulling the dark thoughts of suicide, his mind was concocting an 'emergency plan' for leaving Vancouver. He knew one day—*if discovered*—he'd have to run.

Clay stared blankly out into the water. A number of freighters sat at anchor, dark and foreboding in the harbor. There wasn't a breeze tonight, but the air was colder than it'd been. Vancouver is a mishmash of conflicting weather in March.

He'd celebrated earlier, a jubilant run and spinning across the empty beach, thanking God for everything He'd accomplished in his life. He'd read scripture and prayed, remembering Brent who'd soon be in Lethbridge. It'd been a wonderful couple of hours. Clay was still struggling to believe he'd helped a thirteen-year old escape the flesh trade!

How do you even begin to celebrate such a thing?

But now, the old thoughts of self-harm were back, like a rotting carcass dragged across his mind. Some of his thinking, especially the rawest edge of his shame, had been down-graded in its severity since that night with the Disciple Riders, but certainly not all of it. Clay wiped his face with the back of his hand, spiraling again into the cesspool of his shame. *Thirty-eight people died! I don't deserve any of this. Why should I live a good life having destroyed so many others?*

With a last look out at the freighters, he turned to head home. *I'm alone. And I'll always be alone with this.* If his thoughts were going to be so poisoned, he might as well drown them in some late night television.

He didn't make it.

There was a streetlight above the sidewalk sixty yards from him, the light falling onto a solitary person. It was Nigel. But this time he wasn't satisfied to wait passively; instead he leapt from the sidewalk and was rapidly pounding across the sand. He'd cast aside his usual elegance and was huffing across the darkened beach like lives were at stake. At the last second, his arms were wide and he pulled Clay into a tight embrace!

"I'm right here, Clay. I'm right here. And you're never alone." His words were emotional, ragged, matching his rapid pulse. "I'm right here! And I'll *always* be right here."

Clay and Nigel walked the length of the shoreline for a long time. Clay poured out the entire story of what had happened with Nasty Dogs. He described the carnage he'd left behind in a slum in Northern India, and his role in the whole mess. His voice stuttered and broke as he struggled through the telling. He left nothing out, including the cash he suspected Eustace Green had used to cover the entire thing up with.

"I never tried to stop him from making the whole thing go away." Clay was staring out towards the water. "I was afraid of what would happen to *me*—far more afraid of *that* than what those hundreds of poor families faced after the building collapsed." Clay finished in a whisper. He hadn't looked towards Nigel for the entirety of the story, convinced that somebody as successful and dignified as Nigel would be horrified at what he was hearing.

"I—I should have told you all this when we first met, Nigel." Clay looked up. "I'm sorry."

Nigel was facing away. He allowed a long silence to hang between them before speaking. "Clay, the building was supposed to be six floors. Two Nepali businessmen paid off a low-level politician for permission to bulldoze a wide strip through a section of a squatter village that had been there forever. A contractor and an army of cheap laborers were hired and the concrete for the first floor was poured. A month into the project nobody'd been paid. That first company could see the writing on the wall and promptly quit. A lot of promises were made to a second company, a different concrete supplier was found, and parts of the second and third floor were poured. To save money they insisted on using off-spec concrete and half the amount of rebar necessary. Again, nobody got paid, all the laborers quit, and the project sat for three years. It was just a weathered framework of rusted rebar and dangerous concrete when somebody else bought it. The fourth floor was started. That company went broke within a month and so there it sat, abandoned. Some local people took it over, pirated some power, constructed some semblance of walls, and started leasing it out. It was about then you arrived looking for an audio assembly facility for Nasty Dogs.

"It collapsed on Wednesday, October 14. A light rain had covered the area earlier in the morning. It was 2:41 in the afternoon when the first pillar fell. The name of the slum is Shiliguri."

Clay would have been surprised except this was *so* Nigel being Nigel. He'd even pronounced the name correctly.

Nigel continued. "We at Thirteen44 Global Investments look at a lot of people in our search for clients. We chose you. And we don't make mistakes. The reason we're so convinced we can work with you is because of what you just told me—or rather, *how* you told it to me." A pause. "You just told me the most horrible thing in your life. And you didn't spend a single breath on aiming the blame in any other direction. You've accepted full responsibility, and acknowledged people died because of your greed."

Clay nodded slowly.

Nigel smiled. "That's quite an admission. And that's what the watch was registering on the floor of that community hall. You acknowledged to God your role in what happened in Asia, and then asked, humbly, for His help to live differently, for Him. You didn't blame anybody else, and so today, you walk free."

Clay looked down at the '5' on the watch. He nodded again.

Nigel locked eyes with Clay. "I can tell a lot about a person by what they include in their stories, but I can tell even more about a person by what they *leave out*. Were you ever going to tell me about the nine-hundred thousand dollars there at the end?"

Another look of surprise flashed across Clay's face. But just as quickly, it disappeared. "It—it should have been more."

Nigel shrugged. "You were listening to a lot of other voices at that point. People who didn't understand how much you cared about what had happened. People who only cared about protecting Nasty Dogs' market share. Your entire senior staff was against you. And so you fought through static and opposition, desperate to not abandon those people. I know the nine hundred thousand you gave to help rebuild the lives of those devastated families helped a lot. The organization you chose to manage the funds did a great job."

"You—you *know* that for sure?"

Nigel smiled again. "I do. I'm in Shiliguri occasionally."

Clay didn't want the night to end. He'd waited so long for some kind of confirmation that his money had helped those people in the slum, but had resigned himself to never knowing. And here he was, listening to Nigel describe individuals who'd had their lives destroyed by Clay's greed, or who'd lost loved ones, who'd now been at least partially restored. Money, even nine hundred thousand dollars, can't repair much, but Nigel assured him it'd accomplished more than he might have imagined, and had certainly given the families hope.

Clay wept as Nigel talked.

After midnight a silence settled on the two of them as they walked. Suddenly Clay stopped. "Nigel, what is the watch *recording*? What does a '3' or a '5' mean?"

There was a pause. "Long or short answer?"

"Hey, I've got nothing but time."

Nigel smiled. "Okay. The Bible says that you, Clay, were dead in your transgressions and sins in which you used to live when you followed the ways of this world and of the ruler of the kingdom of the air, the spirit who is now at work in those who are still disobedient. That's a fancy way of saying that, unknown to you, you were following the ways of Satan. The watch simply records it as a negative number. A hundred thousand in the negatives is no better than one or two. Neither matters, if you're in the negatives you're dead spiritually and the wrath of God remains on you."

"Okay."

"But that same passage goes on to say because of His great love for you, God made you alive with Christ even when you were dead in your sins. And God raised you up with Christ and seated you with him in the heavenly realms in Christ Jesus in order that in the coming ages He might show the incomparable riches of his grace. The watch records *that* moment of making you alive as a '1'. And it's quite a moment. As you knelt on the dirty floor of that community hall, millions of angels, the *entirety of heaven*, fell to their knees in celebration of what Jesus had done for a guy who certainly didn't deserve mercy, but found it anyway."

"I *don't* deserve any of this."

Nigel smiled again. "Which brings us to the positive numbers shown on the watch. The passage continues, saying that it is by grace you have been saved, through faith. And that you, Clay, are God's workmanship, created in Christ Jesus to do good works, which God prepared in advance for you to do. And *that's* what the watch is recording in the positive numbers, your good works accomplished for God's glory."

"Good works? Like—like my helping Brent escape the streets and return home to a relative?"

"Yes, but remember it only records good works that are *for God's glory*. There are lots of nice people in the world who could've paid for a ticket on that Greyhound. Always remember good works done for God's glory will move people closer to a relationship with Jesus Christ. Or build them up in their knowledge of God."

Clay nodded.

"So based on that, why did the watch increase your numbers as you sat in that café with Brent?"

It took Clay a moment to mentally replay the entire incident. "I—I told him what Jesus had done for me. I told him how to find freedom."

"Right. And what you told him helped him move closer to a relationship with God. Every time you do a good work for God's glory, or help a person move closer to a relationship with Him, the watch celebrates by adding another digit. But remember, often your part is simply to give *opportunity* for people to move closer to a relationship with God. If and when the person finds salvation is always *God's* business. He accomplishes it. Which means you can share Christ with the most hardened of people, and get nothing but abuse and profanity in return, and the number on the watch will still click forward another digit."

Nigel smiled. "And the numbers can get crazy. Because the watch records *every* person your life touches for the glory of God, even people you've never met, but were moved towards a relationship with Him by another person your life *did* touch. Does that make sense?"

"Yeah, it does. Like Brent's uncle and aunt. I never met them, but they'll hear what I said about freedom being found in Jesus, from Brent."

"Exactly. The watch will keep recording every person touched by an individual good work until the day you step away from this life" Nigel shrugged. "Live the right life, and your numbers can be huge."

Clay stared down at the watch. Until recently he'd been eighteen thousand in the negatives, wishing only for the courage to jump from a bridge. Now a bold, digital '5' stared back at him. He was being given a second chance.

It was time to live a different life.

Clay wasn't ready to accept that rescuing Brent had been a fluke. And hadn't Nigel said God had prepared good works for Clay to accomplish? If this God he now followed knew him so well, then it made some kind of sense that He'd chosen thirteen year-old Brent as a display of what He was capable of. Clay whistled. *Whoa. Rescuing runaway kids from the streets. Was this really a possibility for somebody like him?* He was a computer geek, not Bruce Willis of *Die Hard.*

There was only one way to find out.

He rubbed his two grains of courage together and was soon meeting with at-risk youth in some of the darkest places in Vancouver. He'd sit with them under bridges and deep into the alleys, often in the most miserable weather, the rain drenching his sneakers and jeans, but always thankful to be there with them. He listened to their stories of abuse and abandonment. And stories of them being exploited in ways unimaginable. But he had his own story, one filled with hope and freedom, and the new life available in Jesus Christ.

He shared it everywhere he went.

The watch went crazy. The single digit in the left column was quickly replaced by double digits and continued to climb. Lonely and hurting youth Clay had shared the message of freedom with were obviously sharing what he'd said with others. He pushed into low triple digits in the third month.

His celebrations on the beach continued.

He was soon a regular late-night customer at several of the below-ground restaurants on Granville Street, the main hub of Vancouver's counter-cultural scene. He'd be surrounded by five or six heavily pierced and tattooed young people in a booth, all of them talking and jostling each other as they surveyed the menus. The food bill was often huge. Clay didn't care.

The watch raced to 155 and less than six weeks later it was lighting up numbers in the low 200's. He was making inroads into the at-risk youth culture of the city, and it thrilled him. He reasoned he had nothing but time, so he learned to be patient. Even the most hardened youth started to trust him and he was able to help some of them escape the streets. Returning them to their homes, which were often abusive, sometimes wasn't a possibility. And so like he'd done with Brent, Clay hunted down relatives eager to have them live with them. He'd arrange for counseling, or for them to enter teen addictions programs. And suddenly, kids who'd survived for years, barely breathing on the ragged edges of society, were finding their way 'home' to places of love and safety.

Clay decided he'd been naïve when he'd put thirteen-year old Bent, *alone*, on a bus to Lethbridge. He wasn't making that mistake again. And soon fourteen, fifteen, and sixteen-year-old teens were strapping into seats aboard Air Canada jets and lifting off from Vancouver International. It was expensive. One look at the watch as his number continued its climb and Clay didn't care.

He thought it'd last forever. Until while taking a shortcut through an alley behind one of Vancouver's youth shelters in the shadowy darkness, he almost ran into Hannah Taylor! Her back was towards him, embracing a young runaway girl. But there in the darkness, he could hear Hannah gently assuring the girl she wouldn't leave her tonight. That together, they'd figure out the girl's future.

Clay was mesmerized. Hannah was good at this, *really* good.

He watched her for a few seconds, wanting to approach her but knew that nothing positive could come of it. So retracing his steps, he slipped from the alley silently.

He blew out a ragged breath. *Why had he been such an idiot during the money days?* Watching Hannah embrace a weeping homeless girl confirmed her spot as the most incredible person he'd ever met. Clay emerged from the entrance of the alley and flopped onto the sidewalk, not caring about the dirtiness of the concrete. Late night traffic on the street continued, the crowds on the sidewalk laughing and jostling as they headed for downtown clubs and restaurants. Clay was invisible to them.

Until from far down the street the high-pitched whine of a motorcycle carving through traffic could be heard. It was a yellow, high performance race bike, its rider also in yellow leathers. The rider accelerated until he was almost past Clay. And then, with two stabs of the gear shifter and a tight clamp onto the brakes, the sleek bike came to a violent stop directly in front of him. The visor on the helmet flipped up in a fluid motion as a helmet was thrust toward him.

"Hop on." Nigel.

"Uh, yeah—who's bike?" Clay pulled the helmet on and tightened the strap.

"A client's." And with that, Nigel flipped down his visor, the revs of the engine climbed to redline, and they rocketed down the street. They cut through several narrow alleys, which Nigel assured Clay were a shortcut, accelerated through Stanley Park, across the Lion's Gate Bridge, and were quickly lost into the fast lane of the upper levels highway.

The Subway franchise in the little village of Horseshoe Bay was empty at a few minutes before midnight. A trim little Hispanic girl greeted them and quickly made up their sandwiches. Nigel flipped her a fifty, declined any change, and they found a seat near the window.

"Yes, you're right, Clay. Hannah *is* really good on those streets." That arrived from Nigel as they took their first bites of the sandwiches. Clay hadn't mentioned her.

"She just seemed to know what that young girl needed to hear."

Nigel nodded. "And she's fearless in the alleys. She's able to trust God in the worst situations. It's quite incredible."

Clay sighed. "So what are we going to do? She won't want me on the streets, won't want me anywhere near her or the youth she's trying to reach. If she discovers me out there we'll have to somehow divide the city in half."

At that moment, the Hispanic girl arrived beside their table, coat in hand, obviously ready to leave. Nigel stood and shook her hand. Clay noticed he deftly pressed a trio of folded hundred dollar bills into the pocket of her coat.

"How's your mom doing, Maria?"

"Still not back to work yet, Senor Nigel. We—we continue to pray."

She and Nigel switched to Spanish for several minutes of emotional discussion. Then Maria smiled and hugged him. "Can you lock up when you leave?"

"Si. Of course."

She crossed the room, the door closing behind her, still unaware of the cash gift in her pocket. Nigel remained standing, watching her go.

Clay smiled. "Okay, help me with the math here. You gave that girl three hundred and thirty bucks tonight. In cash. So was that another investment by Thirteen44 Global? Is *that* what we do?"

Nigel turned from the window and sat down. "Her mom lives in a miserable barrio outside Mexico City. She's very sick. Five of Maria's younger siblings still live with her in Mexico. The dad ran off years ago." Nigel took a bite from his sandwich. "And no, that's not what we do. That's what *you* do.

She'll discover that money in the morning when she's looking for her keys. All she'll remember about tonight is she had a single customer who came into the store. He arrived late, bought a sandwich, and left her a large tip. That money will soon be in Mexico, purchasing a medicine they haven't been able to afford."

"What are you talking about? Maria talked to you. You shook her hand and hugged her."

"She won't remember any of that. She's a client. And I'm her investment broker."

"Like you're *my* investment broker—? But I know everything you've done in my life since we met."

Nigel smiled. "Are you sure?"

Clay sank back against the plastic of the seat. *No. He wasn't sure.*

Nigel set down his sandwich and wiped his mouth. "We're not like other investment firms across the city, Clay. We only invest in one thing. We invest in people. That's it. People like Brent and Maria and her mom. And all those runaway youth that you've been hanging out with. Hurting people. Broken people. People who know they won't make it through this life by themselves."

"People like me."

Nigel smiled. "Exactly. And we invest for the long term. The *really* long term. I promised you wealth beyond measure, and we can deliver on that. But you won't see it in this life. Investments made with us won't pay a return until that first moment just beyond this life. And then, surrounded by every person who's ever lived, the final tally of your investments will be declared and you'll enjoy those returns—forever."

"Forever?"

"Yeah. For all of eternity." Nigel smiled again. "I know it's hard to think in such terms, because most investment firms care only about your next sixty years. They build their reputations by creating wealth for their clients that can be seen and touched in the here and now. A comfortable life of ease and luxury while you're living *here*. But we want so much more than that for you, Clay. We want to prepare you for the millions and millions of years that follow this life. And so I'll be encouraging you to invest everything you've got *now* so you're ready to step into an eternity you couldn't possibly imagine."

Nigel leaned back in the plastic chair. "Clay, at Thirteen44 Global Investments we step past what you can see today and deal in the forever after."

Clay stared at Nigel. "So none of this falls easily onto one of those colorful investing scenarios where a fictitious Pam and Sam both invest ten grand, both with seven percent interest compounded annually, but Sam starts twelve years before Pam, so how much will each of them have on their sixty-fifth birthday?" He smirked. "It's obviously not like that."

Nigel laughed. "Actually, it's more similar to that than you might think. Like every other investment firm we encourage people to start early. Look at what you've accomplished in four months. If somebody were to start today, they'd really have to hustle to catch up to your numbers."

Clay was silent for a few long seconds. "Yeah, but I'm losing minutes again. Every time I go into the dark places of the city trying to reach at-risk kids my minutes are spinning away in a blur. I've already lost eight years of my life."

"Clay, most people don't ever think about eternity. The watch is making sure you don't make that mistake. And your other number is climbing nicely. I'd say you're setting yourself up for a perfect eternity, something neither Pam nor Sam were encouraged to think about as they invested in hopes of a few years of secure retirement."

"But nobody's keeping track of any of the stuff I'm doing."

Nigel gave one of his mischievous grins. "Actually, they are." He pulled out a folded sheet from inside his leathers. He laid it onto the table and pushed it across to Clay.

What was on the sheet changed everything!

Nothing should've surprised Clay after all the time he'd spent with Nigel, but this one floored him. For there in carefully aligned columns was an itemized list, starting with Brent at the café, of every person he'd met on the streets, what they'd talked about, the length of their time together, and finally the amount Clay had spent during their time together. It was a long list. He just sat and stared at it. Completely overwhelmed that something like this existed.

Nigel leaned forward. "There was some discussion about line sixty-one. We're quite aware that you didn't pay for Brian Forster's seat on that WestJet flight, but you were prepared to pay what would've been $241.75, so that amount was entered into your account."

Clay looked up to stare at Nigel. Brian Forster had been a seventeen-year old from Toronto. He'd barely survived two years on the streets. Clay had been standing at the WestJet counter with Brian in the last moments before paying for his ticket, trying to assure him for the hundredth time his step-father would be waiting at the airport when he landed. And then, just when he should've been paying for his ticket, the WestJet counter attendant had been joined by a well-dressed, older man. Turns out he was some kind of senior executive with the airline. His words to Clay were easy to remember. He'd simply pointed at Brian and smiled. "There won't be any charge for your friend's flight today. All of us here at WestJet would consider it a privilege to play a small role in helping you get him home."

Clay leaned back, his breath coming out in small gasps. "It's all being written down. Everything I do—it's being recorded. It's... being... recorded." He looked at the sheet again. A week earlier he'd sat on the floor of a filthy laundromat with a sixteen year-old girl he knew was selling herself. They'd talked for almost an hour. That was recorded on the sheet. 68 minutes. He'd shared Christ with her. That was on the sheet. They'd gone to the Denny's on Jackson Avenue where they'd both had the French Slam and Pepsi. With the nine dollar tip, the bill was $27.65. All of that was on the sheet. Clay stared at it.

"Of course it's being written down. We keep very accurate accounts on you as our client." Nigel was serious again. "One day everything's going to come down to what's recorded on your sheet. The scriptures say one day you'll stand before your Savior and hear Him say 'I was hungry and you gave me something to eat. I was thirsty and you gave me something to drink. I was a stranger and you invited me in. And you'll ask, 'When Lord? When did I invite you in?'" Nigel pointed at the sheet. "Right there. At a Denny's on Jackson, you invited Him in."

Clay wasn't sure if he'd read that verse; he still had a long way to go to finish reading the *whole* Bible, but he nodded anyway. In front of him was something he couldn't pull his gaze from. The sheet was incredibly detailed, and precise. Notes had been made of young people he'd wept with and those he'd embraced. Line after line after line. He was surprised at the number of people he'd met.

"Currently you're at $4987.12." Nigel recited the number without effort.

"Is—is that my total?" There was no final number at the bottom of the sheet.

"Yeah. And I've must say that it's quite impressive. Your take home pay from Circuits Circus isn't that high. Depending on your hours, it's usually around $1721 after taxes, and on an average month you're giving away almost six hundred dollars. I'm incredibly proud of you. One of the hardest things to do as a believer in this country is to escape the materialism that rages all around you. To step past the constant North American mantra of 'I want—!' That's a tough thing to do. But you're learning to avoid it."

"Thanks. I'm just—I'm just *really* grateful to God for what He's done." Clay wiped his face with his arm. And then he pointed at a narrow column on the sheet. "Nigel, what does GMP mean? And here's a YPP. What are these and why are they highlighted?"

Nigel got silent again. And after a long moment he looked at Clay. "You want to get as many of those onto your sheet as possible because they play the biggest role in the person finding freedom, and in them living out the life God always hoped for them."

"So what are they?"

"GMP means grandmother praying. GFP is grandfather. YPP is youth pastor praying. There's a code for almost everybody. It's the powerhouse of everything else on your sheet. No prayer, no power.

Unfortunately, your sheet has only a smattering of them."

"CRP. Is that me? Clay Rawlings...praying?" He swallowed. There were just twelve of them.

"Yeah, that's you. And I don't usually talk about other clients, but Tagger, the leader of the Disciple Riders has a sheet with almost three hundred thousand lines. And almost every entry was recorded onto his sheet alongside a half a dozen codes, including DRP, which is Disciple Riders praying, and his own personal prayer code. His sheet is one of the best I've seen in a Western nation."

"So when you wrote down the address of that community hall, you knew you were sending me to a heavyweight."

Nigel paused again, as though he'd waited all night for this moment. "Yes. Tagger is truly a heavyweight in the things of God. And you, Clay Rawlings, can be just like him."

Chapter Ten

Clay was stunned. Right there in a sandwich shop in Horseshoe Bay, Nigel had stated the impossible. He'd said Clay could one day become a heavyweight follower of God like Tagger, the leader of the Disciple Riders. Immediately a leathery voice roared from deep within Clay. "*You—a man of God? Ha! You know that's not possible!* And in a consuming rush, his mind was again flooded with feelings of self-hatred. He was immediately ashamed of himself.

The venom of the voice continued. *You're a killer of Asian mothers and children, and that's all you'll ever be. You're worthless to the—!*"

And right there, mid-sentence, the voice came to a strangled stop. And Clay was again embraced into a calm he was just learning to recognize. And that's when he noticed Nigel had reached out his hand, as soon as the voice raged, to grip Clay's shoulder.

"Don't listen to that voice, son, I'm right here! It's speaking lies to you. The truth says you're one of God's chosen saints, an adopted son, holy and dearly loved."

Clay couldn't believe the peace that had exploded within his mind. The windblown prairie field was back. The voice hadn't just fled. Instead it was like it'd suffered a lightning strike as soon as Nigel touched him. The voice had been vaporized! *Gone.*

"You okay?" Nigel's voice had returned to its usual level of concern.

Clay tried to accept what had just happened, but it was beyond anything else Nigel had ever done. *The voice was afraid of Nigel!* Was that even possible? It seemed like crazy talk.

"Yeah, yeah, I'm okay." He tried to keep his tone level. "Hey, we were talking, uh— about our need to have people praying for the street youth I'm trying to reach. GMP and YPP." He pointed to the few codes on his sheet. "And of course, *my* code when I pray for them, CRP."

Nigel smiled. "Yeah well, we're definitely going to have to get more of that code onto your sheet. Like I said, it's the main trunk line to where the power comes from. Your investments won't mean a lot without it. They'll look good, but they won't accomplish a lot."

"No prayer, no power—right?"

Nigel's stare got that faraway look. "Yeah, but I don't think you'll be easily convinced."

"I'm convinced. I need to pray more. Got that."

Nigel leaned back in his seat. "No, you aren't convinced. You've seen some success in reaching at-risk youth and you're already growing confident in your own abilities. I need to break that. This'll demand something—unique."

Clay swallowed. The last time Nigel had talked like this, he'd shot Clay with a handgun.

But there was no handgun this time. Nigel reached into his leathers and pulled out a piece of note paper and a pencil. "Okay. I think we'll use the prison system of Indonesia for this little exercise." He wrote that onto the paper.

"The prisons of Indonesia—?"

"Yeah. They're perfect. They're half a world away. Any abilities you think you have *here* are worthless to your brothers and sisters in Christ who are imprisoned *there*."

"Wait. Followers of Jesus are being held in prison?"

"Thousands of them. It's a crime to convert from Islam, the religion of the entire country, to Christianity. And so Indonesian pastors and their wives and church leaders are thrown into overcrowded cells where they're beaten and tortured, often by other inmates." Clay had never seen Nigel so serious. His words were like steel. "Many of them don't survive it."

Clay breathed out. "So—you want me to pray they'd be released. That they'd be freed, right?"

A long silence arrived to the table. Nigel gave a thin smile and closed his eyes. "No. I don't want you to pray that they'd be freed. No."

Clay sat quietly while Nigel worked through whatever was going on in his mind.

"The decision of if, and when they're released, is God's alone. And you could pray for that, yes, but across Indonesia the followers of Jesus consider it a privilege to suffer in those filthy cells for their King. They know they've entered into what the scriptures refer to as the 'fellowship of their Savior's sufferings', and they do so with great joy. Already the halls of heaven are alive with their songs as they sing out in worship. It might be hard for you to understand but their burn scars and their blood, staining the concrete of their cells, is an offering to Him who sits on the throne."

Clay swallowed. *Whoa.*

"So no, right now I don't want you to pray they'd be freed." Nigel opened his eyes and he wrote several short lines on the note paper. "Instead, I'd ask you to pray they'd stand firm through their trials. That they'd have perseverance and great faith. That they'd be dressed fully in the armor of God. You'll find the list of armor in Ephesians 6. Most of Paul's letters, the epistles, were written from prison, so you'll find a lot of applicable passages to use in your prayers there." Nigel pushed the note across the table.

Clay looked down at the note, his mind blank.

"You're thinking prayer is for old women who talk to the ceiling. A bit of spiritual foolishness that isn't worth the effort." Nigel tapped the note. "*This*—this might change your thinking on that."

"Sure. But what's this—?" Clay pointed at the third line. "Pray they be filled with the Holy Spirit. You say here to read Acts 2. And after that, you've listed eight things: love, joy, peace, patience—"

Nigel pulled a thin New Testament from his leathers and laid it on the table. "Satan hopes in their imprisonment, with everything stripped from them, they'll discard their allegiance to God and return to the usual thinking and actions of the world. Fear, hatred, anger, and a desire for vengeance against those who've hurt them."

"And I'm going to stop that?"

Nigel's stare got that faraway look again. He smiled. "Hardly. Your job is simply to ask God the Father to release the most powerful, spiritual being in the universe on their behalf. And I can assure you, Clay—" He smiled again. "—not a lot stands in *His* way. What He wants done, gets done."

Clay leaned forward, not sure what to make of this. "You're— you're talking about the Holy Spirit?"

"Right." Nigel stood. He laid his yellow leather jacket and the keys on the table. "You can drop off the motorcycle in the parking garage where your

Porsche is sitting. I'll pick it up tomorrow sometime. Wear my jacket. It'll help cut the wind."

"Where are you going? We're a long way from a bus stop here in Horseshoe Bay."

"I gotta go." His eyes flicked to the note on the table. "I think it's going to be a busy night for me. I'll see you later." He crossed the room and was about to exit when he stopped at the last moment, the door already open. "Oh, and Clay—" Another of his mischievous smiles arrived. "Take a glance at the watch when you call upon the Spirit to invade those prisons."

Clay remained sitting for a few extra minutes in the little Subway outlet. It'd been an incredible night, absolutely mind-blowing. And yes, he wanted to thank God for everything, but— what was this? He glanced at the note with Nigel's handwriting. *Okay, everything else he could handle, but this was way out there. Crazy stuff.* Clay smirked. He was supposed to pray, and something was going to happen ten thousand miles away in Indonesia. *Yeah, yeah, sure it is.* He stood up, stuffed the note and keys into a pocket, shrugged into the leather jacket and exited, locking the door behind him.

He left the motorcycle where it was parked, and headed towards the waterfront. Without any wind the water was calm, flat. Along the edge of the bay, docked at the government terminal, one of the massive Vancouver Island super-ferries sat silently. Rugged mountains rose up all around the sheltered bay.

Clay's mind was conflicted. He glanced down at the watch. 322. It was a good number. He smiled. It was a *huge* number! "322—" He whispered it aloud. Was it even possible such a number could be credited to somebody like him?

He knew he was grinning. Tonight he'd seen his sheet! *He'd seen it.* He'd never heard of anybody having seen their eternal balance sheet, but tonight, he'd seen his! *He'd had some influence in 322 lives.* Everything within him wanted to explode, his insides bursting with an aliveness he could barely contain. Tonight was a night for celebration! For cartwheels and laughter.

He kept walking. It was a night to celebrate, not to be wasted on crazy stuff like praying for people ten-thousand miles away. That was foolishness.

He followed a path along the water's edge. His mind couldn't let go of the hundreds of lines on his sheet! His whisper was lost into the night air. "God, you've used the worst of sinners in all of this. You've allowed me, by your grace, to help lost young people find their way to safety."

Clay arrived to the government wharf and wandered along its length. He then continued down the steep ramp onto the wooden planking at water level. Several small powerboats were secured to the dock. He stared out into the shimmering blackness of the water. *Prayer is for old women.*

Talking into the air to change things in Indonesia? *C'mon, be serious.*

Sure, God was probably listening, but He'd answer decades from now.

Prayer is for old women in rest homes.

Praying for people somewhere in a prison was stupid. Nothing would be accomplished. Prayer was just flinging words at the sky. And oh yeah, God might listen, but He wouldn't do anything about it.

Clay yanked out Nigel's rumpled note from a pocket. He was just about to chuck it when something stopped him. Hadn't he once promised Nigel he'd follow his instructions regardless of what others around him said? In fact, hadn't Nigel warned him that many of his ideas would sound crazy, but he'd need to trust him? And Clay had agreed. *Crazy as the instructions might sound.*

So with a grimace of frustration, Clay smoothed out the note. *The prisons of Indonesia?* "C'mon, Nigel, this isn't gonna work."

He took a last glance at the '322' displayed on the watch.

And he bowed his head.

"Father God, I've—I've never had an evening like tonight. Thank you for everything You've done in my life. And for the numbers You've given me. I—I come before You, grateful and knowing

I deserve none of this." Clay breathed out again, fearful he was about to step out into empty air. *Okay, bring on the crazy.*

"Father, there's people…uh, there's people in Indonesia who've trusted you. People like me who had nowhere else to go. Now they're in prison."

He looked again at the note. "Lord, I'd ask that they'd be able to stand firm there in…uh, in their cells. Regardless of what's being done to them, or if things are miserable."

Clay cast a quick glance around to be sure nobody was listening. It was midnight and absolutely silent. "I ask they'd stand firm through whatever they have to endure. And I ask they'd—" Another quick glance at the note. "I ask that You, in your goodness, would fill them with your Holy Spirit. Fill them with Your love and joy. And peace. Give them Your gentleness and kindness when faced with hatred and anger. Allow them to stand against whatever Satan is telling them, to discourage them, by the power of Your Spirit. Dress them fully in the—"

Clay was going to say 'armor of God'. He didn't get to say it. His focus was instead pulled to the watch.

324…328…358…378…411…465…501.

He stared at the blur of digital light. The numbers were speeding up!

584…668…781…804…872… 988…1054...

Clay stood there, not breathing, until the numbers slowed in the thirteen hundreds, and finally came to rest at 1407. He stared at the number, his mouth slack. Everything around him went silent, like the entire universe was in awe of what it'd just witnessed. *Was this possible?* He looked around, desperate, floundering for an explanation! Nigel had said his Christian brothers and sisters were being beaten in their prison cells. Had he somehow helped them, and if so, how?

Every circuit in his mind was blowing! Was this actually happening?! He was on a dock in Canada and—*he could barely say it, let alone believe it*—he'd somehow touched the lives of men and women held in prisons across Indonesia. A country he wasn't sure he could find on a map!

Clay grabbed his head, pressing against his temples. He took jittery little steps in tight circles on the wooden planks. *No!* There had to be *another* explanation. There had to be! Prayer was for old women who made quilts and sipped tea from delicate, saucered cups.

He whispered it. "Lord God, there's gotta be another explanation. Prayer isn't like this."

But what if it is like this? He shook his head. *No! This isn't possible.* But something within him wasn't resting easily with that answer. And there was nobody to ask.

So he did the only thing that would settle it. He looked at the instructions on the note again. They were quite clear. Clay pulled out the New Testament and, in the little bit of available light on the dock, he read the passages Nigel had included. The first two chapters of Ephesians. The sixth chapter of Ephesians. First chapter of Colossians. The first chapter of both First and Second Thessalonians.

It didn't take long for a common theme to leap out at him. These passages were all written to people who were enduring great suffering. And over and over again Paul encouraged them with a version of the same words: 'With this in mind, we constantly pray for you, that our God may count you worthy of his calling, and by his power He may fulfill every good purpose of yours and every act prompted by your faith. We pray this so the name of our Lord Jesus may be glorified in you.'

Clay leaned against the railing and considered the last part of it. 'We pray our God may fulfill every good purpose of yours, and every act prompted by your faith.'

He imagined an Asian man, a pastor, held in a dirty cell, surrounded on every side by people who hated him. What would be his *good purpose*? And what *acts* would his faith prompt?

Something Nigel had said arrived with great clarity to Clay's mind. This pastor's good purpose would be to *stand firm*, to continue trusting and praising God, even when he was brutalized. To sing the praises of the King of heaven, even while being held in prison unjustly. But why—*why* would he do such a thing? Wouldn't that just bring only more abuse from those around him?

An answer arrived to Clay and it knocked the air from his lungs. Was it possible prison hadn't changed anything for these people? That his Christian brothers and sisters in Indonesia hadn't let go of their hope of seeing everyone around them come to know salvation in Jesus Christ! It remained the only goal in their life. They weren't allowing being thrown into prison to slow them down. Instead, they were enduring all forms of savagery. They were singing while being brutalized, and exuding joy, peace, kindness, and love in the swamplands of hell, that they could be *living examples* of Christ. And they did it so they could demonstrate the power of Christ in their lives—whatever the cost—that other inmates would embrace Jesus.

That was their good purpose!

Clay sat down on the dock, stunned. And where was this power coming from for his brothers and sisters to live like that, to endure such savagery? He looked at the watch. For eleven *hundred* of them tonight, it had arrived from the Holy Spirit, in direct answer to Clay's prayer!

The dull, grey bench had been there since the town had been incorporated. It was identical to hundreds of others in parks across Vancouver. Concrete end supports with heavy wooden slats that could handle the harsh wet of the west coast. There had never been anything unique about the bench.

Not until tonight.

For tonight, for three hours, it was the staging grounds of an assault upon the prison system of Indonesia the likes of which had never been felt out of Horseshoe Bay before!

Clay accelerated past a tractor-trailer unit as he raced across the Lions Gate Bridge, the whine of the bike's air-cooled engine at redline. He couldn't get the smile off his face, couldn't silence the joy bubbling from within him. Nothing he'd ever experienced came close to what had happened tonight—nothing! There'd been a time, at the very peak of his wealth, when the entire world and all of its pleasures were at his fingertips. Compared to what he'd been part of tonight, sitting on a little concrete bench in an obscure town, that all seemed like shredded paper. Isn't that what Nigel had once said to him? "While others are investing in shredded paper, we're going to be piling up gold bars!"

Gold bars. He loved that imagery. Here he was, at four-thirty in the morning, serving the One who'd rescued him. Serving the One who'd died a violent death that Clay could know freedom forever. This was life! The only life Clay wanted.

The bike was at full throttle, laid almost onto its side, careening through the twists of Stanley

Park when he glanced at the watch. He smiled. The number 2027 stared back at him. If the Holy Spirit of God was going to battle within the prison system of Indonesia, Clay Rawlings wanted to be along for the ride!

Chapter Eleven

At quitting time at Circuits Circus, Clay pushed through the exit doors, fired up the Porsche, and raced home. There he changed into a pair of weathered jeans and a San Diego Chargers sweat shirt. Three packages of Kraft dinner and a bowl of Raisin Bran were dinner. And then he was back in his car heading downtown. He found free parking on a side street, and headed on foot towards Granville. He smiled. He always felt energized as he approached the streets of Vancouver. *Who was God going to bring across his path tonight?*

But something quite different had arrived tonight. On every street, he found yellow T-shirted young men and women talking with the street population of young people. And they were everywhere! Granville Street was like a moving montage of energetic yellow. He moved west to other streets, but there were more of them. They were leaning against the buildings, or kneeling on the sidewalk, listening intently to some of the city's most hardened youth. He heard a lot of laughter between the two groups, but also some serious conversations. He was impressed. Whoever had trained this army of volunteers was good at this. *Really* good at this.

Clay went into restaurants where he knew he'd be recognized as a late-night regular. They were all hopping, crowded and loud. And again, the yellow brigade was busy! Most of the stools at the counters, and a lot of the booths, were deep into conversations about hurting lives and freedom. Young people with tongue studs and sleeve tattoos, some still wrapped into filthy blankets, were ordering up steak sandwiches and burgers. Waitresses hustled from the kitchens with huge platters of food, and nobody seemed to care what this was costing. He didn't see a tip left on a table of less than ten dollars.

He left the restaurants and sagged happily against a chain link fence. *Whoa.* God was at work! And not at all subtly. His presence was being felt tonight across Vancouver. Clay had no idea where somebody had been able to recruit all these people, but they were high caliber.

Hoping to escape the crowds, Clay headed for the alleys. The night was closing in, the darkness arriving. But again, the yellow shirts were ahead of him. At the entrance of the first alley, a yellow-shirted girl was stationed, nervously shuffling from foot to foot, obviously waiting for something. Several others were directing traffic. And then Clay could hear the wail of an ambulance racing through the city. He moved into the alley and there, wedged into a narrow space, sprawled onto the dirty concrete, was a young girl in a dress far too short. Her dress was soaked in blood, her hands holding her abdomen. *Gunshot wound!* She was barely coherent, mumbling gibberish, her face ashen. But what stopped Clay was the person leaning over her, asserting pressure to the wound with a wadded up yellow shirt, her arms covered in blood, assuring the girl help was coming, trying to keep her awake until the ambulance arrived.

It was Hannah!

Clay stared at the entire scene. He'd never seen Hannah as such a hero.

The ambulance arrived, doors flew open, two young paramedics emerged at a run with their jump kit, and the group of yellow shirts moved back. And then, with everyone's attention directed towards the girl on the ground, a third person exited from the back doors of the ambulance.

Nigel.

He stepped out in a charcoal suit, like a movie producer exiting a limousine. He barely acknowledged the action around him, as though he were directing it. Paramedics worked feverishly on the girl lying on the ground. Yellow-shirted volunteers held back spectators and directed traffic. A life was at stake, and guessing by the tone of the paramedics, not doing well. The stress levels among the inexperienced volunteers was spiking.

Nigel stepped towards Clay as though none of it was happening. "We need to talk."

Clay had been standing by, eager to help, but feeling quite useless as a dozen of the yellow-shirted young men and women took control of a bad situation. When he addressed Nigel he was almost shouting. "Nigel, we've gotta stay and help this girl—!"

Nigel didn't even glance in her direction. He smiled. "She's going to be fine. I know she looks bad right now, but it was necessary. Something drastic was needed to allow her to escape these streets. And to get her home."

"What—?!" Clay stared at him.

"C'mon." Nigel placed his arm around Clay's shoulders and led him from the alley. "We need to talk."

FlipJacks was a pancake place on Seymour Street. When the waitress arrived, Nigel very pleasantly ordered French toast, bacon and a three-egg scramble, but couldn't decide on a fruit topping. He and the waitress, a middle aged bottle blonde, laughed together as they went through all the options. He finally settled on strawberries and whip cream. Clay abruptly pushed his menu at her, "Just coffee. Thanks."

Clay leaned forward in the booth. "Okay. What did you mean out there? How could you *possibly* know—?"

Nigel cut him off. "I'm pulling you off the streets of Vancouver for a while."

"What—?" Clay felt like he'd been torpedoed.

"Something's coming. And if we want you to be as successful as possible, then you've got to know how to pray." Nigel had lost his easy-going manner. He wasn't smiling. "An opportunity to get your numbers into a league of their own is coming, but you'll have to be ready."

"What's coming?"

Nigel avoided the question. Instead he pointed outside. "Hannah is the one who trained the yellow shirts. She's the leader of the entire team out there. She's been involved with at-risk youth on these streets since before you knew her in high school. She's fearless, trusting God to direct her." Nigel's smile had returned. "She's learned to let the peace of the Spirit settle her in stressful situations, so she makes excellent decisions under fire. She's waded through some horrible stuff. Tonight wasn't the first gunshot wound she's seen. She's had kids die in her arms."

Clay leaned back. "Kids have died in her arms?"

"Two of them. One was eleven, the other sixteen." Nigel paused, and then he locked eyes with Clay. "That's the quality of the girl you're in love with."

Nigel said it so matter-of-factly. Clay wanted to deny it. He wanted to deflect Nigel's words, but there wasn't anything to say. He *knew* Nigel knew the truth. He was, and always had been, madly in love with Hannah Taylor.

Nigel smiled again. "Somewhere in the future I'm thinking you'd make great partners. You've both got the same heart, the same zeal, but that's all somewhere down the road. For now, I'm pulling you away from these streets."

"So what am I going to be doing instead?" Clay tried not to focus on what Nigel had said about one day partnering with Hannah. It made his heart race.

"You're going to pray. The letter to the Hebrews says, 'Remember those in prison as if you were their fellow prisoners.' You, Clay, are going to be encouraging the Holy Spirit to continue battling within the prisons of Indonesia. And then to keep it interesting, you're going to join Him in His efforts across China. Millions of your Christian brothers and sisters are suffering in the prisons and work camps, *the laogai*, of China. You're not going to let them suffer alone."

Spring weather in Vancouver is often synonymous with drenching rain and deep puddles. Clay didn't let it stop him. He was usually out walking on the beach at three-thirty or four in the morning, lifting up to God the pastors and church leaders imprisoned across Indonesia and China. He barely noticed the rain as he celebrated what the watch was allowing him to see. He'd spend two or three hours in prayer, and then allow himself to look at the new numbers on the watch. His numbers were climbing. The sight of higher numbers never failed to fill him with gratitude. And so there in the solitude of the morning he'd dance and spin, his face turned up towards the falling wetness.

"How could God have chosen *me*—" He asked it a thousand times in reverent awe. "—for such a task as this?" And there wasn't a good answer. So in celebration Clay would fall to his knees in the sand, and thank the One who'd rescued him. They were amazing, and soggy, times.

One morning, at about five-twenty, he was making his way around the darkened curve of Spanish Banks. It was pouring out. The beach was shadowed in a thick mist, a wind coming in off the water. It'd been a great morning, truly incredible, his prayers flooding out easily. There was nobody around and Clay was about to launch into one of his dance celebrations.

And that's when he saw a lone figure through the mist. Whoever it was faced away from him, sitting alone on a bench. It made no sense. It was pouring out! Who'd be sitting in the rain, at this time of the morning? Clay was wary, so he cut a wide arc around the bench.

"Morning, Clay." Nigel. He was completely soaked, puddles forming in the folds of his jacket. He didn't seem to notice.

"Hey." Surprise didn't register anymore.

"Congratulations on getting to 12,000. Not bad."

Clay laughed. The display on the watch had reached twelve thousand *just* the night before. His number was climbing by about seven hundred most mornings on the beach. Which he easily translated to mean his prayer life was making a difference in seven hundred lives within the prisons of Asia. It was hard to even consider.

"I'm certain you didn't come out here to congratulate me on that. You're drenched."

"You need to be somewhere on Sunday morning at nine-thirty." He handed Clay a card. The name of a church was embossed on it. "There'll be a guest speaker. You'll want a good seat."

With that, Nigel stood and headed off the beach.

Sunday was overcast but dry. The Porsche roared into the narrow parking lot of a medium sized church in south Vancouver. Or it almost did. A young girl in a flag vest stopped Clay and, with a friendly smile, asked him to park instead on one of the tree-lined streets that bordered it. The church lot was already full and the streets around it were quickly filling as he climbed from his car. *Okay, who was this guest speaker? Somebody special, obviously*. Clay grabbed his Bible and headed for the entrance doors.

The speaker's name was Francis Chan. Clay had never heard of him, but then he wasn't familiar with most big-name church leaders. Francis was Asian, dressed in khaki slacks and a collared golf shirt. Somehow the leather flip flops seemed appropriate. He had the bearing of somebody comfortable with large crowds. As the senior pastor introduced him, Clay glanced through the bulletin that had a short bio on him.

This guy had supposedly planted a church somewhere in California. It'd grown from a few people in his living room to almost seven thousand attenders every week. *Okay, so this guy was once a major player in the Christian world.* Clay wasn't sure why Nigel would have gone to such lengths to be sure Clay was here, but the next line—well, it wasn't at all what he expected. Francis had walked away from it all, at the height of his success. He'd quit the church and sold his home. He'd given all his stuff away, to travel with his wife and family of five children to some of the worst slums in the world. *Whoa*. He'd gone into the worst places to minister the love of Jesus to people who'd known nothing but poverty and oppression. To reach out to hurting people that they could find freedom, and the forgiveness of God. *Alright!* Clay liked him already.

He set aside the bulletin and glanced around. There wasn't an empty seat.

Francis had finished his opening comments and was already plowing headlong into his sermon. "The world keeps encouraging you to look at your past." He paused. "Yeah, well you keep looking at your past and you're gonna get depressed. And then in your depression you're going to get stuck in your past. Instead, look to your future. Look towards that moment when you stand before Jesus, that moment when you stand before the Judge of all the earth. Oh man, what is *that* moment going to be like?"

Francis smiled. "A lot of the things I do are simply because I'm thinking about my future."

Clay relaxed. Francis was easy to listen to.

"I'm thinking about that moment when I first see Jesus. Because I realize everything I do is going to bring either reward or regret. It really is." He paused. "Everything I do. Reward or regret.

"So let's say I've got an extra thousand bucks." Francis held out his hand as though holding a big wad of cash. "On that day, in that future before me, that day when I first see Jesus, what's going to bring reward and what's going to bring regret?" He paused again.

"I could buy a lot of fun things for myself with that thousand bucks. But on *that day*, the apostle Paul's saying, if I just keep looking towards *that* day, maybe I just give it to the poor, because on *that* day I'll be rewarded for it." Francis stopped and stared out towards the audience. "Everything I do. Reward or regret.

"Hey, we've all bought stuff we regretted. Stuff that was a waste of money, right?

"Think about what we're going to say at the end, when we stand before God. Are you going to regret the car you drove, the house you lived in, the clothes you wore—? What about your time and the way you spent it? Man, I'm so glad I watched nine thousand movies!" A nervous laughter rippled through the crowd.

"I think you'll regret that." He paused, allowing time for the audience to consider his words.

"Instead, Paul wants us to think about our future. He wants us to think of *that* moment, that *very first moment*, of seeing Jesus! And for us to live with an eye on rewards."

He paused again.

"Let me give you an illustration. Probably the best illustration I've ever used." Francis moved to the far corner of the stage and picked up the end of a rope laying there. He pulled about sixty feet of it along with him as he returned to center stage. It was obviously spooling out from somewhere behind the stage.

He held up the end of the rope. "Pretend this rope goes on forever, that it loops around the world several times, and doesn't have an end. Got that?"

Clay smiled. *Yeah, got that. The never ending rope.*

Francis continued. "Now imagine this rope is a timeline. Of *your* existence. " He pointed out at the crowd. "A timeline of *your* existence."

Clay leaned forward. *Okay, the rope is a timeline of my existence.*

Francis then held up the end of the rope at eye level. "Do you see this little red part?"

Clay could barely see a little section at the very end. It was about three inches long, wrapped with red tape. *Yeah, I see it.*

"This red part represents your time on earth." A silence had settled onto the crowd.

He held up the rope, wiggling the little taped end. "You've got a few short years here on earth and then you've got all of eternity somewhere else." As soon as he said that, he held up the lengths of rope higher to show its length. The contrast between the three little inches of tape and the rest of the rope was staggering.

Clay smiled. *Okay.* This is why Nigel had gone to such lengths to have him here! He'd never seen such a powerful demonstration of eternity. This is what Thirteen44 Global Investments was about. This is what Nigel was about. *And this is what Nigel wants me to be about.*

Preparing people for eternity!

"Think about this." Francis pulled on the rope so another forty feet arrived from somewhere off stage. It continued to spool out without any hint of an end. "This is your existence. We're all going to live forever. All of us." He allowed another pause.

"What blows me away is that some of you, all you think about is this red part." He held up the three inches of tape, his finger resting on it. "It's all you think about. You're consumed by it! 'Oh man, I can't wait until *here.*'" He barely moved his finger to point near one end of the red tape. "I'm gonna save, save, save, so I can really live it up during this part *right here.*" Again, his finger barely moved.

The audience laughed, but he'd gotten their attention like they probably hadn't allowed in a long time.

"You're consumed with this little red part right here. This tiny section, barely wider than my finger, consumes your thinking! It's all you think about. 'Oh man, am I going to get to travel? Am I going to eat at great restaurants and play golf during this time?"

Francis stopped again, a look of shock scrawled across his face. *"Are—are you kidding me?!* What about *this and this?!*" He started pulling at the rope. Another sixty feet arrived, making a deep, jumbled pile in front of him. "What about *all of this*—? And *this*—?" He kept yanking more rope onto the stage.

Francis paused, staring down at the long coils of rope. And then, holding up the little red taped end, he faced the crowd. "It drives me crazy because the Bible teaches what I do with this little red part here, determines how I'm going to spend millions and millions of years. So why would I spend this little red part trying to make myself as comfortable as possible, enjoying myself as much as I can? Why would I do that?

"Instead, the apostle Paul says, 'Look guys, I'm going to live my life building the kingdom of God. I'm going to spend my life, invest my life, for that moment when I cross the finish line. I'm going to forget about all the stuff I *could* enjoy and I'm not going to look around. No, I'm going to be like a runner looking ahead, focused intently towards the moment when I'll face God. Because when I face Him, I don't get this opportunity again. We get one chance at this life on earth.'"

Francis slowed his words. "It can end at any time for any of us. And then comes eternity. And people look at some of my decisions and they say, 'Oh, you're so stupid because your decisions are going to affect *this*." He pointed his finger to a tiny section of the red tape.

Clay he knew he was referring to his abandoning everything to minister in the world's slums.

"And I respond to them, 'No, you're stupid, because *your* decisions are going to affect *all of this!*'" He leaned down and lifted up a hundred feet of rope. Another smattering of laughter.

He continued. "I look at the way people live and I say, 'wow, that is so crazy. You are so crazy. You're going to do *that* just to enjoy *right now*, not even knowing if you have tomorrow. And you think *that's* smart and I'm dumb.'" Francis shook his head.

"Instead, Paul is saying here, 'I'm not going to look around at all this stuff. I'm not living for what everybody else lives for.'"

Francis's words slowed. "Look at our lives. It's crazy. But we're surrounded by the craziness on every side. And it tempts all of us because *everybody* lives this way. Everybody lives for the little red part. Nobody's thinking about the millions of years after this. My friends, it's a deception—an *evil* deception we can't get out of our minds.

"And Paul flatly states, 'I'm not doing that! I'm keeping my eyes on the finish line. I'm going to forget what's behind me and not look at what's around me. Instead I'll be straining forward for that mark. I'm going to face the Judge of all the earth and He's going to hand me that trophy. You can believe I'm using every muscle in me to finish well.'"

The parking lot of the church was empty now. The street was empty. Clay sat in the Porsche, replaying the whole thing in his head. Wasn't this everything he'd wanted since he'd gotten off the floor of that community hall, since he'd been embraced by Jesus? To live a life that allowed people to find freedom in Christ? He wiped his eyes. He knew it was.

He started the Porsche, dropped the clutch and roared away. The beach, and another invasion of the prisons of Asia, awaited him. But what had Nigel said? *Something is coming.* Something that Clay needed to be *ready for.* Somehow he knew it had something to do with what Francis Chan had talked about. He wanted to be ready.

Chapter Twelve

During the money days Clay had never gone grocery shopping. Life was frantic and so meals were a scattered affair. If he was eating alone, either at home or at the office, he'd order in food. And if he wasn't alone, then meals were a perfect opportunity to impress corporate clients or the latest, arm-candy girlfriend. An executive assistant named Kim had proved rather adept at getting tables at the most exclusive, eating hot spots in Vancouver and across the globe. It simply hadn't made sense for Clay, whose time was easily worth thousands of dollars an hour, to be pushing a shopping cart across a grocery store.

At his new, current wage of $11.40 an hour, Clay was happily wheeling through Green Tags Market, trying to navigate a cart with a bad rear wheel. It'd been three weeks since he'd heard Francis Chan. But even now, moving along in the breakfast cereal aisle, if you watched closely, you'd notice Clay's lips were moving. He was muttering something quietly about Liuzhou, a city in China. It was the site of a prison.

A gum-chewing, middle-aged woman checked his groceries while Clay bagged them. He paid the total and was about to put the full plastic bags into his cart when the lady asked if he'd like assistance in getting his groceries to his car. Clay almost laughed. *Wasn't that a service for pensioners and the disabled?* He smiled and was about to assure this misguided woman he was fully capable of—

But she was already on the intercom, calling for 'assistance at checkout two'.

The store wasn't busy and it was only a few seconds before Clay heard a voice behind him. "Are these your groceries, sir?" Clay turned expecting to see a teenaged bag boy. Instead, there stood Nigel in a collared shirt and the green apron of Green Tags Market.

Clay shook his head. "Somehow I doubt you're moonlighting as a bag boy. So I'm guessing that you want to talk." Clay glanced over at the gum-chewing checkout woman. She was staring at him oddly. Nigel winked at him, lifted his bags into the cart and wheeled them out into the parking lot.

They settled into the Porsche. Nigel had left behind the apron just inside the entrance to the market.

"It's time." That arrived without expression. "Everything we've been working towards is ready. There's a FlipJack's on Cameron Avenue. Let's go there. We have a lot to talk about."

They settled into a booth near the back and ordered. Nigel surveyed the menu as he spoke. "There's been a lot of positive activity within the prison systems across Asia. It's obvious you're taking this seriously."

Clay glanced around the restaurant. He spoke quietly. "I did some research about China. Everything you said is true. No lawyers. No trials. Torture is common. But the most incredible thing is the believers in China actually refer to prison as *God's seminary.* They've embraced it as a part of God building His kingdom, and consider it a privilege to suffer for His sake." Clay's words were now arriving at a bare whisper. "This is pretty humbling work you've given me. I'm—I'm not worthy of these people."

Nigel got that faraway look. "Clay, scripture says that 'these trials have come so their faith may be proved to be genuine.' And so, yes, your brothers and sisters in Asia are being tested by persecution and suffering, through which they must persevere. But don't underestimate Satan. Could it not be he's using a different tactic *here in Canada* you simply don't recognize?"

"What's he using I wouldn't recognize?"

"Wealth and comfort."

Clay stared at Nigel, struggling to consider such a thing.

"I know the idea of wealth and comfort being *a tactic of Satan* is hard for you to wrap your mind around because you're immersed into a culture that holds up comfort as the highest goal. North America sees it as something to be celebrated, when maybe it's actually a carefully camouflaged trap."

"Yeah, okay. I can see that. It—it *can* be a trap." Clay nodded.

"Just remember Satan is all about the end game. He doesn't care what path he has to use, so long as he destroys you. That at the moment of your arrival to eternity you arrive with nothing. That you arrive with negative numbers."

They paused as the waitress set down a couple of clubhouse sandwiches. FlipJack's was generous with the fries, so a deep puddle of ketchup found its way onto both plates.

"Clay, I've been your investment broker for a while now. It's time for you to take what you've learned and strike out in a specific direction. I once told you Thirteen44 Global invests in some really ugly places across the planet. I think your efforts with at-risk youth and the prisons of Asia have given you an appreciation of what I meant. You've made investments in some nasty places that are securing huge returns. But I'd like to see more of them."

"Okay. Where?"

Nigel set down his sandwich. "The world's a big place. There's no lack of people who need to find the freedom and forgiveness of Jesus. And I could suggest places where people sell their children into sexual slavery. Or places where civil war is tearing families and communities apart. And of course, there's inner-city violence across the globe. But we always match our clients with investments that resonate within their heart. Places that grip them emotionally."

Clay leaned forward, a narrow smile already forming.

"So is there anywhere in the world that you—?"

"The slums of India." Clay cut him off. No hesitation. "The slums in northern India."

Nigel was nodding. "I thought that might be your choice." He pulled a brochure from his pocket and laid it on the table.

Clay picked it up. "GraceUnfathomable—?" What's this?"

"Probably one of the best investments I know." Nigel spoke like a collector with a rare art piece. "India's own believers are reaching out into the slums of India. Your brothers and sisters who've lived their whole lives in poverty are now journeying into other slums and villages to proclaim the freedom and forgiveness they've found in Jesus Christ. Think of it as the poor reaching the poor. Often travelling from place to place on foot, or on bicycle. And this brochure is simply an invitation for you to partner with them in prayer and finances."

"They minister in the slums?" Clay's mind was racing.

"Yes."

"And so I'd be helping the poor discover what I've found?" Clay's eyes were riveted to the brochure.

Nigel leaned back. "That's what we do, Clay."

Clay looked up. "I want in."

The waitress returned to offer dessert, which they both declined. Instead they asked for coffee. She disappeared and returned with two full mugs.

"What's the watch at now, nineteen thousand or so?" Nigel added creamer to his coffee.

"Yeah—almost." Clay glanced down. The digital display added another digit while he watched. 18,921. He stared at the new number; his breath coming in short puffs. *Was a prisoner somewhere in Asia able to stand firm while being brutally beaten?* Had he been strengthened to not deny his Savior because of Clay's prayers? Or was an at-risk youth somewhere telling another teen what Clay had told him about freedom?

He could barely contain what was bubbling within him. *Was this really happening?* Out there on Jericho beach, during those early morning hours, swamping through the rain with his voice lifted up to the heavens, he was playing a small role in something enormous. The Holy Spirit of God was changing lives for eternity! Clay looked at the number again. Every minute he'd spent out there on the beach had been worth it—*so worth it!* He'd never done anything that filled him with such joy.

"Clay, we've got to talk about money."

"Money?"

"Yeah." Nigel took a sip of coffee. "You've been pretty generous when it meant getting at-risk youth home. You've never hesitated to lay down the cash if it would help a teen find safety. But you were *with them* on the streets, listening to their stories." Nigel slowed his words. "You were with them at bus stations and airports, helping them get to places of safety. What I'm saying is you were *there.* You could see what your money was accomplishing,"

Clay nodded. "Okay—?"

"But in Indonesia, you weren't there. You didn't need to be in those prisons. That's why I chose a situation so far away. Prayer is a worldwide currency. You stood on a dock in Horseshoe Bay and helped release the power of the Spirit into the lives of nineteen hundred of your imprisoned brothers and sisters. Most of whom felt alone and forgotten. And of course, a lot more since then, even though they were half a world away. " Nigel paused.

"I'm suggesting you put the two situations together. Yes, that you'd continue to spend hours in prayer, but that you'd also begin directing a substantial amount of your financial resources—your cash— to Indian pastors and missionaries. That they could continue to take the message of freedom into some really hard places." Nigel smiled. "Clay, I'm offering you the opportunity to become a valuable partner with people who are already hard at work amongst the poor of India."

Clay leaned against the counter in the kitchen of his condo. He'd been flipping through the three-page brochure from GraceUnfathomable for half an hour. It was incredible.

The founder of the ministry had journeyed to India during the 'hippy era' in pursuit of spiritual enlightenment. While there, in a village on the banks of the Ganges River, he'd been befriended by several Australians who'd found Jesus earlier in their own pilgrimage. Within a week he'd embraced the salvation in Christ and been baptized. But rather than returning home to the States he and this little ragtag group journeyed across India together, sharing the message of forgiveness of sins in Jesus Christ. What they'd discovered in their travels was an endless sea of rural villages where the name of Jesus had never been heard. He'd returned home, enrolled in and graduated from Bible School, and then returned to India. His rather ambitious hopes, as laid out in the brochure, were that he could find more people who'd join him in reaching the eighty-thousand slum villages of northern India.

The ministry plan was simple. India had its own believers, many of them eager to share the message of Christ with their people. He was offering Western Christians the opportunity to supply the rather meager finances needed to keep one of these missionaries on the field. It was a great plan because they already knew the language and culture, and they'd lived their entire lives at the economic level of the people they were trying to reach.

This guy wanted to reach the poor! Clay could feel himself smiling.

The main thrust of the brochure was to sign up monthly sponsors for these Indian missionaries. That was thirty dollars a month, an easy number based on a-dollar-a-day. The *full support* of $200 was suggested several times as the amount needed to completely support a Bible-school trained young man or woman for a month.

To graduate, each one of these young men and women would've already planted a church in a neighboring village, a fledgling church comprised almost entirely of ex-Hindus and Muslims. Then they'd have secured a part-time pastor for the church. When that was accomplished they were ready to *walk* to the next village; and the village after that, fanning out across India. Or they'd travel by bicycle if they owned one, which was unlikely. Bicycles were a hundred and thirty dollars each, and Clay was encouraged to supply as many of them as possible. On a bicycle a missionary could reach more villages, not having to walk.

Clay stared at such low numbers for full support of a native-born missionary. Two hundred a month? *Just seven bucks a day?* Clay frowned. Was such a thing possible? It seemed like an impossibly small amount. But he'd seen the harsh living conditions of Asia. Yes, he had to admit, it *was* very possible.

On the back page was a list of things you could donate money for. Paperback New Testaments were on the list. They were just fifty cents each! Clay smiled. If the missionaries he wanted to sponsor were going to be effective they'd need a good supply of those.

He pulled his checkbook from a drawer. With a flourish he wrote out a check for $600. Two missionaries, full salaries for a month, and 400 New Testaments. And then he sat and stared at the check. Who knew how much these two Indian missionaries could accomplish in a month? The possibilities were staggering.

He grabbed an envelope and addressed it. And then he was running to find his sneakers and a jacket. Mailing the money would come later. Right now he needed to get out onto the beach to pray for those missionaries!

A man dancing and spinning along the streets approaching Jericho Beach hadn't been seen until several months earlier. And it'd seemed weird the first couple of times the upscale residents witnessed it. Now, the residents in Clay's neighborhood were growing used to it.

On Clay's way home from work the next day, he parked outside a tiny pharmacy that had a postal outlet. He purchased stamps and affixed one of them to the envelope. Then with a final look at it, he dropped it into the outgoing mail slot. And then he glanced at the watch. His number hadn't changed. He inwardly laughed at himself. *C'mon, Clay. Your money hasn't even left Vancouver, yet. Give it a chance.*

He exited the postal outlet and made his way back across the street. Nigel was leaning against the Porsche.

"You were right to look at the watch, Clay." His expression was unreadable. Clay recognized this as Nigel at his most serious. "You just provided the funds for two graduates from an Indian Bible school to continue ministering in the slum near the airport of Mumbai. Their funding is running out. The little village church that sent them has no further money to help them, so there's been a concern they'd be returning home."

Clay stared at Nigel. "The slum near the airport?"

"Yes."

"You mean Dharavi?" Clay swallowed. "So I just put money in the mail to fund two missionaries in the first slum where Nasty Dogs had their audio assembly facility? Is that what you're telling me?"

Nigel allowed a thin smile. "Yes. And so I'd keep an eye on the watch. Your numbers are about to climb."

Clay was stunned.

"Oh, and those 400 New Testaments—" Nigel stopped. His eyes were alive, reflecting something wonderful. "More than half of them will be given to new believers who've *never* held God's Word before." He paused. "You have no idea how much good will be accomplished throughout the life of each of those copies. And you'll have played a role in all of it."

Clay barely heard any of what Nigel said about the New Testaments. Instead his mind was far-away in the slums of Dharavi. He'd been there on six occasions. He'd seen the grinding poverty of thousands of families struggling to survive on a dollar or two a day. He swallowed. He'd once ruthlessly laid-off three hundred of those people. He'd canned employees making a dollar seventy-five a day, in pursuit of even cheaper labor further north. His mind was immediately blank, his throat dry.

How merciful was God that he should be given an opportunity to finance an effort to bring the message of freedom and forgiveness to people who should hate him? Clay sagged against the Porsche and allowed his thoughts to praise his Creator. He felt like crying. *How much goodness is God willing to pour into my failed life?*

Nigel seemed perfectly content to wait as Clay closed his eyes and thanked God. He waited several minutes before quietly asking, "Still in the mood to invest your money?"

"Why—? Who needs money?"

"Hannah's struggling. Her car insurance is going to lapse at the end of the month. She won't have the cash to pay it."

"What about the ministry she's working with? Can't they—?" Clay blurted the words out, but knew he'd gladly pay anything to help her.

"Oh, they try. But Hannah's like another certain young man I know. Most of her support money gets gobbled up in restaurant meals and travel costs getting kids to safety. And the leadership of her ministry has just broken ground for a teen recovery center on one of the small islands off the coast. She's investing heavily into the construction of it."

Clay smiled. "How much does Hannah need?"

"Her insurance will be $684.90. So a nice, even seven hundred would be perfect." Nigel handed him a card. 'Children from the Dark' was boldly declared across the front. A mailing address for financial contributions to the ministry was handwritten on the back.

Clay kicked off his sneakers. He leaned against the kitchen counter and yanked out his checkbook.

Wrote in the sum of *Seven hundred dollars.* He signed it. Dated it. And then he wondered if he should include a note. But what would he say? He quickly discarded the note idea. He found an envelope, inserted the check, addressed it, and affixed a stamp.

It was ready to send.

Hannah Taylor. He sat and stared at her name on the envelope. Not for the first time did it cross his mind this might be Nigel bringing them together. Somehow that sounded like Nigel. He pulled on his sneakers, exited his condo and ran the two blocks to a postal box. He'd let Nigel do whatever he had planned. He certainly seemed to be a master at rescuing destroyed relationships.

Chapter Thirteen

Over the next few months Clay's life fell into a predictable rhythm. He was up and onto the beaches at four every morning. During the day he continued at the checkout counter of Circuits Circus. And then at night he usually studied his Bible, or returned to the beach for another time of prayer. At one point he threw out his television when he was conflicted about *if he should pray that night* or watch a sitcom. The television lost. It wound up in the dumpster.

At the end of each month, he'd pour over his financials and celebrate how much he could give away. He was now one of the sponsors for three young missionaries in Mumbai for thirty dollars each. Their ninety dollars was handled by automatic withdrawal on the first of every month. But after that it was open season on the rest of his available cash. He'd sit in view of a big map of Asia he'd tacked onto his wall, checkbook open, with five or six hundred dollars ready to change lives.

And he'd have a ball!

Two or three hundred dollars were often directed towards 'under-supported' missionaries, those who didn't have enough monthly sponsors to remain on the field. The thought of a missionary leaving the slums of Mumbai or a poor area in northern India because of a lack of financial support was enough to keep Clay awake at night. So he made them a priority. The rest of his cash went for Bibles, at three dollars a pop, New Testaments at fifty cents each, and single-sided, literature sheets the ministry referred to as tracts.

The text on a tract was usually a story describing the life of a fellow slum-dweller changed by faith in Jesus Christ, and then a short explanation of the Christian faith. They'd be written in the common language of the area. It was explained to Clay that across Asia tracts weren't casually discarded as they might have been in the West. Instead, they'd be passed around, often read by as many as ten people.

They were only half a penny each!

Most months he'd include at least fifty dollars for tracts, as they truly gave the biggest bang for the buck. He'd been shocked the first time he'd done the calculation. Fifty dollars invested in tracts allowed for *ten thousand* of them to be ready for circulation! Clay hoped that each of them might be shared with just a single friend or another family member. That brought the exposure of the Gospel message, within a population of devoted Hindus, some of whom may have never heard of Christ, to *twenty thousand* individuals! He dismissed the popular opinion that each tract might be read by eight or ten people. That bordered on crazy talk.

The watch seemed to disagree.

The LCD digits were hard to read now, rolling over in a steady, upward climb. Clay watched his number roll past 45,000 late one night on the beach. That, of course, spurred an enthusiastic praise celebration that went on until the early morning. 60,000 arrived six weeks later.

Yes, he had tough days when his mind and heart felt blank, when his prayers seemed empty. On those days he had to give himself grace and not push. He discovered, as had a lot of people before him, that writing the checks is easy. The hours in prayer are the real work.

But there were also the days when prayer came easily. He'd be checking sales through the register at Circuits Circus while he silently muttered the names of prisons across China. Or lifted up his three missionaries in Mumbai. He'd be asking they be filled with the love and peace of the Spirit, regardless of the difficulties they faced. Or asking that the tracts he'd supplied would find fertile soil. And that thousands of people would come to faith in Jesus.

Some nights, while listening to the slap of the waves against the shore, he'd stare at the numbers scrolling upward on the watch. He knew he'd once asked God, at the very beginning, to give him opportunities to share the Gospel throughout his lifetime. He always smiled at the memory, because he'd asked for a *specific* number of opportunities.

The number he'd asked for had been sixty.

Somewhere during this time, Clay chose a church. *Oakdale Baptist.* It was there he met some great people, enjoyed the pastor's sermons, and became a regular attender. It was a great place in every way, except one. The watch started *subtracting* numbers as soon as Clay pulled into the parking lot. He probably wouldn't have noticed, but one week he'd just pulled in, not having even turned off the ignition of the Porsche, his hand still resting on the steering wheel, when the watch went down three numbers.

He'd sat there, flabbergasted. *He was in the parking lot of a church!* It brought a flush to his cheeks, reminding him again of when his numbers had been in the negatives. He sat there, embarrassed, watching his numbers going down! Hundreds of other happy attenders were passing by all around him, and his numbers... were... going... down.

And it happened every Sunday. The watch subtracted numbers every time he pulled into the parking lot. Sometimes it was just four or five digits, but one weekend it was twelve. He visited a different church the next week, and there he lost nine. Six vanished within seconds of pulling into the parking lot. He'd immediately returned to Oakdale Baptist, and lost another three. They weren't huge losses, but it was evidence that something was definitely wrong.

He hadn't seen Nigel lately, but he knew these losses wouldn't have gone unnoticed by him. He was almost expecting a visit.

Clay was running late on a Sunday morning. He wolfed down a piece of toast, grabbed his Bible, and hustled out the door. The night before he'd had a productive time huddled against a tree at Spanish Banks, the only shelter available as a storm pounded the shoreline. The wind had ripped at him, the rain drenching him while he prayed. He hadn't cared, his numbers had been climbing steadily in the last few days. The display on the watch was approaching 80,000.

He was four blocks from Oakdale Baptist when he saw a lone figure standing near the curb. It was Nigel. Clay anchored the Porsche to a stop beside him and buzzed down the passenger side window. "Hey, Nigel. I'm in a hurry, jump in."

Nigel didn't respond. He obviously wasn't in a mood to be rushed. When he did move towards the car, his words were deliberate. "Clay, I need you to park your car here, and walk the rest of the way to church. Can you do that?"

"Uh, sure—I guess so." Clay pulled the Porsche to the curb, shut it off, and climbed out. He hesitated. *Was Nigel serious? Walk to church? Why?*

"Thank you for trusting me." Nigel smiled and leaned casually against the Porsche. And so, leaving Nigel still standing beside his car, Clay started hoofing it towards the church.

He was late, as he'd known he would be. It was just an average service and nothing happened to explain why Nigel had him walk. Nothing about the sermon jumped out as being directly related to *walking*. It seemed random, the whole 'walking to church' thing. But during the closing song, Clay noticed something. His number hadn't gone down. He hadn't lost even a single digit!

"Okay, what does it mean?" Clay was back beside the Porsche, facing Nigel. "Why do my numbers not go down if I *walk* to church?"

Nigel remained silent, delicately moving his fingers across the roofline of the Porsche.

"I can walk *every* Sunday if—" Clay stopped. And focused on Nigel's fingers. And their reflection in the glossy paint of his car.

It was quiet for a long time. Finally Nigel spoke, but it was in the quietest, saddest voice Clay had ever heard him use. "Think about your life now, Clay. What part doesn't fit?"

Clay immediately exploded in a hot defense of his Porsche. It literally flooded out of him! He pummeled Nigel's question with loud, angry accusations against other believers—*the whole lot of them*—judging him because of his car! He had the right to own whatever kind of car he damn well pleased. Nobody had the right to judge him! There was nothing wrong with having nice things. If he wanted to drive a Porsche, then he had every right to drive a Porsche!

He had a lot of ammunition and he unloaded all of it.

Nigel remained silent, his back to Clay now. "Are you done?"

"Yeah—"

Nigel turned around and his next words were barely audible. "Some of the kids and families you're trying to reach won't eat today. They won't… eat… today."

That torpedoed every one of Clay's arguments. He felt foolish.

"Clay, this isn't some kind of middle-class parlor game I've invited you to. There will be real losers at the end of this, and they'll be lost forever." He paused, allowing Clay to consider such a scenario. "But that's not what the watch was signifying when it subtracted those numbers."

"No?"

"No. The watch adds numbers in recognition of your good works for God's glory. When you move people closer to, or build them up in, a relationship with Christ, it adds numbers. But it also subtracts digits when your life moves individuals *further* from that relationship. It *subtracts* digits when your life encourages people to embrace the thinking of the world, when it encourages people to live for themselves. Do you understand?"

There was a long silence until Clay sighed. "Yeah, I get it. A Porsche does that." He knew he'd purchased the Porsche as a symbol of his elite status. It was the ultimate look-at-me toy.

"Actually, luxury vehicles, all of them, when seen in a church parking lot, are hurting people. They're a stumbling block to other believers. Because *those* people, people of lesser means, will want one. And so you're building an unholy lust for *stuff* in other people. And suddenly, their giving money to rescue the world's poor takes a back seat. Giving, to build the kingdom of God, is derailed." Nigel paused.

"Lots of things are like that. Fancy homes. Extravagant weddings. North American culture thrives on it, and the church is being destroyed by it."

That night, in his kitchen, Clay had a good old fashioned, no-holds-barred, interrogation of himself. *What's the most important thing in the world to me? And am I willing to sacrifice everything to accomplish it?* Within minutes, the Porsche was pushed off its rather lofty pedestal into its proper place in Clay's thinking.

But rather than feeling like he was losing something, he actually felt like he'd taken a huge step *forward.* He'd chosen to give something up, in pursuit of God. It felt good. He imagined such a moment was worthy of being celebrated, so he raced the three blocks to the beach.

A week later, a thirties-something young lady arrived to Clay's condo with a well-dressed boyfriend. She worked into the conversation, at least four times, that she was a thoracic surgeon and this was a reward to herself for her hard work. Clay simply smiled and showed her the Porsche. She was a terrible negotiator and paid the full asking price, without hesitation. He went with them to a bank and then to an insurance place. Within two hours she owned a Porsche Carrera. And Clay was aboard the bus, heading home.

Three days later he bought a three-year old, Honda Civic.

Jim Patterson Honda was a busy dealership. Clay had cash and the little silver Civic was in immaculate shape. Ownership papers and insurance were handled efficiently. The salesman handed Clay the keys and shook his hand.

"Mr. Rawlings, I've got someone putting on the plates and topping up the gas tank, right now. He'll deliver your new car to you outside the main entrance." Another handshake and the salesman returned to his cubby-hole office. Clay went outside to wait for his vehicle.

The Civic rolled up and Clay approached the driver's side. But the dealership employee didn't exit. Instead, the window buzzed down and Nigel grinned up at him. "C'mon, let's go for a ride."

Clay went to the passenger side, got in, and they raced away. He'd been pleasantly surprised at the snappy performance of the little coupe earlier, but with Nigel at the wheel it responded like a true hotrod.

"Okay, let's review. You got $42,000 for the Porsche." Nigel downshifted as they accelerated past a tractor-trailer rig. "This Civic cost you $8500."

"Yeah, so I came out ahead by $33,500. A nice little chunk of change." Clay laughed, surprised he wasn't missing the Porsche at all.

"Any idea what you might want to do with that money?"

"Not a clue." Clay looked across at Nigel.

Nigel smiled. "It's probably time for you to meet some people." He wrenched the wheel and there was tire squeal as they roared into a 7-11 convenience store. Nigel shut the ignition off, pulled out a card and handed it to Clay. An address was handwritten with a time and date. "You'll like them. And you're definitely one of them."

Clay had a lot of questions, but he knew there'd be no answers.

Nigel stepped from the vehicle. "You can drive. I'm getting a chocolate bar." With that, Nigel headed towards the 7-11.

Clay went around the car and got into the driver's seat. He didn't wait. Instead, he just drove away. He knew Nigel wouldn't be returning from the 7-11. He was probably already in Argentina or Algeria. Or Alaska. Somewhere with another client.

Saturday morning. Clay was in the fast lane heading east out of the city. He passed the exits for a dozen suburbs. He kept driving. Soon cows peeking out from behind barbwire were watching the little Civic race past. He exited from the freeway and most of what surrounded him now was farmland separated by thick stands of Douglas fir.

Where am I going, Nigel? Clay mentally asked the question, but knew the drive would be worth it. He kept going.

The address was for a campsite.

Clay stopped the car and stared at the entrance sign. *Kitty Coleman Municipal Campground.* No other information was given. There weren't any 'Triple A' or 'Good Sam' endorsements in evidence. In fact, there wasn't anything to encourage travelers to choose this location. It certainly didn't look like much. The entrance was pot-holed gravel, and the road disappeared into a dark forest of trees.

He pulled out the card again, thinking it might be a mistake. *No, this is it.* Okay, so he needed to find number 22. Clay had assumed the number indicated a condo or townhouse unit. He certainly hadn't expected a site in a campground. It seemed weird.

The campsites were a pleasant distance from each other, surrounded by trees, and nicely graded. But if there were any electrical or water hookups, Clay couldn't see them. And through the trees he was sure he saw what looked like outhouses. *Ooh boy.*

There were six vehicles already parked at number 22. Clay pulled to the edge of the gravel and stopped. A young girl and boy barely missed taking off his mirror as they went racing past on bicycles. Their younger, blonde haired sister, maybe three or four years old, rolled past on a tricycle. Clay took an extra glance in the mirror before stepping out.

"Ya got a watch, too, Mister?" The girl and boy had returned on their bikes.

Clay hesitated. "A watch? What d'ya mean?" He'd never told anybody about the watch, and now he faced a curious eight-year old and her younger brother.

"One of them fancy watches like Nigel gave my dad."

Nigel. Hearing an eight-year old mention his name floored Clay. "Uh, yeah. I've—I've got one of those watches." He said it quietly, hoping his voice wasn't carrying to other campsites.

"C'mon. They're this way." The younger brother had laid down his bicycle and was heading past the other vehicles. Clay took a quick survey of site 22. At the center of the site sat an older travel trailer, probably a twenty footer. A large canvas tent draped in blue plastic filled the rest of the available ground.

In fifteen hesitant steps Clay was pushing past the blue plastic and entering the tent.

"Hi. My name's Clay." Six men and seven women looked up from cheap folding chairs. They all rose to shake his hand. He hesitantly added, "I've—I've got one of those watches from Nigel." Immediately there was a collective laugh, introductions were made, and then questions arrived about how he'd met Nigel. Clay's answer resulted in a lot of nodding and them each adding their own stories.

The group was made up of people from all over the province. They met several times a year. Gary and Pam were hosting, and yes, they'd chosen to move into a travel trailer in a campsite with their three kids. That got a good-hearted laugh. The kids were homeschooled. The trailer was borrowed.

Gary was an electrician with BC Tel, which would later become Telus, Vancouver's phone company. Seven months earlier, he and Pam had moved out of their rented home in Surrey, wanting to be involved financially in one of the largest, illegal shipments of Bibles into communist China, ever. Pam and Gary both talked excitedly about what they considered to be the greatest decision of their lives.

"Rent on our house was eight hundred a month. Heat and hot water added another seventy. Add a few more dollars for insurance. The total was pushing thirty-four bucks a day. Thirty-four dollars *every single day*. In contrast, this place costs us seven." Gary laughed, as though the decision had been a no-brainer.

"Our contribution to the shipment of Bibles into China was fourteen thousand dollars. We sent the money through a group in Holland." He smiled and met his wife's eyes. "It seemed like a lot of money at the time. But within a month the numbers on the watch started spinning. We couldn't even see numbers. It was just a blur." He slowly held up his watch so Clay could see it.

Clay could barely believe it. The digits were still rapidly scrolling upward. Gary and Pam, living with their kids in a borrowed trailer, in a campsite, were approaching a million.

971,033…971,493…971,998…972,443…

"So, do you pray?" The question blurted out of Clay before he could stop it.

That got a laugh. "Yeah Gary, do you *pray*?" Several others asked, good-naturedly.

Another glance at his wife. "Site number 41 is empty most nights. I sit at the picnic table with my Bible and a flashlight. I bought a Gortex rain suit at the beginning, for the rainy nights. I usually start about nine—"

"And he's often not back to the trailer until one." Pam finished.

Now Clay truly felt he was among people who understood him.

They went around the circle, each of them telling their own version of meeting Nigel and then of how their relationship with the Lord Jesus Christ had taken off. Clay noticed many of them shared a similar story—they'd been zealous for Christ early in their lives, and had then walked away. Or somewhere in their relationship with Christ they'd been reduced to simple church attenders where they'd become satisfied to just follow the ways of the world.

It had been Nigel pursuing them that changed everything!

Kim, a slim blonde, had been an exotic dancer before meeting Nigel during the first week of a drug rehab program. She was now the director of the women's program at the Kamloops Mission. Her number was in the low sixty-thousands. She told Clay quietly her number when Nigel first gave her the watch had been twenty-nine thousand into the negatives.

She too, had learned to pray.

Chapter Fourteen

Clay looked around. He was sitting on a plastic folding chair inside a canvas tent having been accepted into a close-knit group who were investing their lives and their cash trying to build the kingdom of God. He allowed himself a quick glance over to where Pam sat, her youngest daughter now nestled into her lap. Pam was mid-thirties, a mom to three kids. *What had it been like for her to leave the normalcy of a house and neighborhood? To leave all that behind?* Clay couldn't imagine. He guessed none of her friends would have understood. He smiled. Of course, now having numbers in the high 900,000's probably took some of the sting out of having to use an outhouse.

Rodney and Ethel were in their late-seventies and had the leathery skin of Arizona farmers. They were both sixty-eight when Nigel arrived into the

Nickel Rock Casino just outside Calgary. He'd found Ethel at the blackjack table where, as she did most nights, she was losing buckets of cash. Rodney was nearby, pulling an oxygen bottle, complaining loudly to anybody who'd listen that he was dying.

It'd been thirty-four years since he and Ethel were active with the Billy Graham Evangelistic Association. They'd been part of the advance team for crusades in nineteen cities. That ended when a corporate headhunter recruited Rodney to a Fortune 500 company and the high-rolling, self-centered lifestyle that went with it. They'd abandoned the church not long after.

And now? Now they were supplying the cash for Chilean believers to build Bible schools and to run children's programs and outreaches across Santiago and Valparaiso, two of the larger cities in Chile. They spoke excitedly about the opportunities in South America like third graders on a fieldtrip.

They didn't mention how deep their financial help went, but the watch on Ethel's wrist was slowly counting upward past two and a half million.

Other than Rodney and Ethel, all the other couples had average incomes. Cement plant workers, plumbers, clerks and laborers. Normal people who'd simply chosen to live on less and to give the rest away. They drove older vehicles and had down-graded their housing. They took modest vacations or by-passed that expense all together.

They'd simply walked away from the thinking of the culture that surrounded them.

And instead, they were supporting nationals who ministered to their own people as pastors and missionaries, in far flung countries like Cambodia and Namibia. Honduras and Vietnam. They'd paid for water wells to be drilled across Asia and Africa, and supplied the financing for brothel outreach in some of the worst hellholes on the planet. And their numbers were rapidly spiraling upwards.

Clay sat and listened to the conversations around him. They'd each learned to pray and they all agreed that was where the big numbers came from. But they also celebrated being *partners* with their Christian brothers and sisters across the globe.

It was a wonderful day.

The rather squalor headquarters of 'Children from the Dark' was actually two rooms on the third floor of a welfare hotel. It sat near the center of the Downtown Eastside. No elevator. The homeless were often found asleep in the stairwells. One of its rooms didn't have a window. The other one rewarded its occupants with a view of a brick wall seven feet away. It wasn't great real estate, but Vancouver isn't an especially affordable city.

Hannah was on the phone when the mail arrived.

Val Burton, a twenty-two year old whom Hannah had found living in the burnt out remains of a torched Taco Bell, plopped four envelopes onto Hannah's desk. Val was one of six interns. Hannah had arranged financial support for her through a variety of churches. Val pulled up a chair, kicked off her sneakers, and rested her bare feet on the edge of Hannah's desk.

The call was from Hannah's dad, and the conversation was an old one. Hannah rolled her eyes, and Val quietly laughed. He was trying to talk her down from what he referred to as 'the ledge'. Working with street kids. Journeying into alleys and other dangerous places. He was a chartered accountant in a respected firm. He was *somebody*. When was Hannah going to start taking life seriously and settle down with a profitable career? How was she even paying her bills? Was she still asking strangers for money every month like a street beggar? That was no way for his daughter to live. Blah, blah, blah.

Hannah listened without comment. He was coming a bit too close to the truth. She knew her car insurance was due in two more days. She also knew she didn't have the money. She and Val and the other interns prayed about it every morning, but so far nothing. Her other bills would gobble up everything that usually arrived to her account. Her dad continued to bend her ear until she ended the call with a curt, "Love you."

Val laughed out loud. Hannah breathed out in frustration. And then, pushing past it, she reached for the mail. On the top was an envelope from the ministry's accountant addressed to *Miss Hannah Taylor*. She ripped it open and a summary of the month's donations entered into her personal account fell into her hand. She scanned it quickly.

The total was higher than usual.

She scanned down the list of donations from family, friends, and a few churches. Twenty-five dollars from one. Fifty from another. A hundred. Another fifty. Seventy-five. Another fifty. There were a dozen other donations. Until there, on the very last line, was a name that shouldn't have been there.

Clay Rawlings. $700.

A thousand thoughts ripped through her mind at once. Angry, bitter clouds of memory. But something else swept that aside. *How could Clay have known she needed seven hundred dollars for car insurance?* He could have written *any* amount, but instead he'd come within fifteen dollars on the high side of what she needed. Fifteen. And the timing? *Whoa.* But she pushed her conflicted emotion and the questions aside and instead jumped from her desk and waved the sheet above her head in celebration.

"The Lord provided car insurance! Yessss!" Hannah danced around the office for a few seconds before letting the sheet flutter to the desk. Val had jumped to her feet to join her celebrations, and she scooped it up, wanting to see how such a miracle could have occurred.

Val scanned the list quickly and an unreadable expression arrived to her face. “You know *Clay Rawlings?*”

Hannah smirked. “He’s an arrogant ass from a different time in my life.”

“Arrogant ass—?”

Hannah’s celebrations stopped. “He lost like a billion dollars and—what?”

Val stared at her. “About five months ago I helped a guy transport a seventeen-year old kid who’d been beaten in a street fight, to the airport. So we get to the WestJet counter and this guy’s ready to purchase this kid’s ticket. But some big honcho from WestJet shows up and refuses to take his money. Says that it’d be a privilege for the company to deliver the kid home. Seems this was the sixth at-risk youth this guy had befriended and sent home on WestJet. He’s got quite a reputation among the airlines. And the stories they told me—” Val whistled. “Whoa. This guy’s as good as you at rescue.”

“Oh yeah, and who was it?”

“Hannah, it was Clay Rawlings.”

The color drained from Hannah’s face as she stared at Val.

Clay roamed the beach, still replaying what he'd seen and heard at the campsite. His prayers were scattered, his mind distracted. He smiled as he walked. *Nigel sent me to the campsite to see the possibilities. The possibilities of what's out there if I let go of my financial future.*

A light wind had come up and seagulls rode the air currents above him. He laughed and burst into a sprint along the edge of the water, his sneakers barely keeping dry. Was he willing to let go? Everything within him screamed out yes!

It wasn't like any other phone call he'd ever made. He dialed a number to somewhere in Memphis. A pleasant woman with a definite twang in her voice answered. "This is the offices of GraceUnfathomable. I'm Melinda, how may I direct your call?"

Clay hesitated, not entirely sure. "Uh, I—I wanted to speak with somebody about giving you guys some money."

"Honey, we'd love to have you sponsor a missionary monthly. Or if you just give me your address I can send you a list of items that are popular to give money towards. Bicycles and chickens. Bibles. Stuff like that."

"Uh, I think I want to make a bigger donation than that."

There was some dead air for a second. "How much were you thinking?"

"Thirty-three thousand dollars."

"Yes sir, let me connect you with someone." The twang vanished, immediately replaced with the crisp urgency of a professional.

Barely a moment passed before a husky voice came on. He introduced himself as Malcolm somebody, and asked Clay's name. He asked where Clay was calling from and seemed genuinely interested in Canada. He was very good at putting people at ease. They chitchatted for a moment about the beauty of Vancouver and then he made a smooth transition towards what GraceUnfathomable was doing currently. He asked about the amount Clay was interested in donating, and Clay repeated the number. And then he asked if Clay had anything specific in mind for such an amount. He didn't, except he wanted to touch as many lives as possible.

Something changed in Malcolm's voice. He liked that answer.

"Mr. Rawlings, we currently have nine Bible schools across northern India. They are the backbone of everything we do. To reach the almost billion people of India we hope to build *more* schools. Every Bible school trains hundreds of young people whom we're preparing to go into the most resistant areas of northern India where the Gospel of Jesus Christ has not yet been preached. The schools prepare them for the persecution they'll find as they travel from village to village. And for enduring the hard missionary lifestyle." He paused.

"Mr. Rawlings, we've been in prayer about building a Bible school outside the city of Raipur. The land is twenty-five thousand dollars. We'd love to accept just the twenty-five we need for the land. Or if you wished to, you could put the rest towards the construction costs of the school."

Clay had expected a bit of hard selling, but it never arrived. Clay had some questions about the number of students, and the length of the program, and Malcolm answered his questions without any push towards a decision. It seemed they were wrapping up when Clay blurted out, "Malcolm, can you tell me about *one* of your students who's on the field."

He could hear Malcolm lean back in his office chair, choosing a student to discuss. Within a few minutes, *Mr. Rawlings* became *Clay*, and Malcolm had him journeying into Hindu villages alongside a recent graduate named Dalaja. They talked together for more than an hour.

Clay wrote the check for $33,500 just minutes after he got off the phone. And then he sat and stared at it. *Nobody would understand me doing this.* He smiled. His stomach wasn't in knots. He wasn't fighting to hold back a few dollars. He actually wished he'd sold the Porsche for more. He looked at the dollar amount. This would be the greatest investment of his life! In three years the Bible school would be graduating students. A hundred more Dalajas would be journeying across the dusty plains of India, sharing the message of freedom and salvation with some of the most exploited people on the planet. And a hundred Dalajas the next year, and the year after that. Clay pulled out a calculator and jumped to ten years in the future, if each graduating student shared Christ with just *fifty* people in their lifetime.

A number appeared on the calculator. Clay whistled. Okay, now he was stacking up gold bars!

He dropped the envelope in the mail slot the next morning. Sleep had been impossible after writing the check and so he'd spent most of the night on the beach. The watch was busy, rolling over steadily. He looked at the numbers.

94,083…94,348…94,999…95,418…96,078…

It was a great pace. But Clay he knew it'd be a lot busier in three years. He laughed and fired up the Civic. His job was waiting.

Actually, his job *wasn't* waiting. He pulled into the parking lot of Circuits Circus, and everything had fallen apart. The place was chaos. The entire staff was outside on the sidewalk. Sheets of plywood had been hastily secured across every entrance, and bulky security guards roamed everywhere. Each employee, as they arrived, was handed a package by a severe looking woman. The store had been closed by its American owners. All employees had been terminated. The inventory would be auctioned off at a later date. She didn't smile or apologize. Instead she looked more threatening than any of the security staff. People milled around for an hour and then slowly wandered away. It was over.

Chapter Fifteen

Clay staggered home from Circuits Circus and was forced to take a hard look at his situation. He knew he'd given away most of his money. There wasn't a big bank balance available to help him weather a layoff. His doubts immediately grabbed the stage in his mind and urged him to put a 'stop payment' on the check to GraceUnfathomable. Common sense trumpeted this as the only responsible course of action. Or could he not just call them, apologize, and *reduce* the amount? A couple thousand less would make all of this easier.

But from somewhere deep inside, a quiet little voice within him was battling back. *This is a test. A test of your faith. You've been declaring as you walk the lengths of those beaches that you trust God; that you've placed your faith in Him! When it was easy you made bold statements of trusting Him—well now the tide has arrived to sweep away your sandcastle. So now is the time, Clay Rawlings! Now is the time when you must stand firm!*

It wasn't crazy talk, and he knew it. Hadn't he prayed exactly *that* for the believers in the prisons of Asia? So right there he sat down and asked God to fill him with the Holy Spirit, and for him to be enabled to stand firm. He'd just sent a check big enough to do some powerful work across India. In three years a hundred eager students would be sharing the message of freedom all across India. A smile unfurled across his face at that thought.

He would not retreat!

Trusting God, he would go *forward*. This layoff would become a rock pulled from the middle of the Jordan River for him.

And it became exactly that. He never missed a payment for his three missionaries. He sent the money for a thousand New Testaments and sixty-thousand tracts, which were celebrated unlike anything he'd sent before. He wrote those checks during a second week of eating nothing but instant noodles and peanut butter toast, but it was one of the best times of his life.

"I will trust you, Lord." He whispered it as he tweaked his resume. He whispered it as he made photocopies. Whispered it while pounding the pavement. And again and again he'd whisper it when he'd feel like an unwelcome guest in the fashionable offices of firms across the city, as he handed out resumes. He was granted several initial interviews, but nobody invited him back.

Clay suddenly had more time for studying his Bible, and of course, with no job to fill his schedule his prayer time on the beaches often ended by welcoming in the morning. He'd sit there, staring at the golden shimmer of the sun playing amongst the waves, and watch his numbers.

126,045…126,243…126,604…127,261…

Whatever else was happening, the Spirit of God was active within the believers of Asia.

Clay visited Gary and Pam several times at the campsite. They'd sit outside in folding chairs, wrapped into heavy jackets if the weather was decent. If not, he and Gary would go to a coffee shop. They were wonderful times for Clay, and he never left before they'd all prayed together. So what he'd whispered throughout the week would be almost shouted as the little Civic raced home. "I will. I will *trust you*, Lord!"

Midway through the second month, some unemployment benefits arrived in an official envelope. Clay sent away $130 for a missionary bicycle and enough for another three hundred Bibles. And then, on the last day of the month, his funds now dangerously low, he sent another $100 addressed for Hannah.

On day 67 of being unemployed, he got a call.

Larry somebody. *High-Q Robotics* was looking for software designers. They were a small firm, but miles ahead of their competitors in the manufacturing industry. Larry repeated this several times as though everybody else was still struggling to understand the cotton gin. Yes, he'd followed the tragic tale of Nasty Dogs, and had a dozen ideas that could have saved the company. He was a fast talker, completely lacking a social filter.

Clay met him at a well-groomed business park in Richmond, a neighboring suburb. Larry invited him inside and then stood back. Clay simply stared. It was like a precursor to the hundreds of dot.com startups that would soon arrive. The work attire was casual, matching the free-flowing, open workspace. Groups crowded together, talking excitedly, different designs being tried, rejected, something else attempted, more excited ideas spilling onto a dozen computer monitors. Clay remembered this from Nasty Dogs, the adrenalin rush of bringing out a new product, trying to be first onto the market.

He would've worked here for free.

In the end he didn't have to. Larry offered forty-two thousand a year. Clay accepted. It was December 16, nine days before Christmas.

It doesn't snow in Vancouver on Christmas, unlike most Canadians cities. Instead, it's usually raining. Clay pulled the Civic to the curb outside his parent's place, the hand-set cobblestones wet from a recent downpour. Their home was in an upscale development designed to showcase the lifestyles of the wealthy. Big, custom homes, built on top of one another, no expense spared, like spoiled teenagers trying to outdo each other at prom. The outside of the house was bathed in light. Clay knew a professional had put up the Christmas lights. It was an ugly neighborhood competition that had raged for years. He shook his head and went inside.

The house was full of relatives. Not a good thing. Most of them had been quite vocal when Nasty Dogs was being dragged through bankruptcy, and with his recent unemployment Clay knew he'd probably gotten a lot more negative airtime. He had only a few quiet minutes with his mom, alone in the kitchen, when she directed him into the living room. A younger cousin immediately faced him.

"So what happened to the Porsche? I saw ya pull up in that Japanese econo-box." That brought all the other conversations to a stop. Every person was looking at him.

Clay hesitated. "I—I got rid of it. Picked up the Civic a month ago. It's better." He didn't make an effort to explain how it was better. It wasn't hard to translate the look on every face. *Only a dumbass trades a Porsche for a Civic.* Clay returned to the kitchen to grab a Pepsi. His mom was still primping the turkey as though it were attending a coronation. His father was leaning against the counter, a wine glass in hand.

"You lost the Porsche." It wasn't a question. Howard Rawlings was a man who cut things into two categories: winners and losers. Clay had been a winner when he had a yacht. Now he was a loser. The Porsche had been the last evidence of Clay being a winner. No yardage would be gained by explaining.

His mom aimed a look at his dad and he backed off. "So, tell me about High-Q Robotics. It sounds interesting." Clay appreciated the change in direction. So they discussed the speed of progress in the world of software development, and the direction High-Q was heading. The software used in manufacturing isn't very sexy, but his father listened intently. For Howard, everything was about one thing. Profits. Hard cold cash. So Clay allowed the conversation to head in that direction. How much would High-Q make after taxes and overhead this year? Next year? Clay hedged high on the numbers, but his father was pleased. His son was back in the saddle. He'd be cruising the skies in a Gulfstream 320 again, soon.

His father poured himself more wine. Clay had another Pepsi. And then he tried something he hadn't completely thought out. He told his parents about the at-risk youth he'd built relationships with on the streets. He didn't tell them about the money he'd spent on them. Instead he made it sound as though he had a wealthy team standing with him, paying the costs.

Clay's family had never been the kind to emphasize helping the unfortunate, but both his mom and dad seemed impressed. His mom asked several questions about Clay's safety among 'those people' and he weaved an answer that downplayed it. And then, because it seemed like a natural opening, he told them about the freedom he'd found in Jesus Christ. He gave God the credit for his new-found abilities with at-risk youth, and for the peace he experienced in places some people would consider dangerous.

The room was immediately quiet, a stunned silence overcoming both parents. Suddenly his dad had an urgent phone call to make, and Clay's mom needed to get the turkey onto the table.

Clay wandered into the living room to face more criticism. But he smiled. He'd breached the subject of his new *spiritual* relationship with his parents. It was a start.

The rest of the Christmas celebrations were about what he'd always known. Big and noisy, with elaborate presents traded among people whom Clay knew could barely stand each other. He'd brought some modest gifts that again signaled his falling status, and there was a comment made about how meager Clay's unemployment benefits must be. That got some hearty laughter.

About ten-thirty the bickering had started among family members, and he left. The rain had stopped. Clay strapped into the Civic, dialed in a radio station that was playing Christmas music, and raced away. He knew his Christian brothers and sisters in Indonesia certainly weren't exchanging gifts in an over-decorated home. It was time to hit the beach.

High-Q Robotics turned out to be everything Larry had promised. It was exciting work, with a great team. Clay loved it. The hours were long; dinner was often a sandwich at eight-thirty or nine. He'd eat while hammering out code at his workstation, but everything about it invigorated him. And of course the higher wages were immediately thrown into action.

He sent $500 for under-supported missionaries, secretly hoping that teams might be descending upon the slums of Shiliguri. Two hundred bucks was sent to Hannah, still without a note. He'd lie awake at night and dream about what he'd write if he *did* include a note. His thoughts weren't especially realistic. He'd fall asleep mumbling out long and windy marriage proposals.

At the end of January he paid for the drilling of a water well in northern India. That was $1,000. He'd read the stories of what Third-world communities endured to supply their daily need for water. A five gallon bucket of water weighs thirty-five pounds, a rather heavy amount for a child, or for a slender woman, to carry upon her head. Especially when carried for miles. And the water was often pulled from a muddy slough where animal excrement and toxic effluent from industry flowed into it. Untold numbers of childhood deaths had been attributed to unclean water.

Worse yet, across India any clean source of water would be off-limits to the Dalits, the Untouchables. They were strictly banned from using community pumps. They'd be beaten if they disputed it because Hindu caste had declared them worth less than the mongrel dogs that ran along the streets. So the people Clay cared the most about, the three hundred million of India's poorest people would be forced to drink the worst of whatever water was available.

GraceUnfathomable offered an inexpensive solution to providing water for some of these exploited people. For his thousand dollars they'd have a well drilled on the property of one of the churches and have a manually-operated pump installed. Being on church property, the water from the well would be made available to everyone, regardless of caste. It was a powerful testimony of God's concern for the poor. And into the concrete base, a message was stamped from John 4.

> Jesus says:
> 'Whoever drinks of this water will thirst again, but whoever drinks of the water that I give him will never thirst. The water that I give him will become in him a fountain of water rising up into eternal life.'

Clay liked that. He stared at the check before he sent it. He was already celebrating the hundreds of opportunities this well would create for the church on whose land it'd be drilled. Clean water, free for everyone! Clean water, supplied by the God of the Christians. Would clean water pumped from his drilled well lead someone to discover the salvation found in Jesus Christ? It was exciting to think about.

Clay bowed his head. "Lord God, who am I that I should have such an opportunity as this?"

At the offices of 'Children from the Dark', a lone figure still sat in her chair. It was late. Hannah would've usually headed home hours earlier. Her shoes were off, her feet resting against a file cabinet. She sat staring at her list of monthly donations. Again, another two hundred dollars from Clay. He hadn't included a note. She shook her head. She'd done some digging since Val had told the story about WestJet. She'd met kids now, hardened kids, who'd verified the WestJet story. An employee at the ticket counter for Air Canada had also been eager to talk about the young guy who was paying for street kids to get home. Hannah quickly hung up when she'd asked for his name.

She breathed out. Clay had blazed quite a trail. She'd met some teens, hard-core street survivors under the Burrard Street Bridge, who'd talked about Clay like they were fraternity brothers.

What happened to the Clay Rawlings who'd once paraded a platoon of half-naked bimbos onto national television while half sauced? This wasn't him. This was *definitely* not him. This guy was showing some serious character. And compassion towards others.

Hannah looked down at the notepaper in front of her. She'd promised herself she'd write a quick 'thank you' note to Clay for the two hundred bucks. A quick note. Twelve words or less. *Crap.* She couldn't do it. She just couldn't. He might be approaching sainthood, but there was still too much baggage between them. She slammed the blank notepaper and the pen back into a drawer, pulled on her shoes, and fled the office.

The wind and rains of February pounded the beaches of Vancouver mercilessly. During an especially bad storm, Clay abandoned his morning routine on the beach and headed towards the Granville Street area. He couldn't admit the truth to himself that it had nothing to do with the storm. He'd made the switch wanting to be in an area where Hannah spent her time. That sounded so pathetic, like he was a lovesick teenager. So he told himself this was a better location to pray for the kids being targeted by Children from the Dark. That it made sense to re-locate to a place that reminded him of what they were enduring every day. It was a lie, but he wanted to believe it.

He wedged himself into a few square inches of dry shelter off an alley behind one of Vancouver's youth shelters. And there, he began his prayer time.

There was something magical about such a location. But not just for praying for at-risk kids. Every door into the alley was reinforced with heavy steel, badly dented, with deep gouges where serious attempts had been made to breach whatever was behind the doors.

It felt like a prison. Like a crumbling, Third-world prison.

And so that morning, after praying for Hannah, he prayed for the church leaders and pastors in prisons across Asia as though he himself were imprisoned. He could see them in his mind, and hear them in his heart.

His numbers jumped by almost eighteen hundred that morning.

Those were the good numbers. Unfortunately, the watch had *two* sets of numbers. And sitting there, in the darkness of an alley, the minutes of his life were spiraling down in a blur. He was there for two hours. During that time he lost five and a half years of his life!

Clay tried to push past the loss of minutes. There wasn't anything he could do about it, so he forced himself to not think about it. Instead, he kept his focus on praising God for the incredible work He was obviously doing across Asia, and in the lives of homeless youth in Vancouver.

Clay moved around after that. He began to seek out the most hardened areas of the city as his places for prayer. Darkened alleys and loading docks. Under bridges and near the homeless camps that sprang up and disappeared constantly around the city.

In these places he didn't dance or spin. The dark places didn't inspire such outward displays of celebration. Instead what these places released within him was compassion. The smells and sounds of destroyed lives are easy to find in Vancouver, like every other urban setting across the globe.

And so slowly Clay became known in the tough areas.

In February he reduced his spending to all but the most basic necessities. He was able to send $600 to India for Bibles. He'd heard they were needed for pastors. And then he drilled another well. That was another thousand.

In March, storm season ended and the beaches were quiet, but his morning routine remained in the dark places of the city. He didn't return to the beaches. Another two hundred pastors were supplied with a Bible. Four bicycles were sent, to speed along missionaries who'd previously been walking. He wanted to drill another well, but car insurance came due.

The number on the watch continued to climb. It was now increasing at a pace that didn't allow him to know what numbers aligned with which activity. It seemed to speed up when he was praying in the alleys, but even that was hard to be sure.

He'd often listen to the sounds of the city during those early mornings and wonder what God was accomplishing in the prisons of China. Or what the messages on those single page tracts were accomplishing amongst the poor of Mumbai. And how many villages had been visited aboard one of the bicycles?

203,224…204,743…205,839…

One morning it was dry, but the rains were threatening. Clay had wandered east into the Downtown Eastside, the worst part of Vancouver. He sat against the exit doors of the Cobalt, a seedy strip club. He'd been there about forty minutes, his head bowed, when he looked up towards a dark, metal-clad wall directly across from him. A number was written, very clearly, in white chalk. It was easily visible in a narrow sliver of light. $54,225.21. Beneath it, Nigel had signed his name.

Clay smiled. He knew what it was. It was the amount locked into his account with Thirteen44 Global Investments, waiting to be celebrated for all eternity. But even as he sat there staring at it, the rains descended in a fury, washing the number away.

Message received—keep going. Clay bowed his head again.

In April, the *Province* newspaper did a lengthy article about the work of Children from the Dark. Alongside it was a low-light picture of Hannah sitting in an alley. Clay's mind turned to mush when he saw it. The tagline under the photo read: '*Hannah Taylor. A powerful example for our entire city.*' Clay read the article and most of it was about Hannah's rescue of a fifteen-year old under the Oak Street Bridge. A known glue sniffer, the young man wasn't breathing when she found him. Clay cut out the picture from the paper and taped it onto his fridge. He looked at it a dozen times a day. And then a week after the article appeared, he sent her $300.

This time he had to fight himself to not include a note.

One Friday he took a call from a local gaming software company. They offered him a contract job that had to be completed over the weekend.

An impatient client somewhere was waiting. It gobbled up his weekend, but paid him $700. Clay added another five hundred to those dollars, and that was turned into New Testaments to be shared somewhere in India. Another thousand was sent for under-supported missionaries.

And suddenly it was end of April. Income tax time. And so for the first time, somebody other than Nigel would have a record of the amount Clay was funneling onto the streets of Vancouver and sending to Asia. He entered his income on line 3 of the federal income tax form. He'd earned $23,841.61 in 1995, but with the sale of the Porsche he'd given away *more* than that. Halfway down the second page was line 46. It was for charitable contributions. He added them up and filled in the number.

His tax burden fell to zero!

That seemed so odd to Clay. He'd once had entire divisions of high-priced accountants working around the clock trying to lower Nasty Dog's tax bill. He'd been desperate to claw back as much of his precious profits as possible. He swallowed. He could remember throwing a chair through one of the floor to ceiling windows at his place in the Bahamas in an angry outburst at tax time.

He stared at the last line on his income tax form. It was for a refund! The government was giving him *all* of his income tax money back. *Whoa.* He sat there for some long minutes before yanking on his sneakers and racing for the door. Eight minutes later he was on the beach. Sure, the filth of the alleys was great for prayer, but for celebrations, especially a celebration to worship the God of the universe, no place was better than the sand and spray of a beach.

Chapter Sixteen

Some homeless camps are situated in highly visible places. The spot will have been chosen as a protest and so the lawn of a federal building is a popular choice. State or provincial law courts are good. Any publicly owned land with enough passer-by traffic to attract the media works. Such locations are chosen to get the protesters onto the 6 o'clock news. So they'll pick a place where you could land a Bell Ranger helicopter, in case a political heavyweight gets involved. And of course, enough space for when the national networks show up with their semi-trailer command posts.

The homeless camp under the Ironworker's Memorial Bridge was four grungy tents barely gripping onto the muddy bank of the Fraser River. It wasn't trying to make a protest statement. It was a collection of six people in various states of addiction, alcoholism, and mental illness. To round out their little community were three dogs of unknown pedigree. The camp had been there for almost five weeks. No news crews so far.

Clay scrambled under the rusted chain link fence that surrounded the area. He carefully lifted the six coffees through the opening and readjusted his backpack. Entering a homeless camp is easy, but the introductions go smoother if you bring some kind of gift. Clay had stopped at the McDonald's on Hastings and picked up eight breakfast sandwiches. And hash browns. He'd been to the camp a week earlier. The hash browns had been a hit.

It was early, but there were six people sitting around a small fire, wrapped into blankets and torn sleeping bags. They'd been quiet the last time he'd visited, subdued, each of them fighting an unseen battle against personal demons. It wasn't like that this time. Instead, a seventh person was telling an animated story that had them all laughing like they probably hadn't in a long time. They were clapping, rocking from side to side, and pounding each other on the back as they listened to the story. Clay wasn't sure he'd ever seen a party in a homeless camp, but there was certainly one going on here!

Of course, he'd never been in a camp where Nigel was the guest speaker.

Clay sat mesmerized. Nigel was a master story teller. He pulled in his ragged audience with situations they could easily identify with, and gripped their attention with a concern that was hard to miss. His stories gave hope to people whom society had written off years ago. Clay had never heard him speak with such love. Every face in his audience held a smile, but was also streaked with tears.

Nigel finished his story and then everyone acknowledged Clay. He passed around the coffees and breakfast sandwiches. The hash browns were a hit again. Homeless people usually aren't that social, but somehow within this little camp there was a level of joy. Nigel brought that out in people.

Clay and Nigel stayed another hour. Before leaving, Nigel pulled each of the weathered men and women into an embrace, addressed them by name, and told them they were loved. Clay followed his example and did the same.

Leaving the homeless camp they had to move across an abandoned industrial area. They were stepping between bent beams of rusted steel; Nigel was ahead of Clay. "I want you to write a short note to Hannah."

Clay wasn't sure he'd heard him correctly. "Write to her—? Now?"

"Yeah. You need to ask her if she's had any contact with a sixteen-year old named Brad Hamilton. You met his dad at a homeless camp under the Ironworker's Memorial. He's worried his ex-wife may have kicked their son onto the streets."

"I met his dad?"

"Third guy you hugged back there. *Jacob* Hamilton." Nigel turned to face Clay.

"And you think Hannah may have met his kid?"

"She met him Tuesday. He's a regular at the youth shelter on Cambie Street."

Clay stared at Nigel. He knew there was no point in asking how Nigel knew that. "So did you tell his dad he's on the streets?"

"How could I tell him that? I wasn't anywhere near Jacob Hamilton this morning."

Clay hesitated. "What d'ya mean you weren't anywhere near him? You were sitting with him before I got there with the coffees. You hugged him. You told him he was loved."

Nigel shook his head and shrugged. "I wasn't at a homeless camp this morning. That was *you*, Clay. You arrived with hash browns and breakfast sandwiches. You told some stories, you hugged some men and women who desperately needed to hear a message of freedom, and *you told them* they were loved."

Clay wasn't sure how to respond, and so he turned to look back towards the camp. But even in that first moment he knew his turning had been a mistake. He spun back, but Nigel was already gone.

The offices of Children from the Dark were running at their usual, enthusiastic pace. Their Thursday night outreach, scheduled for midnight, was only fifteen minutes away. The leaders and four interns were still hustling to be ready. Hannah looked down at her watch, and shook her head. Seventy-six volunteers were probably already at the corner of Nelson and Richards, eager for another night on the streets. *C'mon, Taylor, pull yourself together! Ya gotta go!*

She threw the strap of one of their big yellow duffle bags over her shoulder, crossed the room, out the door, down the stairs two-at-a-time, and swung into the rear seat of a waiting rental van. The door was barely closed when the driver pulled from the curb and accelerated west. Inside the van the frantic pace continued as last minute details were hammered out. Six excited young people were talking over one another.

Hannah never knew who handed her the envelope. It just appeared. Or why she took the time, in the midst of everything else going on around her, to open it. But she did.

Dear Hannah,

I apologize for this letter. You certainly don't owe me anything after the way I've treated you. I am so very sorry for all of it. But I need to ask for your help. I need to know if you've had any contact with a sixteen-year old named Brad Hamilton. He's supposedly a regular at one of the youth shelters on Cambie. I met his dad,

> *Jake Hamilton, at a homeless camp under the Ironworker's Memorial Bridge. His dad was asking if I'd ever met his son. I haven't, but I knew that you probably would have. If you do, could you pass on a message from his father? It's really simple. 'I love you son, and I'm so sorry for not being there for you. I miss you. Love, Dad.'*
>
> *Hannah, I'm ashamed of the way I've treated you. And I can only ask that you might one day forgive me. You deserved the wonderful write-up in the Province newspaper. It was great to see the entire city acknowledge you as the hero you are.*
>
> *Clay Rawlings.*

The van may as well have stopped and everyone climbed out. Hannah could no longer hear anything going on around her, her mind instantly blank. She was stunned. What could possibly have happened in Clay's life that he was now reaching out to people at a homeless camp? And under the Ironworkers Bridge— she blew out a ragged breath— a dangerous spot to be slumming. But there was so much more to it. How had he been able to gain this depth of trust from a homeless father? It was an incredibly personal message. *I love you son. I'm so sorry for not being there for you. I miss you. Love, Dad.*

Hannah knew the power of such words on the streets. They were like diamonds.

She read the letter a dozen times. Maybe Val *was* right. This new version of Clay Rawlings might be better than her at this.

High-Q Robotics wasn't a poor company. And their sales were climbing. Clay's initial hiring salary of forty-two thousand a year made him the lowest paid employee within the software development division. Not that he was complaining. Clay knew he'd been hired without a college degree, which often decides what's included in a compensation package.

Late in May, Larry invited him into his office. They engaged in some breezy chitchat about the project Clay was currently working on, and then Larry asked several questions about specs they both knew. Clay gave the answers and Larry nodded as though they were news.

"You've been doing great work. We're raising your pay to forty-eight a year."

That was it. Larry didn't reach to shake his hand or smile. He was immediately buried back into whatever he'd been doing before, oblivious to Clay still standing in his office. Clay said thank you, but all it got was a muffled grunt.

But then, as he turned to leave, Larry suddenly looked up. "Ever been to Vegas?"

"Yeah. I've been there. Twice"

"I love Vegas. Best place in the world." And with that, Larry launched into a full blown infomercial. He started listing all the shows and nightlife available, and how Clay wouldn't get the opportunity to see these performers anywhere else. And tickets for all the shows could be purchased for half, or even a third, of their real value if you knew where to look. Larry, of course, knew where to look. Heck, he'd seen Cirque de Soleil for twenty-two bucks! In his little sales spiel he highlighted the discounted airfares to get there and hundreds of restaurants where "you're eating almost for free". He insisted emphatically you didn't need to gamble, or even enter the casinos to have a good time. But from the sounds of things, Larry did a lot of gambling. He recounted some substantial losses, laughing that it was part of the charm of Vegas.

"Ya gotta go to Vegas, Clay. Perfect place to celebrate your raise. You should head down there this weekend." Larry extended his hand for a handshake.

"Yeah, I'll think about that." Clay shook his hand and exited his office.

Actually he didn't think about it. Because two days later his income tax refund arrived in the mail. And Clay went on a buying spree.

He'd heard of villages in India where almost every person was illiterate. Places where tracts were useless because they were written in words. Words that a village full of illiterate people can't read.

So into such places missionaries were taking an Indian-made version of the *Jesus* film. Often many of the audience had never seen a film of any type. And suddenly they'd be witnessing a professional re-creation of the Gospel of Luke. On a large sheet hung between two poles, they'd be hearing the Savior of the world speak in their own language. Watching him embrace lepers, heal the sick, and walk on water. And sitting there on the dusty ground, staring up at the screen, they'd see him die for their sins. From all reports, at that moment, tears would flood down their cheeks.

But then just as powerfully, they'd burst into applause when Jesus rose from the dead.

The film had been on Clay's bucket list since the first time he'd heard about it. How many of India's poor could hear the Gospel of Christ, in their own language, in the lifetime of such a film? How many villages? But another question hid deep within him. Could such a film ever make the journey to the slums of Shiliguri? It was more than Clay could even imagine or hope for.

The digital video projector to show the film, and the film itself, was $1700. But it would be worthless in many villages because they lacked electricity. A gas-powered generator would be another $1850. That brought the package to $3550.

It was one of those great moments. Such a price tag could now easily be covered by his income tax refund check. But to finish his shopping list he decided on a couple of bicycles, and another $500 for under-supported missionaries. He leaned against the kitchen counter and wrote out a check for $4270.

Clay knew it was pure Hollywood to imagine the generator on the back of one bicycle, the video machine on the back of the other, with the missionaries being supported by his cash riding together into the worst slums of India. He knew each piece would probably wind up hundreds of miles apart, but he was confident they'd accomplish everything he was hoping for.

He was overwhelmed by what the film might accomplish. He slumped down right there, on the floor against the kitchen drawers. The thought of hundreds of people finding forgiveness from their sins after watching the film was too much for him. He started to weep.

It was a Thursday when Hannah and Brad Hamilton approached the Ironworker's Memorial Bridge. They were hoping to discover the homeless camp Clay had visited, but Brad wasn't in great shape. Several butterfly Band-Aids across his nose were smeared with dried blood. The rest of his face showed evidence of having endured a savage beating. He'd been banned for a month from all Vancouver shelters for fighting. He hadn't showered in four days. Hannah had found him panhandling on Richard's Street and had sat down on the sidewalk beside him. She'd shared what Clay had told her, the message of love from his dad. He'd fallen apart emotionally right in front of her. He was trying to hold up a façade of toughness for the streets, but inside he was just a scared, emotionally fragile, sixteen-year old.

Hannah knew the landscape around the bridge, and so she was leading. Brad had gone silent as they'd gotten closer, the bridge looming large in front of them. But when she pushed through an opening in the chain link fencing, the ash from a campfire was ribboning the air.

"I think we're there, Brad." She pointed to the ridge of a low rise where the upper corner of a tent was visible.

Brad met her eyes for just a fraction, and then he was running. He was pounding across the uneven ground towards where she'd told him his dad was.

Hannah took a breath and waited. *C'mon Clay, be right about this.* She wasn't entirely sure what kind of reception Brad was walking into, but if his dad was here she wanted to give them a few seconds together, alone, before she arrived. She gave them four hundred Mississippi's, and then headed into the camp.

She'd been right to give them some time. They were embracing. The tears were streaming through the dirt and sweat on both their faces. Father and son, reunited. The kind of scene Hannah never tired of. She flopped down into a bent lawn chair next to the fire, a grateful sigh escaping her, and reached out a hand to the ragged woman next to her. “I’m Hannah Taylor. About a week ago, a friend of mine arrived to your camp here. His name’s Clay. Clay Rawlings—”

The woman remembered him. They all remembered him.

Chapter Seventeen

Summer arrived to the city with its early morning sunrises. And though Clay knew of no more beautiful place to worship than the beaches, he kept his morning prayer times amidst the discarded needles and graffiti of the Downtown Eastside. And that decision was costing a huge number of minutes of his life. He did the calculations several times a day and they weren't encouraging. A bit of simple division translated minutes into hours. More math got him to days, and then to months, and finally a dividing of the months by twelve arrived him to the loss of years. He could do the numbers in his head now. Currently he was scheduled to enter eternity somewhere during his fifty-first year. April or May.

Fifty-one years old. Not old enough to get the senior's discount at Denny's. He wouldn't make it to retirement.

He sat leaning against the rusted cladding of a Chinese market and stared at the numbers. He'd lost seventy-eight days in the last three mornings. He tried to smile, tried to make a joke of it like he always did, but this morning it didn't seem very funny.

Fifty-one years old. He blew out a frustrated breath and stood up. He brushed off his jeans and headed out of the alley, stepping into the shadows of a side street. Clay was about to head south towards his vehicle when the diesel rumble of a garbage truck could be heard approaching. He took a step back as it careened towards the sidewalk. The hiss of air-brakes cut through the morning air and the heavy truck lurched to a hesitant stop. The passenger door was shoved open, and someone swung down from the cab. Nigel. The driver remained behind the wheel, patiently waiting.

Nigel stood facing Clay, an unreadable expression on his face. "What if *all* your minutes were taken from you, right now? What if you had only *today* to live, what would you do?" Nigel was serious.

"What would I do if I had only today? Just today?" Clay's mind went blank.

"Just today. That's it."

"I guess I'd call in sick from work and—"

Nigel cut him off. "What's your number right now?"

Clay didn't have to look at the watch. "A little over two hundred and seventy thousand."

"And how did you get it there?"

Clay got quiet. He knew what Nigel was aiming at. "I—I trusted that God knew what He was doing. That He loved me and had a plan for my life. And so I did what His Word says to do."

"Is that the *usual* way of living a life in this society? Waking up every day trusting God knows what He's doing, and then spending every dime and minute you've got, doing what He asks?" Nigel leaned against the fender of the garbage truck.

"No, probably not. Not for most people."

"Look around you, Clay. It's six-thirty in the morning. Your jeans are stained with the dirt of a Vancouver alley where you've been sitting since scrambling out of bed at four. And you're happy here. You're the happiest when you're sitting in places that would've scared you two years ago." Nigel smiled. "Because these places— these ugly places— are a reminder to you that you're partnering with people in similar places. In slums and prisons and rural villages across Asia. And you care about those people."

Clay nodded. "I do."

"So, what would you do if you had only one day left?"

He smiled. "I guess I'd live it just like yesterday. And like I'm living it today."

"Exactly. You want to live a life *every day* that makes sense on the very last day."

Clay looked down at the watch. 270,221. He knew what he was doing wouldn't make any sense to the people in the modern, digital, entertainment-soaked culture that surrounded him. But on his very last day, and for a million years into eternity, it would make all the sense in the world.

Nigel got that serious tone again. "You're at $69,418.62. That number certainly wouldn't make sense to the culture around you either. But the psalmist says, 'Blessed is the man who fears the Lord, who finds great delight in his commands. He has scattered abroad his gifts to the poor, his righteousness endures forever.'

"And that's exactly what you're doing, Clay. You're scattering abroad your gifts to the poor. The psalmist would tell you that your righteousness will endure forever."

Clay nodded, not sure how to respond. He'd certainly *tried* to scatter his gifts amongst the poor overseas.

Nigel turned and climbed back into the garbage truck. After settling into the seat, he rolled down the window. "Clay, that elderly woman you met at the campsite, Ethel, passed away yesterday. Her final number was almost four million. Her investment account with Thirteen44 Global closed with a total of $2,650,281.22. She considered her days as precious only because they gave her opportunity to praise her Savior. And all of Chile was changed by what she accomplished."

With that, Nigel nodded to the driver who found a gear and pulled the truck from the curb.

The staff of Children from the Dark had been run ragged all summer. They'd had help from an army of volunteers. It'd been a summer that had stretched the little organization both spiritually and financially. Hannah was alone this afternoon in the office when the mail arrived. She immediately rifled through it, absent-mindedly. Some of it was bills. Some was junk mail. But the very last envelope was different. It was hand-addressed, in pen, to *Miss Hannah Taylor*. There wasn't a return address.

It was from Clay. She knew it.

How she knew she wasn't sure. It'd been more than a month since he'd written to her. His monthly donations had kept her afloat financially when she wouldn't have made it, and she was grateful for his money. But there was something more. She'd had her scouts out on the streets all summer. What they'd reported to her was startling. Clay was seen regularly in the alleys of the Downtown Eastside, sitting on the asphalt of the alleys behind the welfare hotels. His head would be down, his lips barely moving.

Clay Rawlings in prayer? Hannah had at first laughed at such a thought. But as the summer continued the reports continued to flood in.

She tore open the envelope.

Dear Hannah,

I know I don't have any right to speak into your life, but I simply wanted to congratulate you on such a great summer. Your team has done really well. I have a friend who's active with believers all over the world and he says people everywhere are talking about what's happened in Vancouver this summer. Some ministry in Guatemala is talking about trying to recruit you. They want you to train an outreach team of nationals. There are supposedly lots of kids living on the streets in Guatemala City. Other people were suggested, but no, they want Hannah Taylor. Anyway, congratulations on your summer. And again, I sincerely apologize for how I've treated you.

Clay.

She sank back into her chair. It had been a good summer, and lives *had* been changed. But the thought that people in other places were talking about what God had accomplished through Children from the Dark was humbling. And what was that about Guatemala City? *Whoa.*

She read the letter several times. And then, a thought arrived to her mind. You should phone him. *No—! No! I'm not phoning Clay Rawlings! He disgraced me on national television. I'm not phoning him. I'm not.* But she kept holding the letter.

I'm not phoning him. I'm not.

Clay's co-workers at High-Q had waited. It'd been eight months, and still they waited. They knew all about Nasty Dogs and the bankruptcy, and when Clay wasn't around those subjects had been discussed to death. They knew the length of the yacht he'd once owned, and the name of the country music star who now owned it. They knew which brokerage firm had handled its sale. They knew how much it'd sold for, and most of the details of the extensive refit it'd undergone later that same year in a San Diego shipyard. The sale of his Gulfstream wasn't so easy to research. They'd drawn a blank on it. His home in the Bahamas was now owned by an aging movie star whose last three action films had lost money. The actor had paid six and a half million. Clay's home in North Vancouver had been resold several times, climbing in value with each sale.

And so yes, Clay had gone through a bankruptcy, but he was making pretty good money now. Not money like the millions he'd had before, but still decent cash. And so they were waiting for him to arrive to work having bought something. Something flashy. Something that reminded everybody he'd once dated supermodels. Something that declared to the world that a little thing like bankruptcy couldn't cripple him.

Eight months had passed and they were still waiting. He'd bought nothing.

So a secret committee was hastily thrown together, and a spokesman selected. His name was Hawk Rambler. He was thirty-seven. It was rumored amongst his co-workers that Hawk still lived in his parent's basement, though none of them knew for sure. They did know his entire working career had been at High-Q Robotics. During college Hawk had held some kind of intern position at Apple when it was bringing out the original Macintosh. He'd been buried away in some isolated division, far from the action, but he still worked it into every conversation.

He had no social skills, so he was the perfect person to ask Clay the big question.

It was about six-thirty at night, Clay concentrating intently on a project approaching deadline. Hawk arrived, flopping down onto a chair opposite him. He immediately launched into some random small-talk as though they were fraternity brothers. He'd probably spent most of his high-school years dusting the library or something, so his attempt at swaggering guy-talk was comical. At one point, Clay looked up and just stared at him. "What d'ya want, Hawk?"

"Nuthin'."

"Ya sure—?"

He waited just a second before bluntly blurting out, "What d'ya do with all your money?"

Clay smiled. Co-workers always know what others around them are earning. Maybe not to the penny, but they have a pretty good idea of each other's take-home. And so when you earn a certain amount, the normal thinking goes, your lifestyle should reflect it. Clay's paycheck wasn't at the same level as Hawk's, but for a single guy he was still making a nice income. So why the plain-Jane Honda? He still lived in a rented one-bedroom. There'd been no mention of any vacations or trips to exotic locations. Clay knew his frugal lifestyle had raised red flags in the minds of his co-workers, and so Hawk had been enlisted to discover what Clay was into.

Clay gave a look around as though the IRS might be listening. And then he moved in so he and Hawk were nose to nose. Another quick glance over his shoulder. "I'm investing it all off-shore." Deadpan expression.

"Oh, right—of course, off-shore. Yeah. *Off-shore.* To keep the government from knowing—" Hawk was whispering now. He gave a conspiratorial wink.

"Something like that."

"Well—thanks, Clay." He looked towards the clock on the wall. "Hey, I gotta go."

Clay watched him cross the room and make a hasty exit. He knew by the end of the week the gossip hounds in the company would be quietly sharing a wildly fabricated version of Clay's investment strategy. He smiled. *It's actually true. My money is being invested off-shore. They're just not thinking far enough off-shore.*

Two days earlier he'd sent a thousand dollars to drill another water well. That money was now recorded on a ledger in an extremely secure account.

Far off-shore.

Chapter Eighteen

Hannah thought about it a lot, but she didn't phone Clay. She wanted to, but she couldn't do it. Instead she wrote him a quick 'thank you' note for his donations. The note was just two stiff lines. Or it would have been two lines, but at the last second she included a question asking where he'd heard about the offer from Guatemala City.

So it was three lines. Then she sat there like an insecure high-schooler wondering if she should tear it up. She fretted about it for three days, the note remaining in a drawer of her desk. And then, just before sticking it into an envelope, she hastily scrawled another question across the bottom:

Could we maybe get together somewhere?

It took another week before she put it into the outgoing mail.

Across America, few headlines have ever launched such grand-scale celebrations as the official ending of the Second World War. The entire Western world danced and sang on every street for days, while aircraft overhead did barrel rolls against a background of fireworks and streamers. Marching bands played while crowds cheered and hugged each other. That was relatively close to Clay's celebrations when he received Hannah's note. Vancouver's beaches got quite a workout. Out there, splashing through the water and running crazily across the sand, he celebrated. *He was being given a second chance with the most incredible person on the planet!* Or so he hoped.

In a phone call, Clay suggested they get together for dinner. Hannah refused, and suggested a coffee at a diner. It went back and forth before they settled on lunch. Clay gave her an address for a place he knew, and told her he'd arrange a table. Hannah set the phone down, already berating herself for agreeing to this. He hadn't mentioned the name of the place, but Clay had built his empire wining and dining clients in the poshest restaurants. She knew he'd lost everything financially, but old habits die hard. It'd be white tablecloths and sterling silver. She shook her head. Would the place have valet parking? Probably. She couldn't imagine handing the keys of her dented Hyundai to some uniformed kid used to parking Lamborghinis. *Darn you, Clay.*

It wasn't a restaurant. Not even close. The address was a neighborhood park, on the corner of Sixth and Arbutus. Hannah pulled up and actually laughed out loud. It was just a park. Just a thin sliver of freshly mowed grass adorned with brightly painted swings and teeter totters. And there, in a collared-shirt and jeans, sat Clay at a concrete picnic table. A plastic vase in the center of the table held a small spray of flowers. And wrapped into their usual wax paper were two Subway sandwiches.

"Is this table okay, or would you prefer one overlooking the teeter totters?" Clay offered as she sat down. He smiled. "I'm sure if I slipped the waiter a fifty he'd get us moved."

Hannah laughed. "No, this table's perfect. You—you must've gotten reservations."

"Oh yeah, I called ahead. This place is usually packed elbow-to-elbow with hedge fund managers and political appointees at lunch time. Not an easy place to get a table." Clay could see she was smiling. Surprised, but in a good way.

"I'm speechless, Clay." She was. And trying to recover. Sitting down to eat sandwiches at a concrete picnic table told her more about this new Clay than everything she'd already heard from her staff. This was not the guy who'd embarrassed her on national television. The arrogant swagger and flamboyant cockiness was gone.

Clay held up both sandwiches. "Now, the food here is fabulous, but the menu, while world-renowned, is quite limited. You have a choice of roast beef or the cold-cut combo."

"Cold-cut combo."

"Pepsi or bottled water?"

She smiled. "Bottled water."

Hannah was just about to open her sandwich when Clay asked, "Do you mind if we thank God for our lunch?"

She nodded and he bowed his head. Hannah didn't bow her head or close her eyes. Instead she listened as a guy who'd once been worth $200 million, and recognized as the most eligible bachelor in Canada, *a guy who'd once disgraced her*, lifted up the name of Jesus Christ in the most humble prayer Hannah had ever heard.

The sandwiches were delicious. They talked mostly about Hannah's work with Children from the Dark and the incredible summer she'd had with volunteers from all over the world. She tried to move the conversation towards what was happening with Clay, but he sidestepped all that. He kept the focus on her and everything she'd accomplished. An hour disappeared quickly and they both had to go. Clay pulled away first, heading for High-Q.

Hannah sat there in her vehicle, the ignition off. Her mind was reeling. *Was such a thing possible? Was Jesus able to change people so dramatically?* She stared at the little park with its swing sets and concrete picnic tables. Clay Rawlings. They'd been high school sweethearts, but she was sure she'd never met this guy before. Not *this* guy.

Thankfulness can't be taught in a seminar. You can read the books and listen to emotional speeches made by those who've been rescued, but the thankfulness they display will always remain the property of those who've experienced it. Rescued people are thankful people. Clay Rawlings was a rescued person. And so yes, he was a thankful person.

The tears were flooding down his cheeks, his entire body heaving with emotion that fought to escape from within him. It was four-thirty in the morning and Clay was leaning against a stack of wet pallets behind a Chinese market, his head bowed.

"Lord God, you rescued me when I wasn't worth anything. I let…I let thirty-eight people die—" He breathed out. "—just to feed my need to be declared a somebody. To fulfill my lust for stuff that would show the world… I was a success. And even today, you're there in Shiliguri, among those two-hundred devastated families… as they struggle with the needs of disabled family members." Clay's words were barely audible now. "I did *that* to them, Lord. I know I did.

"And yet, you rescued me. When everybody else would have run *away from me,* abandoning me for what I did, you ran *towards* me. You ran to me…

when I couldn't live with myself anymore." Another wave of emotion sagged Clay to his knees.

"I won't—I won't ever understand it, Lord, but you chose me. There were other people, *far better people* than me, whom you could have chosen. But you didn't choose those people. For reasons I will never understand, you chose to work in *my* life. You chose *me*. You rescued me. From suicide. And self-hatred. Though it cost you the life of your Son, you— you chose me. I don't deserve any of this. I could never deserve any of this." He stared down at his hands in the half-light of the morning. "Thank you, Lord. Thank you."

Far away, in the brightness of heaven's throne room, a million angels on their knees looked towards the One who sat upon the throne. Their king had a special smile when He was pleased, especially when a son of Adam recognized and declared His amazing grace. He wore that smile now.

Chapter Nineteen

Fall arrived, with every intersection full of school buses and crossing guards. Clay had never noticed the flurry of school-aged children before. But on the third morning of September, something changed. Two little girls, probably in grade three or four, obviously twins, were hurrying through the school crossing with their mom. They wore new clothes with matching sneakers and backpacks festooned with the latest Disney movie characters. Clay wouldn't have paid them any attention except one of them stopped right in the middle of the crossing. And she waved at Clay. *She waved directly at him!* Her mom instinctively reached out to stop her, probably repeating past warnings about 'stranger danger', and hustled her through the crosswalk.

Clay sat there for an extra moment, long enough to get a blast of horn from the car behind him. He continued on towards High-Q Robotics, but his mind was now elsewhere. Had the girl in the crosswalk simply been a coincidence? Or was she a messenger?

GraceUnfathomable had just sent him an exciting write-up about their new child sponsorship program! For thirty-dollars a month, Clay was offered the opportunity to pay for an education, in English, for a child struggling to survive somewhere in a slum. And with *that* education, an entirely different life would be available to the child. A far better life. But more importantly, the child would be taught about the freedom found in Jesus Christ.

He swallowed. *How dare he think about this?* He'd once paid kids not much older than the little girl who'd waved at him. But it wasn't for an education. No. He'd invited them to join the almost slave-like conditions at his crumbling factories. For the princely sum of a dollar-seventy a day he'd stolen any hope of a better life for children just like the little girl in the crosswalk!

Lots of them.

And then, when his business partners had tried to get those kids into school and away from Clay, he'd shut down the facility and abruptly fired them all. He'd stripped them of even that meager income! That thought was like broken glass washing through is mind. He wanted to scream. *What kind of monster does that to a bunch of half-starved kids?*

He was slowing at another crosswalk where a group of older students slouched their way across the street heading towards a brick senior high. Suddenly the passenger door on the Civic was violently yanked open and Nigel pulled himself inside.

"You're listening to the enemy." Those were Nigel's first words. He wasn't smiling.

"But I *did* do that. Nigel—I *am* a monster."

Nigel was shaking his head vigorously. "Not even close. Not anymore. The Word of God declares that 'if anyone is in Christ, he is a new creation. The old has gone, the new has come.'

"You, Clay, are a new creation! An heir of God and a co-heir with Christ. You are the adopted son of the Lord of glory. And He's extremely proud of what He's accomplishing in you."

Clay kept looking straight ahead, quite sure none of this was true.

"You have a voice in your head that sounds like you, and you've been listening to it for so long you're convinced it's you. But it's not you." Nigel paused. "Clay, you're listening to the voice of a demon."

"A demon?" Clay wasn't sure if that was possible. Wouldn't there be a hissing in its words and the smell of sulfur?

"Demons are easy to identify because their message is always for you to give up. For you to quit. For you to abandon anything that's moving you closer to, or building you up in, a relationship with Christ. And of course, to quit anything that's building the kingdom of God." Nigel looked at Clay. "Does any of this sound familiar?"

Clay glanced towards Nigel. He shrugged. "Okay, yeah—it does."

"Your past is a well-travelled path to destroying you. Believe me, they know that. 'You've failed before so there's no hope of victory now. Quit! Take the easy road and live like everybody else! You've failed at other things, so you'll fail at this, too. Quit now!' It's always the same message." Nigel was gritting his teeth.

"But what if what it's saying is true?"

Nigel gave a narrow smile. "Oh, you can be sure what it's so elegantly spewing into your mind will almost always be true! Or at least it was *once* true. That's what makes the strategy so effective."

"So we just lose every time?" Clay swallowed.

Nigel leaned back, and smiled. "No, my friend, we don't lose. We fight! That voice in your head is the killer of faith. The only weapon forged to stand against it is the Word of God."

Clay groaned. *Well, that's going to be a quick battle. They'll be celebrating in the locker rooms of hell within two downs.*

It was quiet for just a second before Nigel started speaking, his words almost inaudible. He wasn't facing Clay.

"Number 47. Jodie Schecter from Dryden, Ontario. $391.88. Pizza Hut, some travel cash, and WestJet airfare. She's now in a youth drug facility near her uncle and aunt's home. She embraced Christ in mid-February.

"Number 129. Randy Broder from Fort St. John. $226.30. Six meals at various restaurants over the course of three weeks and then bus fare. He's now working through his anger issues with a church counselor. He's returned to high school. He embraced Christ on March 21."

Nigel continued, his voice gaining some volume. "37,537. Balagari Raju in Mumbai, India. Alcoholic. He read a tract given to him by a neighbor in the slums of Dharavi. That tract was a small part of an $800 donation. He was freed from addiction by prayer. He and his entire family are now Christian believers. His wife no longer having to endure beatings, and his children, they no longer beg on the streets—"

Clay wrenched the wheel, barely avoiding a collision with a bus, the little car squealing into an empty parking lot. The Civic anchored to a violent stop. "What are you doing? Whose numbers are those?"

"They're yours. 284,221 thru to 284,589. A single showing of that 'Jesus' film in a slum near the rail yards of Bilaspur, India. And yes, the generator and the projector were kept together, so $3560. That night forty-eight people came to faith in Jesus Christ. A church has since been established.

Numbers 231,092 thru to 231,324 are from that same film team, two nights later. It was a village six miles further north. Eighty-five people came to faith."

Clay dragged his hand through his hair, overwhelmed. And then, throwing open the door, he leapt from the car! Nigel waited a moment before exiting the Civic. Clay was sitting on the ground, leaning against the front fender, his knees pulled to his chest. His eyes were glistening, his entire body slowly rocking back and forth. Nigel lowered himself to the asphalt next to him.

"That film team is seeing incredible results everywhere they travel. More than nineteen thousand people have been given the opportunity to hear about the God of heaven arriving in the flesh to rescue them. A dozen churches have been established in places where the name of Christ was unknown even six months ago."

"Why—why are you telling me this?"

"Because a guy who ate peanut butter toast for three weeks while unemployed so that he could continue funneling cash overseas to keep missionaries journeying onto the next village shouldn't believe the lies he's listening to. Instead, he should trust what the scriptures say about him—are true."

Clay looked over at Nigel, who was staring away at the traffic. "Okay. And what does the Bible say about me?"

"That your life is evidence the kingdom of heaven has arrived."

Clay shook his head. "It doesn't say that."

"Actually it does. Clay, we named our investment firm very specifically. The name is a reminder to us of the kind of person we're looking for." Nigel paused. "And it describes the kind of person you've become."

"I don't get it. Thirteen44 Global—?"

"Yeah. 13:44. The book of Matthew, *chapter* Thirteen, *verse* 44 says, 'The kingdom of heaven is like treasure hidden in a field. When a man found it, he hid it again, and then in his joy went and sold everything he had and bought that field.'" Nigel gave a knowing smile. "In an old community hall you discovered treasure. And right there, on a dusty floor you embraced it. You embraced mankind's greatest treasure, the Lord Jesus Christ."

"I did. I discovered treasure."

"I'll never forget watching you celebrate that night in the parking lot. And your celebrations haven't slowed since then."

"You know about that?"

"Let's just say your joy often rattles the windows of heaven."

Clay stared at him, waiting for him to insist he was kidding.

"Your account is currently at $76,144.74. The verse says that in his joy the man *sold all he had* and bought—"

"—the field." Clay finished for him.

"I'd say that Matthew 13:44 describes you perfectly."

"Nigel, I'm just trying to say thank you for what He's done for me."

"I can assure you He hears that. And more importantly, He sees it."

Clay was again seated in the Civic, about to pull away and continue on to work when Nigel reached in and gripped his shoulder. "Oh, and Becky and I both think you should go ahead and sponsor one of those kids in an Indian slum."

"Becky—? Who's Becky?"

"The little girl in the crosswalk. The one who waved at you." With that, Nigel turned and walked away.

The envelope arrived to the offices of Children from the Dark with the usual mail. It was rumpled like the voyage hadn't been easy. A dark smear discolored the face of it. Two strips of tape now held it closed. There were three Guatemalan stamps in the corner. Hannah smiled. *Third-world postal services.* She knew the letter would've been shuffled across Central America in every assortment of vehicle imaginable, and whatever was inside would've already been rifled through repeatedly. If there'd ever been anything of value inside, like cash, it'd be long gone.

She ripped it open, a single page tumbling out. It was written in English, the name and logo of a Central American ministry spelled out in Spanish across the top.

Dear Miss Taylor...

Hannah raced from the office after reading the letter, jumped onto a bus, and headed for Stanley Park. And there, on the grass looking back across Coal Harbor towards the finance district, she read it again. It was, as Clay had told her, an offer for her to come to Guatemala City to train and co-ordinate a team. They wanted to reach the thousands of kids who called a piece of dirty cardboard on the sidewalk, home.

They'd heard about her at an international conference in Madrid, Spain where supposedly everyone was talking about what was happening in Vancouver. And like Clay had said, they were quite emphatic *she* was the person they wanted. They'd prayed. They'd fasted. They'd heard from God. Hannah Taylor was the only name that had arrived to over forty Guatemalan church leaders.

She sat there on the grass. And worried.

High-Q Robotics was full of computer geeks. It was full of people who lived their lives on the digital edge. Engineers of every stripe were on the payroll: mechanical, software, and networking. Scattered among them were degrees from Stanford and MIT, and past gigs at places like Hewlett Packard and Atari. High-Q's research and development division was spread across two floors. It was basically a sixty-thousand square foot playground for a bunch of social-misfit, technical wizards. The thought of having a computer problem they couldn't solve was unthinkable.

Until it happened.

Every second screen on Clay's entire floor went blank. Not every screen, but every *second* screen. There was nothing random about it. Every second monitor was completely dead. There wasn't an easy explanation for it, and at first it just seemed weird. Even when two monitors sat beside each other, sharing cables and a power source, the second one would be unresponsive. Or even if the second screen was a laptop.

The network guys immediately dismissed it as an unusual anomaly and scattered across the floor in search of the problem. A quick fix was promised. An hour passed. The monitors remained dead. Two hours came and went. The network guys had lost their unflappable demeanor and were barking at each other. Calls were being placed to other IT specialists. Suddenly at three hours, the situation took an even weirder twist. The screens did a flip. The ones that had been dark now came alive, and the ones that had been alive went blank. No explanation was even suggested. The situation was building its own momentum. A meeting of the bosses was convened and, behind closed doors, a yelling match erupted.

Clay and his team were inconvenienced by the problems, but they tried to stay focused. All around them a crisis was brewing. They continued to plow ahead, using the monitors and laptops that were still responsive.

It was just after the screens did their flip that an outside IT team arrived. They met with members of the senior management of High-Q before being dispatched loudly, "to just solve the damn problem!" With that, three of the high-paid visitors, each paired with one of High-Q's own network guys, disappeared in different directions.

A fourth member of the visiting team headed across the upper floor of R&D with a practiced casualness. He moved as though on a grade-school fieldtrip. He stopped at a number of work stations, introduced himself, and then asked people how they were doing. And then he listened. He listened as people poured out frustrations about areas of their lives that had nothing to do with work. Marriage issues and financial struggles. Relationships. He laughed with some people and encouraged others. And as he crossed the floor, in a widening wake, he left behind only a calming peace.

All the way to Clay's work station.

"Nigel—! What are you doing here?"

Nigel casually lifted the laminated visitor's security card slung from a lanyard around his neck. "I'm here solving a tech problem."

"No you're not. You don't know anything about—" Clay stopped. "Wait a second. This is *you*, isn't it?" Clay was whispering now. He glanced around furtively. "*You*—you're doing this."

"Maybe." Nigel shrugged. "Anyway, I've got a message for you."

Clay barked out a nervous laugh. "What—? You can't call me on the phone like anybody else?"

"What fun would that be?" Nigel smiled. "And besides, I thought this message would carry some urgency for you."

"Okay—?"

"Hannah's going to be at MissionsJam at Willingdon Church next Saturday. She'll be speaking twice, her second session finishing at eleven. She'll then check back with her team at their booth, and after that she'll be free for lunch."

"She'll be… free for lunch. Okay."

"Yeah, there's a little place called Fresco's, two blocks north of the church, right on Willingdon Avenue. Excellent beef dip. You might want to suggest it, as it's her favorite."

"Beef dip. Sure. And how are you so sure she'll agree to lunch?"

Nigel smiled. "She's interested in the new Clay."

"The *new* Clay?"

"Yeah. That person you're becoming." Nigel shook his head. "Y'see, during the summer, the wharf rats come off the waterfront docks and they breed in the alleys of the Downtown Eastside. Thousands of them. So late at night they move like a dark, carpeted mass across the stained asphalt of the alleys. It'd be considered by most people a good place to avoid, anywhere near such a swirling migration of filth." Nigel paused. "And yet this summer, in the shadowy light of the early morning, a solitary figure was often seen sitting on that asphalt, head down, Bible out, in prayer."

Clay swallowed. "Does she know it was me?"

"Oh yeah."

"Did she—" Clay hesitated. "—did she think that was a good thing? Does she understand why I'd be—?"

"I guess you'll have to ask her." Nigel smiled. He turned to look across the floor. Dozens of young, frazzled engineers were still scrambling in an effort to solve High-Q's network problems. He nodded towards Clay. "Once I'm gone, go onto any computer. Type in Hannah's last name and your system will be restored. And don't worry, no data's been lost. Anyway, I gotta go."

Nigel had already turned, heading for the entrance when Clay blurted out, "Are we— Hannah and I—are we ever going to work together? Are you going to bring us together on the streets as partners?"

Nigel gave him a wink. "You never know what I might do."

Nigel arrived to the reception area just as the entire High-Q computer system was restored. He joked with a young intern who took his security card and signed him out. And then, just before heading for the elevators, Nigel looked back. Clay was again surrounded by his team, hard at work creating the next big thing in robotics. He smiled. "What you haven't realized, Clay, is that you and Hannah have been working together for almost seven months now. Her success on the streets of Vancouver was only realized because of you."

Chapter Twenty

MissionsJam was its usual success, spilling out from Willingdon Church onto the BCIT campus next door. It had again attracted thousands of believers from all over the Pacific Northwest to hear about the global effort to build the kingdom of God. All the big-name players in the Christian missionary world had arrived. And they arrived with literature and representatives, ready to sign up people for a weekend, a week, or a lifetime of service. Some of the booths were huge. They'd been professionally designed, and would spend a lot of the year being shuffled onto and off aircraft, travelling the missions trade show circuit. Expensive literature and books written by their founders were backstopped by high-budget videos highlighting the incredible work of the organization. Thousands had been spent to declare they were taking a lost world by storm.

Amidst all of that was a little booth that wasn't much more than a folding table and some badly photocopied literature. 'Children from the Dark' sat between two of the behemoths, definitely the low-heeled little brother. Underfinanced and struggling. But things are not always as they seem.

Clay arrived in what he considered plenty of time to attend Hannah's first speaking session. He was wrong. He and two hundred others in line were turned away for lack of seating space. Her second session was moved to a much larger room and there was talk of her being invited onto the main stage during the evening plenary session. For Clay, he knew an unforeseen wrinkle had arrived to his plan when Hannah was swamped with questions during her final few minutes of Q&A. Few people budged from the room until almost noon. And then, to return to her booth, she shuffled along, barely moving, surrounded by a crowd eager to talk to her.

"Thanks for rescuing me." Hannah exclaimed as she and Clay headed away from the church. She ran her hand through her hair. "People want to talk to me, but I'm as mystified as anybody else to explain our success this summer."

Clay tried hard not to stare when she ran her hand through her hair. She was stunningly beautiful. "I don't think you're giving yourself enough credit. I think delivering a beat-up teenager to a homeless camp to re-unite him with his dad might be evidence that you're really good at this. God's given you some special abilities."

She stopped and looked directly at him, a smile forming.

He continued. "C'mon Hannah, you're willing to wade into the murky places to find these kids. And then, when you arrive, it's like every ounce of heaven's love and concern explodes onto the scene. It simply floods out of you, into lives that have only experienced abandonment and abuse."

Her mouth dropped open and she covered it with her hand. "Clay—."

"Oh wow. I'm—I'm sorry." He could have kicked himself. "I didn't mean to say all that."

"No, it's quite all right." She laughed. "It's probably not true, but I love the sound of it."

The crowds on the sidewalk continued to swirl past them.

They got to Fresco's and without looking at the menu board Clay ordered two beef dips and iced tea for both of them. He led her to a narrow table near the back.

She laughed. "Okay, how do you do that?"

"Do what?"

"You just ordered me a beef dip. Dozens of things on the menu and, without looking at it, you order my favorite. And last time, you invited me to the very park I played at as a child."

Oops. Clay shrugged. "Would it be okay if I told you I was trying to impress you?"

"Yeah. Yeah, that'd be okay."

"Hannah, I don't deserve to be sitting here. I know that." Clay breathed out. "I've hurt you, and embarrassed you. On national television, no less." He shook his head at the memory. "I was a pompous ass when I was flying high. And now, after a pathetic flame-out where I ran my company into the ground, I can see the carnage I left in my wake. You were one of the people who got hurt by my arrogance, and I'm sorry."

She was leaning towards him now, so he continued.

"Recently, I've taken a few feeble steps towards trying to do better." Clay allowed a self-deprecating smile. "I'm probably still a pompous ass. And I can never undo the hurt I've caused you, but I still want to ask that you could, one day, forgive me." He met her eyes. "I know I don't deserve it, but it's all I've got left. It's—it's pretty much all I live for."

Hannah slowly leaned back in her chair. An unreadable expression crossed her face. She stared across at Clay for several seconds. "Wow. Well first of all, I know about the kids you've sent home on WestJet and Air Canada flights. And having talked with dozens of waitresses, I know about the meals and the cash you sent them home with. And for the past three months, I've arrived to work every morning hearing reports about a guy who spends his early mornings in the alleys of the Downtown Eastside. The rumor is that you're praying. You're out there, praying for broken people. For homeless youth, under-aged prostitutes, and drug addicts."

She hesitated. "I hear all this stuff, Clay, and I gotta tell you it's impressive. But this apology—what you've just said to me—I think is the most impressive thing you've done." She smiled.

"Thanks—"

"Clay, you're not the same person. You're not. And I'd love to hear how it happened."

There it was, just like Nigel had said. Clay was stunned, and his mind went blank. Fortunately the waitress arrived with their order, buying him a minute to consider a response. He knew he couldn't tell her about the watch. That'd be too much crazy, too fast.

He took several bites of beef dip before starting with, "I wasn't doing well after the bankruptcy of Nasty Dogs. The company had hurt people in its final days. I'd burned every bridge in my life. Not just with you, but with lots of other people." Clay's words slowed. "For three years it was a struggle to get out of bed. Or to go outside. To talk to anybody. I truly felt my life was over. You could say I know what an abandoned kid living on the streets feels like. I don't have to guess. I know the gut-level emptiness of not wanting to live."

Hannah had set her sandwich down and was leaning forward.

"And then I met a guy. His name's Nigel. He gave me some convincing proof... that I was dead inside. And he challenged me that if I was going to survive, if I was going to find life, I'd need a new heart."

"A new heart?"

"Yeah. He convinced me that my current heart was so clouded by the thinking and norms of our society it'd need to be junked."

"Junked? He actually used the term *junked*?" She smiled.

"Okay, he didn't use that term, but he said my current heart was thinking like everyone else. Its tastes and desires had been too badly influenced by the society around me, and it'd be worthless in accomplishing what he wanted for me."

Hannah's eyes got big. "Wow—"

"Yeah, I know. He said a new heart was the only thing that would save me. I'd need radical surgery if I was going to see life, and nothing else would allow me to stand firm in the places I was going to find myself once I embraced his plan for my life."

"His plan being for you to reach out to lost kids, and journey into homeless camps?" She smiled. "To stand firm in the dirty places of the city?"

Clay nodded. "Yeah. And he said only with a new heart would I understand what's truly valuable."

"Valuable?" Hannah leaned back again. "You mean like befriending an under-aged prostitute. And then driving her to New Hope Ranch outside Calgary. That kind of valuable?" Hannah paused. "I hear she's done well in her first three months."

"Wait. You—you know about Cheryl?"

Hannah smiled. "I do. Her parents wanted me to thank you if I saw you."

Clay nodded, not sure how to respond to such a thing.

"I owe you an apology, Clay."

"For what?"

"In highschool I pushed you away because you weren't excited about Christ. And I know I hurt you."

"No. It did hurt me, but you were right in ending it." Clay stared at the table. "I started out well, but as we moved closer to graduation I knew I wasn't willing to live for Christ. Instead, I wanted money and a fancy lifestyle. And I probably wouldn't have admitted it then, but I was just playing a game. I talked about Jesus, but my priorities had already changed towards everything that, ultimately, Nasty Dogs enabled me to experience. I was completely absorbed into my own selfish pursuits." He paused. "You deserved a lot better than that. And so did God."

Hannah was quiet for a few seconds. "Well I've gotta say your friend Nigel brings out the best in you. That sounded like repentance to me. And not the forced kind, but like you've worn those words smooth with a lot of humble repetition."

Hannah waited unto Clay met her eyes and then she pushed her open hand across the table. With a racing heart, he reached out and laid his fingers lightly into her palm.

Answering machines hear some of the most life-changing news. Early morning calls from relatives to report the birth of a baby. Or that a work promotion has been secured. There'll be the caller's initial disappointment, and then a moment of decision. Should the caller talk to a machine or call back? A decision is reached and there's a brief, disjointed summary of what's happened. But the last two words of the recording are always the same. 'Call me.'

Clay's machine received the call from his father, Howard, early on a Thursday. The message was short. "It's your grandpa. Something's happened." And then, as with thousands of other messages, it ended with the iconic, "Call me."

Clay arrived home from his early-morning prayer session, pushed the button on the machine, and his heart stopped. 'Something's happened' seemed so cryptic. Clay took a ragged breath. His grandpa hadn't won an event on the PGA tour; that much was obvious. He was eighty-seven, and lived alone in an upscale retirement village in Monterey, California.

He quickly phoned his parent's home. His mom picked up.

"Hey, this is Clay. What's happened to—?"

"Grandpa suffered another stroke early this morning." His third. The line was empty for a few seconds and when she spoke again her words were brittle. "Your grandpa's gone, son." Clay didn't hear much after that.

Jericho Beach had been the stage for many of Clay's celebrations. It was where he'd gone to rejoice the greatest moments in his life. It'd been his place of victory, dancing and spinning across the sand. And then of splashing through its clear, blue waters. And so in the minutes after a call that had announced such a tragedy as the death of his grandpa, it seemed strange his thoughts directed him towards the beach. He knew with the death of his grandfather, the beach wouldn't be the same.

The dance floor would've been stripped out, and the band sent home.

He went anyway. He laced his sneakers and slowly made his way to the beach. A lonely wind was rippling the waves at the edge where several hounds were barking and chasing sticks into the surf. But standing just off the sidewalk, patiently waiting for Clay's approach, was Nigel.

He didn't talk. Instead he pulled Clay into an embrace as the first of Clay's tears arrived. And then Nigel stood silently beside him as they stared together out at the water. The morning became afternoon, and then afternoon became evening as they walked the empty beaches, silently. Together.

Clay placed his carry-on luggage into the overhead compartment. Both of his parents had encouraged him to book a flight with them, but he'd declined. After four days he still wasn't ready to talk to anybody. He noticed the window and middle seat beside him were already filled. Middle-aged executives in suits, bulky laptops out, sleeves rolled up, busily furthering their careers. *Perfect. Weathered road-warriors who wouldn't probe him with a lot of throw-away questions.* Clay slouched into the aisle seat just as the seat belt sign illuminated. The stewardesses went through the usual safety routine, and they were soon taxiing towards the runway. The cabin shuddered as the engines ramped up, there was a deafening roar as the pilots pushed the throttles to maximum, and then every passenger was pushed into their seats as flight 761 to San Francisco rocketed off the tarmac.

Clay stared down at the watch. And thought about his grandpa. *When the minutes of his life hit zero, what was his worth number at?*

It was an agonizing question. He'd died of a stroke. No time for a last minute Hail Mary pass. No time for anything but to step into eternity with whatever numbers he'd held.

Clay had always thought of his grandpa as a salt-of-the-earth type. A good person, generous and kind. He'd spent his life as a maintenance supervisor for CN, Canada's national railroad, living in various small towns across the prairies. Married to the same woman for more than forty years before cancer took her. They'd attended some type of mainline church together, off and on, until her passing, though Clay couldn't remember which one.

But right now, the question that mattered to Clay was, had his grandpa ever sunk to his knees on a floor in repentance somewhere, and then lived his life in thankfulness for what Christ had done for him?

Eternity had begun for his grandpa. He'd had eighty-seven years to prepare for it. On that last morning, was he ready?

Chapter Twenty-One

The plane made a graceful landing in Monterey, California. The weather was perfect. Seventy-eight degrees and sunny. Clay took a taxi to the funeral home, a sprawling white structure surrounded by acres of manicured lawn. As he entered through the huge glass doors of the main building, a tuxedoed older man directed him towards the Seaside Room. In hushed tones he explained that there a 'celebration of life' had been prepared for James Floyd Rawlings. Clay continued on down the hall, polished marble beneath his feet.

At eighty-seven years old, Grandpa Jim had outlived most of his friends in Canada. The ones he hadn't outlived obviously weren't able to make the journey to California. And his friends in Monterey had made other plans, too. That left thirteen members of family. The spacious Seaside Room was almost empty.

The 'celebration of life' involved a lot of solemn words spoken by a willowy man who hadn't known his grandpa. Clay ignored most of it. A graveside service followed where more heartfelt words were shared. Again by somebody who'd never known him.

They returned to a reception hall where a huge spread of food and beverages was waiting. Jackets and ties were removed, plates filled, and people made their way out onto the patio. Clay had just poured himself a Pepsi when his uncle, Louie, approached him. Two of his cousins, Jeff and Patrick, both in their late-twenties, were with him.

"Clay, I need you to follow us."

"Sure, what's up?"

"Let's go next door and we'll talk." Uncle Louie was already heading towards the entrance.

Clay looked at Jeff and Patrick, "What's this about?" They both shrugged.

In the next room was a long table surrounded by leather office chairs. Another cousin, Wendy, was already seated. "Grab a chair, guys." Uncle Louie placed a briefcase onto the table and sat down. He opened the briefcase and pulled out a file folder.

"Okay, first of all, the four of you are mentioned in your grandfather's will." Louie slid out four envelopes from the folder. "He left each of you a specific amount of money."

Jeff, Patrick, and Wendy leaned forward, eyes locked onto the envelopes.

"As executor, I began working on your grandpa's estate within minutes of his first stroke, almost five months ago. As you know, he survived that first one. I've still got some tax stuff to calculate and a bunch of—" Louie stopped, knowing they wouldn't care about the details. "Anyway, your grandfather requested I get your money to you as soon as possible. And I guess that's today." He smiled.

"Are—are they all the same amount? Does each of us get the same?" Patrick was almost salivating. They all knew he had huge school debts, but also that little of the money would be aimed in that direction. A horrific spender, nobody doubted Patrick wouldn't burn through it within a month. Regardless of how much it was.

"No. They're not equal amounts. Sorry."

That news wasn't easy to hear, but Jeff and Patrick shrugged it off.

"Any other questions?"

There were no other questions.

"Okay, then enjoy." Uncle Louie handed them each an envelope with their names typed on the outside.

Patrick's envelope had barely arrived into his hands before he ripped it open. A check fluttered to the table. He scooped it up, took a quick look, and triumphantly exclaimed, "Twenty grand! I got twenty grand—Yeah!" He kissed it.

Jeff quickly tore his own envelope open. Another $20,000 check landed onto the table. "Whoa. That looks like a new Polaris snowmobile and one of them new, big screen TV's for me." He laughed. Patrick reached over and they did a celebratory high-five.

Wendy opened her envelope, but didn't announce the amount. Instead she leaned back and gave an airy sigh. "Guess I'll be spending Christmas on one of those cruise ships in the Mediterranean. One of the serious party boats."

Clay got up, shook Uncle Louie's hand, thanked him, and returned to the reception hall. He pocketed his envelope, but didn't open it.

Clay got a window seat on his return flight to Vancouver. His mind was still adrift, trying to sort out everything that had happened. He reclined his seat and stared at his hands. A lot of religious-sounding words had been thrown into the air during the memorial service, but that didn't calm the knot in his stomach. Wherever his grandpa was, he'd been there eight days now. If he'd found the forgiveness of Christ, and simply kept it a secret from his family, then he'd just spent eight of the most incredible days ever.

But there was another scenario. Not a nice one.

Clay had once spent four and a half minutes in another place. A place of darkness and loneliness. A place of terror.

He'd only been there four and a half minutes.

His grandpa had now been gone eight *days*.

Chapter Twenty-Two

The envelope from Uncle Louie remained on Clay's kitchen counter, unopened. Clay knew it probably held twenty grand, but somehow that didn't make much difference. One of the most wonderful people in his life was gone. At first he'd willed himself to believe his grandpa had embraced Christ, and his had been a secret faith. That his grandpa had privately spent hours celebrating everything Christ had done when nobody was around. But as the days piled up he gradually let go of such a hope. Was it possible for someone to have met the living Savior and for their life to not reflect it? For them to not live differently?

Clay couldn't imagine such a thing.

He'd walk the beach and stare down at his numbers rolling over.

364,312…364,951…365,712…

He knew his numbers were being multiplied in prisons cells and in work camps across Asia, and in the lives of troubled youth across Canada. Clay's finances and prayers were touching lives. Those lives were then touching other lives. It was simple multiplication.

He was pretty confident four or five hundred Indian pastors were using their new Bibles to teach entire congregations, and to lead slum dwellers to faith. He couldn't even guess how many of the numbers represented people hearing the message of freedom as they viewed the Indian-made 'Jesus' film.

Clay knew each digit was another person being given an opportunity to move closer to the salvation found only in Jesus Christ. Or to be built up in Him.

But since the death of his grandpa, one thought haunted him. He knew other believers had their own numbers. They were being recorded in an account similar to the one Nigel had established for him. So how many of the numbers of other Christians were them inviting his grandpa to consider the claims of Jesus? In eighty-seven years there had to have been lots of them.

And had he rejected them all, or had he believed at one point and then allowed the thinking of the world to influence him until he no longer lived out the message of the cross?

It didn't matter now. He was gone.

Clay didn't celebrate anything for several weeks. And the letter remained unopened.

On the corner of Blenheim and Norton Avenue, wedged between a dry cleaners and comic book shop, sat a café. The narrow little café certainly wasn't much to look at, with just four tables along one wall and a long lunch counter. But it was the kind of place where they'd refill your coffee cup endlessly. Hannah had found it during her early years in ministry, and it'd easily become her Saturday morning oasis. She'd grab a table, order breakfast, and read the weekend edition of the newspaper from cover to cover. Now, with the crazy hours and responsibilities of running Children from the Dark it'd been a while since she'd visited the place.

She pulled open the door, a tinkling bell announcing her entrance. Clay was already seated at one of the tables. Hannah slid in across from him, smiled at the middle-aged waitress, and requested a coffee.

"Sorry I haven't called." Clay gave her a quick smile. "It's been hard since my grandfather died. I never would've imagined it to be like this."

"Clay, I'm sorry about your grandpa." She reached across the table to grip his hand. "It's only been a couple of weeks. You need to give it some time."

They discussed Clay's grandpa until the waitress arrived with their coffees. They both ordered the French toast. The waitress thanked them and headed towards the kitchen.

"Clay, I wanted to get together for a reason." Hannah hesitated. She pulled a rumpled letter from her jacket. "I got this a couple of weeks ago, and I don't know what to do."

He read the invitation for her to train Guatemalan young people on the streets of Guatemala City. "So you finally got the invitation?"

"Yeah, but I don't know—"

"Have you given them a response?"

"I emailed them I wanted to pray about it."

Clay smiled. "And have you? *Prayed*?"

"No." She rolled her eyes. And smiled.

"So you don't want to go?"

Hannah leaned forward. "It's not that. I'd love to help them reach those kids."

The waitress was back with their French toast. She topped up their coffee cups and moved away again.

Hannah took a sip of coffee and then continued. "I'd love it if I'd been invited as part of a team, but they want—"

"They want you to teach them. To work your magic across Guatemala City. Like you've done here."

Hannah frowned. "Yeah, but I've got no magic." She set down her coffee cup. "I'm not sure *why* what we're doing is working. Nobody could be more astounded than me what's been happening across Vancouver. And yeah, okay, I know God's powerfully at work among hardened youth here. But I can't teach what I don't understand."

"But you gotta admit that your fearless attitude is part of it. There isn't a situation you won't—"

"No, that's not it." She shook her head. "C'mon Clay, there's street ministries in the big inner cities of the United States who've got people roaming deep into situations a hundred times worse than anything here."

"And nobody's talking about them at the big international conferences?"

She gave an awkward smile. "Exactly."

It was quiet at the table for a minute. Hannah picked up a fork and took her first bite of French toast. Then setting down her fork again, she said, "Late at night, when I'm honest with myself, I often wonder if it's somebody on my team. That God is blessing our efforts because of something that somebody on my team is doing. It's something *they're* doing. And it has nothing to do with me."

"What could they be doing you wouldn't know about?"

"I don't have a clue."

"And you're getting the credit." Clay smiled.

"Unfortunately, yes." She frowned again. "And so I go to Guatemala. But the person who's responsible for God's blessing doesn't go with me. And so nothing— absolutely *nothing* happens for those kids."

"No. I don't think that's gonna happen." Clay set down his fork and picked up the letter. "It's right here. Forty Guatemalan church leaders have prayed. They've fasted. They've heard from God. And the only name they heard was—?"

"Mine."

Clay set down the letter. "Sorry. No mention of a partner. God wants you."

The next morning Clay awoke, dressed, and exited his building. It was frigid. The entire neighborhood was sparkling and rigid with a glaze of frost. It was beautiful.

Another blessing of being up so early. Clay smiled. While warming up the Civic he decided against heading for the alleys of the Downtown Eastside. Instead he wound his way through the frost-covered neighborhoods towards the Granville Street area. There he found an empty parking garage, parked, and exited his car. For Clay, it reminded him of where he'd first discovered Brent wrapped into his torn blankets. He sat down on a ledge of concrete and pulled the hood of his sweatshirt up. It was cold. He rubbed his hands together, pulled out his Bible, and began.

"Father, I humbly come before you, to give you praise. I was nobody you should have cared about and yet you, in your amazing grace, ran to the end of the road to rescue me—"

Thirty-five minutes of celebrating what God had done in his life disappeared quickly. Repentance. Thankfulness. Worship. Clay admitted the sins in his life, asked for forgiveness, and for the strength to live differently.

Then he pulled out his list. Written on it were thirteen brutal locations where the Spirit of God was working hard to penetrate the hearts of men. Working to replace their fear, anger, and selfishness with joy, peace, and love. To bring them to salvation and transformation.

North Korea had been added to his list several days earlier. His research had revealed a level of persecution against his Christian brothers and sisters there that could only be described as barbaric. A lot of them were in prison. He knew that only filled with the Spirit of Christ would they stand firm when facing the brutality of prison. Especially if they were tortured, or lined up to be executed.

Clay swallowed. Filled with the Spirit, the church in North Korea could thrive regardless of what was thrown at them. Those who were afraid could find peace. Those who'd been worn down, their spirits crushed, and were readying themselves to embrace their government's ideology, could discover the courage to remain true to their faith.

And then, when given the opportunity, they could share the freedom found in Jesus Christ. With cellmates and guards.

He prayed. He asked that thousands of lives would be changed today. That the Spirit of God would descend like a blanket across all of Asia. He lifted up the pastors and churches across India. And that hundreds of native missionaries who were sharing the Gospel of Christ among India's three hundred million Untouchables could see visible evidence that God was with them. He remembered the graduates who would soon journey across India from the Bible school being built near Raipur. He prayed for the students currently in the other Bible schools. He lifted up the sites of his six drilled water wells.

One of his favorite focuses during prayer were the ragged little villages where the video bicycle team was showing the Indian-made 'Jesus' film. He didn't know where the film was, but God certainly did. He prayed for every person on that team, and for every audience of the film.

He moved upward through his list until he got to the first line.

The first line was special.

It was for Hannah's work among the at-risk and homeless youth who made their home on the streets of Vancouver. Clay smiled. He ran his finger across her name, allowing a ragged breath to escape him. Then, with the excitement that always flooded his heart whenever he mentioned her name, Clay lifted up Hannah Taylor to the throne of God.

"Father God, I approach you humbly, and ask that You would fill Hannah with the Spirit of

Christ. May she roam the streets of this city filled with Your Spirit. Filled with Your love, joy, and peace. May every hurting young person be convinced, within minutes of meeting her, that You're pursuing them. That the most hardened youth would somehow know You've sent her as a messenger of Your coming rescue."

Clay swallowed. "And Lord, regardless of how violent any situation gets, or if her life is threatened, give her the strength to respond with gentleness and kindness. Replace her fear with boldness and courage.

"And Father, may the Spirit enable her to love these kids with a depth of love they've never experienced before. A love that would encourage them to trust her with their fragile lives. And with their hurt."

Clay continued for another forty minutes.

Directly across the street from the parking garage where Clay was sitting was the Reimer Building. Within its twenty-seven floors were the offices of some of Vancouver's most prestigious corporations. But, at five-thirty this morning, what set it apart from every other building in Vancouver weren't the wealthy clients who'd leased space within its iconic structure, but rather the person who now stood three hundred feet above the sidewalk on the darkened edge of its flat roof. For there, with a frosty wind swirling around him, Nigel stood calmly looking down. He was, again, watching Clay.

But more importantly, he was listening to his prayers.

He smiled. "Oh yeah, Hannah. You might not know it, but yes, you've got a partner. And he's going to assure that you accomplish more than you can imagine in Guatemala City."

Another smile, a last glance towards Clay, and Nigel vanished.

Chapter Twenty-Three

Things experienced during childhood often set a pattern for the rest of our lives. We'll see something, often even for the briefest of moments, and it's engraved upon our minds. We *want* that. Or we want to *do* that. Or we want to *be* that. It could be at an airshow or on the back page of a comic book. It could be at a rodeo or an opera. For Clay, the experience that set the die for his life happened in a single bay garage on his grandpa's property outside of Saskatoon. He was nine. Grandpa Jim had taken him across his yard, unlocked the heavy padlock that secured the door, pushed it open, and then switched on the lights inside the garage.

There wasn't a car inside. Or even a motorcycle.

Instead, the space had been converted into an extremely well-equipped workshop. Clay had hesitantly stepped inside, removed his shoes and stepped onto polished floors that reflected the bright overhead lights. Well-labelled cabinets filled an entire wall with all sorts of electrical gizmos and gadgets that Clay couldn't have named. Along the other three walls were clean work surfaces with their own overhead lights. Across the back, rows of books were neatly arranged. A large chalkboard covered one wall with electrical diagrams and random calculations.

But in the middle of the room was a wide table, upon which sat some sort of half-constructed metal device about the size of a Kleenex box.

That was the moment in Clay's life when everything changed.

The moment of magic arrived for him when his grandpa handed him the unpainted, metal-sided box containing dozens of electronic components connected by thread-like paths of silver solder.

"What you're holding is going to allow people to bring the arcade games you see at the mall, into their own homes, to play them on their televisions."

Clay's wide-eyed response had been a certified "Whoa. That's so cool."

The device certainly hadn't been much to look at. Its metal cover had been hand-fabricated and then discolored by soldering burns. It looked homemade and amateurish. And being an early prototype, it didn't work. What his grandpa hadn't told Clay was that he was in a frantic race. And it was a race against some of the biggest names in electronics and dozens of talented startups, to create the first computer gaming console!

It'd been eighteen days since the funeral. Clay sat on a chair in his kitchen holding the unopened envelope from his grandpa. It was time. He slid a knife under its flap and gently worked it along the seal. Inside was a folded sheet of paper. He pulled it out and a check fell from inside to land face-down on the counter. Ignoring the check, he unfolded the letter.

Dear Clay,

I want you to know I'm proud of you. I always was, even as Nasty Dogs was being torn apart by creditors. I know it hurt to lose everything, but I want you to keep going. Keep dreaming. Keep working on projects that have the possibility of changing the entire world. I have great confidence that you'll discover another idea, an idea better than what you created in Nasty Dogs. An idea that will change everything for millions of people. Don't give up. Don't ever give up!

Always remember, the prize is not for those who sit on the sidelines, but for those who struggle in the arena. Those who risk everything in the hopes of great victory.

You know I lost the race to bring out the first home gaming console. I lost to the Atari 2600.

And yes, it hurt to watch other people create gaming empires across the globe while I continued on at CN Rail. But ninth place, or twenty-ninth place, or in whatever place I finished, still paid pretty well when I sold my version to Magnavox. I've included a bit of that cash for you here. Use it on whatever your current project is. And know that I always loved you. And lived every day proud of you.

Your Grandpa Jim.

Clay leaned back in his chair and stared at his grandpa's words. They seemed somehow prophetic. Clay had certainly discovered something that would change everything for millions of people. In just a few years, the half-constructed Bible school in Raipur would graduate its first class of a hundred missionaries. And with them, the Gospel would be journeyed into some of the poorest places on the planet. And with another hundred graduates the year after that. And the year after that.

He reached out and flipped over the check. One look and he almost fainted.

It was for fifty thousand dollars!

Clay pulled the Civic off the road and rolled through the treed entrance of Kitty Coleman Campground. With it being winter there weren't many campers.

Gary and Pam were standing outside drinking coffee as he pulled up. Their kids swooped past him on their bikes as he exited the car. Clay waved to them. Then he was eagerly invited into the tiny trailer for coffee. Just before he went in, he grabbed his portable DVD player.

Some conversations build us up and refresh our vision. They encourage us to push aside the earthly struggles we all face, and to set our eyes firmly on Jesus. They bring into sharp focus again what our lives should be about, and equip us to move ahead with confidence. Gary and Pam, living with their three kids in a borrowed travel trailer, were champions of such conversations with Clay.

Gary and Pam had just sent three thousand dollars to help pastors in northern Sudan who'd had their homes and churches burned to the ground. They discussed the persecution in Northern Africa for a few minutes. And then Pam looked across at Clay. "How are you doing since your grandfather's passing? Have you been okay?"

Clay took an extra second before answering. "It's been hard, but the death of my grandpa has cemented into my mind what we're doing with our finances, and with our lives, is real. And it's important. It isn't foolish or risky. Real lives are at stake. The Bible repeatedly tries to remind us our lives are short, but we don't see it. And suddenly, without warning, somebody we know takes that step from this life into eternity." He paused. "Their minutes spiral to zero, and all they've got is the numbers they held in that last moment."

"Yeah. And suddenly how we're living our lives doesn't seem so crazy." Gary laughed as they all glanced around the narrow trailer.

With that, Pam got up to refill their coffee cups. "So what did you want to discuss with us?" Gary nodded towards Clay's portable DVD player. "You didn't drive for an hour and a half without a reason."

Another brief silence. "My grandpa left me fifty grand."

"That's—that's pretty nice."

"Yeah. And he invited me to spend it on my latest project."

"Your latest project—?" Gary leaned forward. "So you're going to spend it in Asia?"

"I am." Clay flipped up the little screen of his DVD player, clicked it on and turned it towards Gary and Pam. He tapped the 'start' button and a short video played. For seven minutes, Gary and Pam sat mesmerized.

"In the note he encouraged me to use the money on a project that would change the lives of millions of people. I'm thinking of purchasing two of these." Clay pointed towards the image on the screen.

Both Gary and Pam whistled.

"I know it's a bit optimistic to think in terms of millions, but it's not unreasonable to think of maybe a hundred thousand. Or they might do twice that."

Gary smiled. "I think it's a great choice."

Pam was still staring at the final image on the screen. She shook her head slowly. "Don't be so quick to dismiss the idea of millions. Yes, in their lifetimes, two of these could help touch the lives of hundreds of thousands. But what God accomplishes through *those* lives, as they devote themselves to Him, could easily reach deep into the millions."

Clay nodded.

"What's your current number?" Pam nodded towards his watch.

Clay held the watch up where she could see it. The numbers were rolling over steadily, the digits never fully forming. He'd just passed four hundred thousand.

"Are your numbers speeding up?"

Clay laughed. "Oh yeah."

Pam smiled. "Well then let's get them going even faster. Let's pray."

Clay didn't make it all the way home. Instead, seeing the exit signs for Surrey, he pulled off the freeway. He continued along one of the main streets through the suburb. The nicer neighborhoods gradually gave way to lower income areas. He kept going until he got to Scott Road. The area hadn't improved since his last visit. The storefronts were still boarded over and streetlights destroyed by vandals were still dark. Clay slowed and pulled into the parking lot of the weathered community hall.

The tilted, hand-painted sign advertising ballroom dancing and a swap meet was still there. What weren't there were the motorcycles of the Disciple Riders. The place was deserted.

Clay shut off the ignition and exited his car.

He moved to sit on the sidewalk outside the entrance. He smiled. So much had changed for him here. The desire to end his life had come to a stop right here. He'd found life, a life he couldn't ever have imagined, right here. A life devoted to God. A life that was attempting to bring freedom and life to people in places where his old self had brought only pain and death.

Clay pulled himself from the asphalt and retrieved his little DVD player from the Civic. He set it on the roof, clicked it on, and played the video again. He never tired of watching it.

The SUV was like a Toyota Land Cruiser, but Indian-made. It was racing down a dusty, gravel road somewhere in rural India. On board were five young men. All of them were smiling, eager to get wherever the little truck was heading. The narrator introduced them as recent graduates of an Indian Bible school. The camera angle pulled back to get a better look at the outside of the truck as it approached the outskirts of a village. Everything was dusty. Tethered livestock and mangy dogs watched as the truck rolled past. The camera rose up to allow an aerial look across the roofs of hundreds of dismal, sagging shacks of torn plastic and mud brick.

The next scenes were filled with laughing, smiling children as the young men unloaded the truck. The narrator added commentary about the plight of these children, most of who would never go to school. Instead, as Dalits, as Untouchables, they'd spend their lives exploited by all the other castes in Indian society. Seen as cursed within Hinduism, they'd spend their lives as virtual slaves, doing the most disgusting jobs imaginable.

To make its point, the camera refocused further along the street where a toothless man carried two buckets supported on a pole across his stooped shoulders. Everyone he passed swore at him and hurried away. For what was in the buckets wasn't fruit or vegetables, but rather, human excrement. This man, the narration continued, probably in his seventies, was part of the sewage system within the village. And had been for his entire life.

The video image changed again to several of the young men setting up a screen and a video projector. Again, they were surrounded by mobs of excited kids. The scene changed again to focus on two of the others from the SUV. They were standing on a dusty street, amidst the bright colors of an outdoor market, handing out Gospel tracts and invitations to the film showing.

And then the images on the laptop grew darker. It was night and Clay was witnessing a film showing of the Indian-made 'Jesus' film. In the middle of a scrabbly field, sitting on the ground, were probably three hundred people of all ages, gripped by the story unfolding on the screen.

The cameraman pulled back so that you could now see the Indian-made sport utility vehicle sitting silently in the foreground. The narrator added, "Tomorrow, this little truck will be carrying the message of salvation in Jesus to another village. And to another village the day after that."

The video ended with a silhouette of one of the villagers praying with one of the young men.

Clay smiled and closed the little DVD player. He knew one of the Indian-made SUVs, fully equipped with a video projector, generator, and screen would cost $24,000. Two of them would be $48,000. That left two thousand dollars from his grandpa's gift for gas, Bibles, and whatever else was needed to get those two teams team headed towards their first village.

He pulled out his checkbook.

This was the perfect location to do this. He smiled as he remembered Eve, with the Disciple Riders who'd given him the Bible just before they'd pulled away on their Harleys. What had she said to Clay? 'Remember your incredible thankfulness of this night— *remember it for the rest of your life*— and live out every minute, proclaiming your thankfulness by what you do. Okay?'

Okay. He pulled out a check and wrote it for the amount of fifty-thousand dollars. He dated it and signed his name.

He'd brought an envelope and a piece of notepaper. He wrote GraceUnfathomable a short note about his desire to pay for two of these fully equipped, missionary vehicles. And then, inserting both the note and check into the envelope, he sealed it.

Clay set the envelope inside his car and then, barely able to contain his excitement, he celebrated in the late-night darkness of the parking lot. The evening ended with Clay worshipping, kneeling on the asphalt. He'd never been so thankful.

But his last words were spoken through tears. "Lord God, these vehicles are yours. They are to be used in your service, and they can be deployed wherever you wish. But Lord, if it's at all possible—" He breathed out. "—could you have one of them journey to the ragged little slum village of Shiliguri?"

Across the street, someone was standing, hidden into the darkness outside a boarded-up supermarket. He'd watched with great interest as Clay had celebrated. He'd listened to his prayers and thankfulness. But those final words, that final request, made him smile. “Well done, Clay.” Then Nigel pulled up the collar of his coat and headed silently back along the sidewalk that had delivered him to that spot.

Chapter Twenty-Four

Hannah had dated a number of different guys throughout the years. All of them had kept to the usual, modern dating protocols that emphasize expensive activities and dinners at high-end restaurants. The new Clay Rawlings wasn't following those rules at all. He invited her out several times, but the bill was always moderate and the atmosphere casual. A low-end steak house. A waffle place. A spaghetti dinner at his church.

Hannah certainly wasn't complaining. There was something wonderfully refreshing about it. But her co-workers at Children from the Dark were less impressed. They kidded her that Clay was cheap. They'd even started a wager about when Clay would invite her for their first big, formal dinner. Something with impressive views of the ocean and a nine-page wine list.

They didn't have to wait too long.

It was a Wednesday morning about ten-thirty when she took his call. "Hannah, are you available all day Saturday?"

"I might be. What were you thinking?"

"I got us invited onto a two-hundred foot vessel leaving at about eight o'clock from a dock south of Vancouver. We'll have breakfast onboard. We'll tour the Gulf Islands for the day, and return late in the evening. They've promised me a table overlooking the water, both for breakfast and dinner. The views are quite spectacular, I can promise that. But there's something on one of the islands I want you to see."

"Are you giving me any hints of what it might be?"

"Sorry, no hints."

"Okay. Yes, I'm available on Saturday." She hesitated. "What should I wear?"

"Well, the captain and crew will all be in uniform, but guests are encouraged to dress casually."

Hannah laughed to herself. This was more like the old Clay. *A two hundred-foot boat? Whoa.* That'd be a mega-yacht! She'd just been invited to spend Saturday touring the Gulf Islands aboard a mega-yacht. And he'd promised dinner aboard, which of course would include a spectacular eight or nine course dinner. This oughta shut up her co-workers.

Actually, the boat wasn't a mega-yacht. It was the *Queen of Capilano,* one of the government-run ferries that gave access to the little group of islands nestled between the mainland and Vancouver Island. Hannah laughed out loud when they passed under the signs announcing the approaching ferry terminal. She punched him in the shoulder good-naturedly. "You promised me a day aboard a mega-yacht!"

"No. I said it was a two hundred foot vessel. And it is."

Within minutes of boarding, Clay and Hannah were outside on the upper deck watching seagulls gliding along on the air currents. If Hannah had been mildly disappointed, it disappeared pretty quickly. She'd spent little time on the water and the views from the ferry overwhelmed her. Especially when it journeyed between the islands. The coastline, with waves crashing onto windswept beaches, was, as Clay had promised, spectacular.

And they saw most of the islands. The ferry was on some kind of milk-run. So Clay had them remain on the ferry as it docked at several of the smaller islands, not allowing them to disembark until they arrived at the northern-most stop, Galiano Island.

They walked down the ramp to an open shelter attached to a tiny post office. Six other walk-offs got off with them before the vehicle traffic disembarked. The other walk-offs rode away on bicycles or hurried towards waiting vehicles. The happy bark of dogs greeted several of them. Clay waited until all the traffic had disappeared before he led Hannah across the parking lot to a waiting, quad-cab pickup truck. It was a work vehicle, the name of a construction company across the door.

"You're Clay Rawlings?" The driver inside wasn't smiling. He wore a jacket that couldn't hide his muscular build.

"I am." Clay offered his hand. The driver didn't reach to shake it.

"Got any identification?"

"Yeah, I do." He pulled out his wallet and produced his driver's license.

Hannah wasn't sure what to think. *Why did Clay need to give this guy identification?*

The driver gave Clay's license a serious examination. Still no smile. "So who do you know? Who told you about us?"

"Nigel Lockheed."

That name obviously meant something to the driver. He quickly handed back Clay's ID. "How do you know Nigel?"

"He's my investment broker."

That was news to Hannah. She'd never heard Clay mention having an investment broker. So she was surprised when the driver broke out into a wide smile. "You're a client of Nigel's?"

"Yeah." Clay nodded.

Hannah was completely floored when the muscular driver threw open the door of the pickup, leapt out, and pulled Clay into a powerful embrace. "My brother. Praise God! Welcome to Galiano Island." He turned towards Hannah. "And who's this?"

Clay reached for Hannah's hand. "This is Hannah Taylor. One of the investors in your project here on the island."

Hannah stared at Clay. *I'm what?*

"Miss Taylor. Of course." He smiled and gently shook her hand. "You've been a huge part of what we're building here. I think you're going to be pleased with what you're about to see. C'mon—" He swung back into the cab of the pickup and started the engine.

"Clay, what's going on here?" She gripped his hand tighter. "What are we doing?"

"I'm going to show you what you're building with your life." He winked at her before sliding into the rear seat. Hannah hesitantly got into the front passenger seat.

The driver's name was Henry. And he was tight-lipped about where they were going. Instead he talked about the efforts of his team to keep security tight. Hannah guessed he might be ex-military. He spoke in a clipped tone, filled with security jargon. She tried to relax. Wherever they were going was a well-kept secret, and rough men like Henry were being paid to keep it that way. And yet, somehow, Clay knew about it. That didn't make any sense, but then, what did make sense about the life Clay lived now? Not a lot. She leaned back in the seat and watched as the beauty of Galiano Island, and its hundreds of sheltered coves, passed by.

The pickup continued until they crossed a bridge. It was like the bridge signified a dividing line. The pavement got worse and the number of homes decreased. Anybody who chose to build a home and live on the northern end of Galiano obviously valued their privacy. Henry kept their speed even and gradually the homes, as few as there'd been to this point, disappeared altogether.

They kept going until Henry slowed and then turned the truck onto a newly paved driveway surrounded by a tall stand of trees. The trees completely shielded whoever lived on the property. Hannah inwardly laughed. *Another island resident with serious privacy issues.*

Forty yards from the entrance, out of view of the main road, Henry pulled the truck to a stop at a heavily reinforced security gate. He swiped a magnetic card through an electronic reader and the gate swung away smoothly. The property was large and relatively flat, the paved driveway continuing towards a ridge line that hid the waterfront.

Henry stopped the truck before they crossed the ridge line. He turned to face Hannah. "Many of those kids you're rescuing on the streets of Vancouver can't go home. They've been abandoned, or their parents are abusive. Or they're fighting the demons of an addiction. So they face significant problems and maybe no relative wants them. There's no safe place for them." Henry's expression had turned to stone. His words slowed.

"Or worse, they've been pulled into the sex trade and some really nasty people have put a price on them. A price they'll never work off. They want to escape the streets, escape the filmstrip of horror their life has become, but where can they go? The city's not that big and they're scared out of their minds. And the animals that'll be hunting them are violent and relentless. So, if they can't go home and they can't stay on the streets, where can they go?"

He put the pickup in gear and idled up onto the ridge. And as what lay beyond the ridge came into view, Hannah's mouth fell open.

Henry smiled. "For those kids we're building *this*. Welcome to Children from the Dark's new island campus."

Clay and Hannah were standing on a narrow pebble beach looking back towards the six majestic buildings of the campus, all in various stages of completion. They'd spent an hour touring the grounds with Henry. The largest building, what Henry had said was slated to become the main dining room, was still just laminated cedar beams and a lot of angular framing. Two cranes were lifting huge sheets of glass into place. Beyond the dining room were the three residence buildings and a classroom building, currently being wrapped in vertical cedar siding. The sound of circular saws and nail guns could be heard across the property. Two slow-turning concrete trucks waited as concrete finishers worked feverishly on the foundation for a gymnasium.

"It's going to be gorgeous. The view from the dining room is going to be incredible." Hannah turned to look towards the little cove that surrounded them. A long, white dock projected out into the water. To the west she could make out the mountains of Vancouver Island. Another one of the Gulf Islands sat to the north. "It's so peaceful here."

"It's the perfect place to bring rescued kids." Clay smiled.

Hannah walked over and sat on the edge of the dock. "I've known about this project for almost a year and a half." She shook her head and smiled. "But it was kept pretty quiet. I was told I'd never know where it was to be built. That the young people who'd come here would be safer if its location was kept a secret."

"That's probably true."

"There was a rumor we'd bought an isolated fishing camp north of Vancouver. The place was isolated, supposedly buried deep into Bute Inlet. It was to be renovated into a rescue station for the street kids. I've even seen the paperwork for the purchase of a jet-boat they hoped to use to transport the kids."

Clay nodded. "The rumors were probably started intentionally. And the bogus paperwork would have added to the misdirection. Good planning on somebody's part."

Hannah got up, kicked off her shoes, and walked to the end of the dock. Clay waited a moment before following her. She was looking out into the water, her arms wrapped around herself. They stood silently for a few long minutes before she reached over and took his hand. "Thank you. Thank you so much for bringing me here."

"You're here because you invested in this project. You invested in a project you knew you'd never see, and somebody thought you should see what faith can do."

"I did give some money towards this—"

"Yeah, you did. If we include the check you sent last Tuesday, your total contributions towards this little rescue station have been about sixty-two hundred dollars."

Hannah stared at him.

"A year from now, this place is going to be home to young people who've never been able to trust anybody. Guys like Henry are going to be protecting them, and befriending them. Those young people are going to be introduced to a life they couldn't possibly imagine today as they're out there panhandling on the streets of Vancouver. A life of freedom in Jesus Christ." Clay paused.

"You were faithful with the money God gave you to invest in His kingdom. And He's going to use it to remove the fear from the eyes of fifteen-year olds. And to remove the shame from the minds of seventeen-year old girls who, tonight, will be selling themselves. Not a bad investment."

Hannah wanted to speak, to say something, but nothing seemed adequate. She could feel tears welling up in her eyes. Somehow he'd expressed exactly what she'd been hoping for when she'd written those checks.

They had dinner aboard the *Queen of Capilano*. It was a rather tasteless attempt at roast beef and mashed potatoes. There wasn't a wine list. No sterling silver utensils or white tablecloths. But she knew that nobody, maybe not ever in the rest of recorded history, would ever top this date. Or this day.

After dinner Clay asked if she'd like to see the lights of Vancouver from the water, and so they moved outside onto the upper deck. The wind was wild on the empty deck and so he moved in front of her in an attempt to shield her from it. His move seemed perfectly timed for what she'd been thinking about since dinner. She grabbed his coat and slowly pulled him to her. Their lips met and for the next two and half minutes they had their first kiss. Or at least since highschool.

November isn't an especially pleasant month in Vancouver. It's cold and wet, with lots of wind.

At High-Q Robotics it was considered an ideal travel month. Spending a couple of weeks aboard a cruise-ship somewhere in the Caribbean certainly sounded better than swamping through the deep puddles and razor-edged winds of the Pacific Northwest. Or a couple of balmy weeks at an all-inclusive somewhere in Mexico. One of those places with a dozen pools, a golf course, and lots of free alcohol. The distraction of journeying somewhere hot, where a smiling staff catered to your every whim, made winter easier to handle. And so among the staff at High-Q, conversations about travel, during November, are constant.

Chad Westbrook arrived to Clay's workstation three shades darker than he'd been just ten days earlier. He'd stopped by to catch up on the technical details of a current project. He stood while he wrote some stuff down and asked several questions, and then glancing around, he pulled up a chair and sat down.

"Hey, I know you used to have a place in the Bahamas—" The standard opening Clay had heard a dozen times before. Guys often approached him with this opening, wanting him to fill in the sordid details of his past life.

"Yeah, I did. It was nice."

"Nice—?" Chad snorted. "I just spent ten days in Jamaica. Didn't want to come back here. Not ever."

"Yeah well, the weather is certainly better than here." Clay hoped that a flat, empty response could stop what was coming, but knew it was probably hopeless. And he was right.

"Man, it was like my ninth time vacationing there, and each time the wife and I just want to ditch everything and stay. This time we got a little place on an isolated cove, with its own private beach. Clearest blue waters. Nobody around for miles. Private, y'know?"

Clay smiled. He was thinking of Children from the Dark's new island campus on Galiano. He looked at Chad. "Yeah, I know about private places on secluded islands. They can be the greatest investment a person can make."

Chapter Twenty-Five

It was another early morning. Clay was back in the Downtown Eastside, leaning against the rear entrance to a bar. His jacket hood was pulled up, his eyes closed, his lips barely moving. All around him, even so early in the morning, the drug trade was busy. Rumpled cash and baggies of product were being traded. Also busy were the desperate addicts who spent hours every day searching the corners of the alleys, poking through the gravel and garbage in a constant search for the tiniest shard of the precious rock of crack cocaine. They moved around Clay like he wasn't there, their glassy eyes riveted to the floor of the alley.

Clay was praying for the two sponsored children he'd added to his list. He knew little about their past life. What he did know was that they were now attending school at one of GraceUnfathomable's

Learning Curve centers. They'd each have been supplied a uniform and would enjoy a nutritious lunch every day. He prayed they'd do well in school and that an education would help them discover a far better life than their parents had suffered. But more importantly, he prayed they'd find an entirely different life in Jesus.

Fifteen emotional minutes passed as he prayed for them, their teachers, parents, and their communities. Then he moved down the list to pray for the thousands of part-time pastors of the churches that were being planted all across northern India. But the lighting in the alley was weak, and as he moved the list into a sliver of light from an overhead bulb, he glanced at the watch.

That brief look stopped him.

The minutes of his life were spinning away again. The numbers disappearing too fast to form proper digits. The minutes of his life were in freefall like a piano thrown from a skyscraper. He stared at the numbers dumbly, his heart-rate increasing. He waited. The freefall continued for what seemed like a long time. The number that was left when it stopped was smaller. It was *a lot smaller.*

Clay held his breath as he did the calculations.

He'd just lost another four and a half years.

He'd now be entering eternity at age forty-six. Somewhere in the month of February. That was only twelve years away! His leg muscles turned to dust and he crumpled to the asphalt. He looked around at the filthy alley and the roaming addicts that surrounded him. *Am I going to* die *in a place like this?*

He hoped Nigel might appear, and he waited expectantly, but Nigel didn't show up. And so instead, Clay pulled out his Bible, and searched its pages for some kind of hope, some kind of reassurance that God knew what was happening. *C'mon, Lord, I need your help here.* He flipped randomly across the Old Testament, but nothing jumped out at him. And then a tiny voice in the back of his mind spoke.

Hebrews 11.

Clay wasn't sure if he'd imagined it. Or if he was remembering a reference from one of his pastor's recent sermons. Whatever. He flipped forward through the pages until he reached Hebrews 11. It was some kind of listing of people who'd followed God by faith. Abel. Enoch. Noah. Abraham. At verse 13 Clay found something that seemed directed towards him:

> *'All these people were still living by faith when they died. They did not receive the things promised; they only saw and welcomed them from a distance. And they admitted they were aliens and strangers on earth. People who say such things show they are looking for a country of their own. If they had been thinking of the country they had left, they would have had opportunity to return. Instead, they were longing*

for a better country—a heavenly one. Therefore God is not ashamed to be called their God, for He has prepared a city for them.'

Clay stopped. He read the passage again. Was he longing for a better country? He wasn't sure. He lived his life wanting only to say 'thank you' for what had been done for him. That wasn't the same as longing for heaven. He was still looking at the passage when he felt someone sit down onto the asphalt beside him.

"So what does the passage mean? And how does it relate to you?" Nigel's question arrived slowly in the shadowy darkness.

Clay read the passage again. "It's pointing us towards eternity. The whole chapter of Hebrews 11 seems to be about people who trusted God even when it wasn't easy. They were doing stuff the people around them told them was crazy. But they trusted God knew what He was doing—"

"Right. And they trusted the words of God rather than the words of those around them."

"Yeah—"

"And what does the Word of God promise for those who live like that?"

Clay read it all again. "He's created a city for them. A better country. A heavenly one."

"So He's promised them a great eternity." Nigel leaned back. "But did the lives of the people of chapter eleven look like victory to those around them?"

"No."

"So what's the message of this passage— for you, sitting right here? Especially knowing you're making the jump to eternity in twelve years."

Clay didn't have to read it again. "I've got a choice. I've got the choice of trusting God, even when He asks me to accept some hard things. Stuff other people won't understand, but knowing I'll spend all of eternity with Him, in the heavenly country He's prepared for me—"

"And the other option?"

"I—I can reject God's plan for my life. And return to the ease and acceptance of the country I left behind."

"So you can stop the minutes from disappearing from the watch? You *could* stop it if you wanted?"

Clay had to think about that. "Yeah, I guess I can. That's what the verse means when it says I have opportunity to return to the country I left behind. I can choose to return to living like those around me." He paused and looked again at the watch. "Like—like I did when I rejected Him back in high school."

Nigel remained silent.

Clay breathed out. "I've noticed the minutes of my life only disappear in huge chunks when I'm living a life of faith. When I'm sitting in places like this. So I'm pretty sure my numbers spiraling downward are linked to my sitting here. And so I'm probably going to die in a place like this, aren't

I?" He took a long look around the darkness of the alley, and then back towards Nigel who didn't respond.

"That's what you meant when you told me the minutes of my life and my worth numbers are related, isn't it?"

"Yes. The two numbers are related. And that's true for everybody. To say you trust God but not act differently than those who make no such claim is foolishness. You understand that. And so here you are this morning, sitting in a place that helps elevate your worth numbers but heavily subtracts minutes from your life." Nigel's words slowed. "You're sitting in a place most people would say is dangerous. And those same people would say your financial giving numbers are impractical. Maybe even foolish."

Clay turned towards Nigel. "And so this passage is reassuring me that this, *for me*, is the life of faith, right?"

"Correct. You've had every opportunity to walk away, but you haven't. Your actions give clear evidence of you trusting in God. You live with a savings account balance that rarely rises above a thousand dollars, and spend a lot of your free time in filthy places like this, in prayer. The kind of place where one day you'll die. So yes, for you, this is the life of faith."

Hannah tried to live like nothing had changed in her life, but it was a failed effort. She was in love and all of her staff knew it. When it was obvious they knew, she allowed herself to place two small pictures of Clay on her desk. They were small, what she considered perfectly acceptable for a professional in the workplace. Her staff disagreed with her definition of what was acceptable, and let her know it. One morning she arrived to find an 8x10 of Clay embracing a homeless man in an alley stapled to her bulletin board. Whoever had taken the picture had caught the full impact and emotional power of the moment. Hannah carefully removed the staple, took it home and framed it.

Three days later another one arrived. Clay kneeling beside a young teen girl on a gurney outside an ambulance. It was a tight shot, taken with a long lens, with just Clay and the girl in focus. The smear of blood and tears across the girl's face gripped your attention. Everything else in the photo was dark and hazy. Hannah allowed that one to stay on her bulletin board. That was a mistake. Her staff took it as permission to have a full blown, Clay Rawlings photo contest.

A black and white of Clay embracing an older, weathered prostitute found its way onto the board. Then three rapid, tight shots of him inside a diner with two teens, their jet-black dyed hair and silver piercings contrasted sharply against the fire-red vinyl of the booth. The three, high-speed photographs had caught them all mid-laugh. They were great pictures.

Slowly the bulletin board was filled. Shots of Clay kneeling in prayer or wandering the alleys in the hazy darkness. Shots of him sitting on the steps of grimy welfare hotels and standing in the rain with addicts. Some of the photos were low quality and hurried, obviously taken with cheap, disposable cameras. Others had the artistic signature of having been shot with highly professional, photographic gear. Nobody volunteered any clues as to who'd taken which pictures and Hannah didn't ask. But she found herself spending more time than she should have, staring at the board. And thinking about Clay.

"I don't know if I can do this." Hannah and Val were walking through Stanley Park, the last of the fallen leaves coloring the lawns. "Everything I've ever hoped for has happened in Vancouver, with hundreds of hurting young people finding real hope—"

"And them taking their first steps towards a life they probably couldn't have imagined." Val finished for her.

"It's been amazing."

"And now, in the midst of everything you've always hoped for, other places are calling. Harder places." Val smiled. "Places a long ways away from Clay."

Hannah stopped and stared out towards the water. "A year ago I'd have loved to hear I was being discussed at international conferences halfway around the world. And that I'd be receiving invitations to work with outreach teams in Third-world cities. And now—?"

"Now you want to be here."

"I do. I want to be here."

Val stepped closer and embraced her. "Holding onto him?"

"And never letting go." A tear worked its way down Hannah's cheek.

They stared out at the water for a long time.

"So when are you leaving?"

"December third. Three weeks from now. My flight will arrive to Guatemala City in the early morning."

An ice storm hit northern India, along the Nepal border, plunging temperatures to levels not seen in seventy years. Within a week everything simply froze. Gale force winds descending from the mountains ripped through the villages without mercy. The poorest people of the area, families huddled together in threadbare clothing, living under bridges and rail overpasses, died first. Then those within flimsy huts of plastic and tin, shelters that offered little protection, died. They froze to death, the cheap materials of their homes scattered across the landscape by the raging winds. The temperatures continued to plummet. Firewood and anything the poor could use as a fuel source ran out. The death toll was soon in the hundreds.

It was late and everything at High-Q Robotics was quiet, most of the employees having already gone home. On the second floor Clay was finishing up a project. At one point, to take a quick break, he checked his personal email. Waiting for him was this message:

> *Dear Clay,*
> *The entire staff here at GraceUnfathomable wanted to especially thank you for the gift we received from you of two thousand dollars. Your generous and timely gift has already been used to provide 166 warm blankets during one of the worst storms to hit northern India in decades. Your blankets were handed out by missionary teams and pastors ministering among the survivors during the storm. You will never know their thankfulness for your gift...*

The email went on to briefly describe the horrific conditions that met the ministry teams upon their arrival. Entire families lay dead on the sidewalks, already stiff and glassy from the cold. Desperate mothers and fathers had dressed their children in their own warmer clothes, in a failed attempt to keep them alive. Burials would have to wait. At this point, with the temperatures still deep into the negatives, keeping survivors alive remained the frantic priority. The email went on to describe how much good his blankets were accomplishing. It ended with another heartfelt thank you.

Clay stared at the message. He swallowed. His gift had been two thousand dollars. Enough for 166 blankets. He grabbed a piece of paper and a pen. *One hundred and sixty-six.* He started slowly to stab out short, vertical marks across the piece of paper, close together. Forty of them…sixty…eighty… a hundred… a hundred and ten… a hundred and twenty-five… a hundred and forty… A hundred and fifty… A hundred and fifty-eight… A hundred and sixty-three. A hundred and sixty-four. A hundred and sixty-five. And finally, the last mark, giving a visual picture of one hundred and sixty-six.

The little lines were all the way across the paper. *Whoa.*

A hundred and sixty-six was a lot.

Every line represented a person wrapped into a warm blanket when their hope of survival had seemed questionable. Every line was one of his Christian brothers and sisters wrapping a frigid person carefully into a blanket, telling them they were dearly loved by God, and embracing them. And so their words had not arrived hollow and empty, but instead had been delivered with both compassion and practical evidence that the Lord of the universe cared very much about the person.

Clay laid down the pen and stared at the number of lines. He'd played a role in this. His life had just touched another hundred and sixty people. Some of those people had been rescued from freezing to death—and knew it. He couldn't have described his thankfulness at that moment. He didn't look at the watch. Instead he lowered his head and worshipped the One who, not long ago, had rescued him.

Chapter Twenty-Six

Clay knew Hannah was leaving. He didn't know for how long but her flight to Guatemala City was getting nearer every day. Any discussion about how long she planned to stay in Central America always ended with her in tears, so Clay didn't push for an answer. Instead he tried to enjoy their time together as if it'd last forever. They took long walks across the city and investigated all-night coffee shops. And then every night, after dropping Hannah off at her place at one-thirty or two in the morning, he'd arrive home to the phone ringing. And they'd talk for another hour.

They both knew she was leaving for an important reason, but it was still hard. After waiting so long for the glorious return of Hannah into his life, it felt to Clay like he was losing her all over again.

On their last Saturday together, Hannah suggested tobogganing on Cyprus Mountain. It would've been a great idea, but the weather didn't cooperate. The mountain was shrouded in fog and wet sleet, and they both got completely soaked. Returning to the city they stopped at Clay's condo for him to grab a quick shower and a change of clothes. They'd run by her place later.

Hannah was about to get out of the car when suddenly she grabbed his arm. "It's not the usual mess of most single guy's places, is it?" She laughed. "Or worse, is it filled with old bowling trophies and outdated movie posters, with just two cans of opened Spaghetti-O's in the fridge?"

That stopped Clay. He suddenly realized she'd never been to his place before.

He grinned. "I got rid of my Pamela Anderson swimsuit poster weeks ago. And nobody touches my bowling trophies."

She laughed. "And what about the Spaghetti-O's?"

"No Spaghetti-O's. I'm a Kraft dinner guy."

"You're making jokes. Your place is obviously a landfill."

"Maybe. C'mon." With that, they climbed out of the Civic and headed inside.

The first thing Hannah noticed was that Clay's condo was clean. It hadn't seen a lot of updates since the seventies, but it was clean. The kitchen counters and sink were both empty, a neatly folded tea towel sitting on one of the surfaces. The cabinets were painted, the flooring faded linoleum. She ran her hand across the cheap Formica of the countertop and turned towards him.

"It's not exactly how I envisioned your place." She smiled. "You haven't left yourself a lot of reminders of your gated mansion in the Bahamas."

"No. I tried not to."

"Do you ever miss it?"

"No. Not ever. I was a different person then. And not a good person." Their eyes met and Hannah thought he was going to say more, but instead he gave a shrug and headed for the bathroom. "I'm—I'm going to take a shower. Make yourself at home."

And so, left alone, Hannah took a better look around his place. A small table and four serviceable chairs sat in the middle of the dining area. On the table was an open NIV Study Bible, a commentary on the book of Matthew, and three lined notebooks. She flipped open the top one and was rewarded with pages of notes in Clay's handwriting. He'd included hand-drawn maps with a lot of circles and arrows to help his explanation of the passages. She closed it again.

The narrow living room seemed empty with just a leather couch and a thick coffee table. No TV was in evidence, which seemed weird to her. Didn't most guys spend their weekends watching sports on the tube?

That ignited her curiosity and so, listening to be sure the shower was still running, she headed towards his bedroom. There had to be a television somewhere.

Hannah didn't find a TV. She found something else.

Clay stepped out of the bathroom in a collared shirt and jeans, his hair still wet. "Hey, I was thinking we might want to go to that Italian place tonight—" He stopped. Hannah was on the couch, an unreadable expression on her face. She was studying him. "What's wrong—?"

She slowly got off the couch, and faced him. She seemed tense, her words stiff. "I—I shouldn't have gone into your bedroom, I know that. I think we both know it's off-limits to me."

"I'm sure it's okay as long as we're not in there *together*." Clay laughed. "Why? What did you—?"

"Clay, I need to know what this is." She cut him off, grabbed his hand, and pulled him in the direction of his bedroom.

His bedroom was as empty as the rest of the condo. The double bed had been made in a hurry. A full laundry basket of dirty clothes sat next to a painted dresser. Hannah ignored all of that. Instead she pointed towards the north-facing wall.

"What is all this?"

Carefully taped to the wall were three sheets of lined paper. They'd been taped together to form a single, long vertical sheet. Across the top, he'd labeled it in big letters: 'My Investments'.

The sheets were divided into two vertical columns. The first column was easy to interpret. It was dollar amounts. Lots of entries, most of them were for hundreds of dollars, but there were fifteen or so entries for thousands. You didn't have to be an accountant to see that a lot of money was leaving this condo.

It was the second column that terrified Hannah. It was a list of numbers and they'd been labeled in Clay's handwriting: 'My current worth'.

The numbers started small and were growing at an alarming rate. An impossible rate. The dollars invested in the first column weren't doubling or tripling; they were increasing at some kind of exponential level. It was the kind of impossible return rate only possible in illegal ventures, like drugs or weapons!

But what had struck Hannah the hardest was the taped sheets were backstopped by a large, detailed map of Asia. And across the map were dozens of sticky notes indicating the prisons of China and Indonesia. North Korea had been circled for emphasis. And then, at the northernmost border of India, a large circle was drawn in thick red felt pen. It circled a village. The name of the village had been scrawled in big letters.

Shiliguri.

"Clay, what is all this? Why are you so interested in the prisons of Asia—?" She paused, her eyes narrowing. "And what's in Shiliguri?"

He hesitated. "Maybe we should sit down for this conversation."

"No. I've got a thousand questions, so let me add another one to the pile." She twisted towards the display again and pointed, her finger punching the paper. "What is *this* number in the second column?"

"I think you'll want to sit down for this."

"I'm not sitting down. What is this?" She spit the words out. "C'mon Clay, I'm not an idiot! Your first investment of six hundred dollars had a return of 2746. I can accept that. That's a nice return on six hundred bucks. But it quickly starts to climb. 4251… 10,926… 19,112…

"And then your investment returns go completely crazy! Look at this. You invested nine hundred bucks and your net worth jumped by almost twenty-eight thousand. I can't even calculate that—!"

She wasn't listening, so Clay just shrugged. She was angry. This wouldn't be a great time to explain the numbers.

"Look, at this!" She stabbed the paper again. "On this day you invested thirteen hundred dollars. But your return was enough for the down payment on a house!" She ripped the sheets from the wall and thrust them towards him. "You're into something illegal, aren't you?"

"No—!"

"Oh yeah? Then how do you explain how fast your worth is climbing? Your last investment was nine hundred bucks and it jumped your total to six hundred and ten thousand dollars! You're pulling out seventy dollars for every dollar you're investing. And it's happening fast. You're either knocking off casinos or you're—" She stopped and stared at him. "And why do you care so much about where the prisons are located?"

Clay led her from the bedroom and they sat in hard chairs, the dining table between them. What the second column was registering would be hard to explain, he knew that. It'd taken a lot to convince him initially. He still had moments when he doubted it. It was a lot of crazy crammed into a three pound box.

So he started at the beginning. The very beginning.

It wasn't easy. He'd waited so long to have another chance with Hannah, and was he now going to risk their relationship by telling her everything? Was there no other option except the ugliness of the truth?

He decided there wasn't.

And so he started slowly with the creation of Nasty Dogs, and within a few minutes he and Hannah were deep into the filth and poverty of the slums of Dharavi. He described the horrific conditions and the meager wages he'd paid his workers.

He described ragged children that played outside in open sewers. He wanted to spare himself the humiliation of explaining how he'd shut down the audio facility, but he didn't. He walked her through how he'd exploited his three-hundred half-starved workers, then hired workers to tear apart the place, thrown a lock on the doors, and walked away.

"Some of my workers were… just kids. I abandoned them and their families when my investment team wanted to send them to school." He stared at the floor, the first tear finding his cheek. Hannah was deathly silent, and he didn't look across at her.

The story had only one direction and so he walked her into the dusty slum of Shiliguri. He described the pitiful construction of the half-completed building with its walls of corrugated tin and faded plywood. And the brutal exposure his workers had suffered as frigid Himalayan winds had punched through broken windows to rage across their work benches.

He kept the story moving until the first pillar collapsed. He hoped Hannah might reach across the table to take his hand, but she didn't.

And so in a voice he barely recognized, he revisited the collapse of the building and the deaths of so many.

She was sitting like a stone, without expression.

He wanted to mention the money he'd sent to help the people in their recovery, but the words jammed in his throat. It sounded so pathetic and self-serving. Instead he acknowledged that he, alone, in a lust for significance, had been responsible for the deaths and crippling injuries of his workers in Shiliguri.

She didn't move. Or look at him.

He waited, hoping for something.

Nothing arrived.

"I've gotta go—" She stood without looking in his direction, pulled her ski jacket from the sofa, and practically sprinted towards the door.

"Hannah, wait. I—I can drive you home."

"No. I can take the bus. I need the air."

"Hannah—!"

"I don't know what you're doing in Asia, Clay. But with returns like you're seeing, it looks like you're still exploiting people."

And with the closing of the door, Hannah Taylor walked out of his life. Again.

Chapter Twenty-Seven

Clay sat at the table and stared at his hands. Had he really expected such a conversation to end differently? He was a monster. He deserved no mercy from good people like Hannah. He deserved only to be branded a killer and dragged through the streets on a chain.

There was no forgiveness for someone like him.

He could feel his tears finding his cheeks. He ran his fingers roughly through his hair, lowered his forehead to the cool surface of the table, and openly bawled.

The promises of God were for good people. And he wasn't good. He'd so hoped for a second chance he'd willed himself to believe that he'd received one. But there were no second chances. If Hannah had abandoned him, then so had God. He'd been a fool to believe what had happened on the floor of an old community hall was enough to erase the evil misdeeds of his life. It took more than a few words of repentance to—

And that's about when the bird collided with the glass of Clay's window. A sparrow of some kind, the thump of his little body smacking the glass hard enough to kill him.

It was a recognizable sound and Clay sat bolt upright.

Had the bird survived? Maybe he was lying on the ground outside, stunned. Clay jumped from his chair and ran towards the door, wiping away tears, hoping to rescue the little guy. He didn't make it. As soon as he opened the door he was pulled into Nigel's powerful embrace.

"I'm right here. I told you I'd never leave you and I won't." Nigel was fighting back emotion. "Rest in what you've been told, and know you're a child of the living God. He will never leave you. Especially not during your hardest times."

Somehow Clay knew there'd been no bird. It'd been another of Nigel's arrival tactics, him knowing Clay wouldn't have answered the doorbell. But it was more than that. It was a visual demonstration of everything Nigel had declared from the beginning, that he'd never leave Clay in the midst of his hurt. Hannah had been gone less than four minutes, and Nigel had already executed a plan to gain access to the condo, embraced him, and disputed every lie Clay had wanted to run back to.

If ever he'd had a living demonstration of the love of God, it was holding him now.

Nigel led Clay back into the condo and they sat at the table. Nigel immediately opened Clay's Study Bible that lay between them. He began in the earliest days of the Old Testament and, using dozens of passages and Biblical stories, he began painting a picture of the God who understands heartbreak. At first, Clay thought Nigel was giving evidence of God understanding what he was experiencing with the loss of Hannah. But that wasn't it.

Nigel, with details pulled from the pages of scripture, was painting a far different picture. He was crafting together the Biblical narrative of the Lord using heartbreak and struggles to build the faith and hope of His children. Ruth. Esther. Isaiah. The entire cast of mongrel characters within the twin books of Kings and Chronicles. Nigel rapidly wove the stories together to illustrate a simple and powerful message from God. 'Trust me through your struggles, Clay. Believe in my goodness, and I will accomplish more than you can believe. For I am with you.'

After an hour, Nigel suggested dinner. He asked to drive and Clay wasn't surprised when they journeyed across the city to the *Electric Hazel Diner.* It was where Clay had taken Brent, the first at-risk young person Clay had helped find safety. He understood immediately why Nigel had chosen here.

He was saying, 'when you can't see the way ahead, look *back* at what God has done before.'

They spent the evening walking along the beaches. They talked some, but Nigel was comfortable with long empty, breezy silences and there were plenty of those.

It was when they returned to the condo, nearing midnight, that Clay noticed Nigel was carrying a sleeping bag. And a pillow. The sleeping bag was one of those weightless, backpacking models. Clay was sure he hadn't had it earlier. Nigel headed straight for the living room and unrolled it on the couch.

"You're staying—?"

"You need to know I'm here tonight." He pointed towards his temporary bedding. "I think a Canadian Tire sleeping bag on your couch is physical evidence I'm not leaving you alone."

"You're not needed somewhere else?"

"I'm needed right here."

And so for the next several days, Nigel didn't leave Clay. He was an easy houseguest. He bought groceries and did the dishes. When Clay wanted to talk, or his sadness threatened to overwhelm him, Nigel was there. He encouraged Clay to look for God's faithfulness in the pages of scripture and they'd sit at the table and pass the Bible back and forth. They wandered along the beaches for hours at night, neither of them saying much. When Nigel did talk it was always to assure Clay that God was actively seeking the very best for him, even if it seemed hidden right now. The painfulness of Hannah's departure didn't hurt less, but Clay was glad to not go through it alone.

And then, on the fifth day of her being gone, Nigel sat Clay down and said something. He wasn't smiling. "You need to set aside your pain. And as hard as it might be, you need to step up to being the person Hannah needs you to be."

"What are you talking about? Hannah's gone, Nigel."

"Yes, she is. And she's about to journey into places that are horribly dangerous. It's Central America, and she'll be leaving behind the touristy areas and stepping into the truly nasty places. I can assure you there are things on the streets of Guatemala City to be afraid of, and she's going to be afraid. Within hours of arriving, she's going to be bawling in a bathroom somewhere, already considering a panicked phone call to her parents, begging to come home."

That stopped Clay cold. "So what am I supposed to do?"

Nigel gave a stiff smile. "You can't do anything about what she's about to face. She's about to stand toe-to-toe with real evil. There's no changing that. But what you can do is equip her with the strength to stand firm when all of hell throws its worst at her. Equip her with the strength to set aside her fears and instead to be armored in peace. I want you to—"

"You want me to do what I do."

"Exactly."

"Okay. Then let's get started. Let's pray."

United Airlines, flight 446 out of Vancouver International taxied towards the runway. A light rain was falling, early morning darkness still wrapped around the aircraft. Onboard, in seat 22A, Hannah stared out the little window towards the city. Her mind was conflicted, her thoughts a jumbled mess. Two weeks earlier she'd allowed herself the first thoughts of a life forever with Clay. She'd spent her days dreamily thinking about becoming Mrs. Hannah Rawlings.

And then he'd told her about Shiliguri. And she'd run from him.

Why had she run? She couldn't even put her reasons into words. He'd left dozens of messages on her answering machine, begging to explain. She'd erased them without listening.

Had Clay done time in prison somewhere in Asia? That scenario certainly made sense. And there, within the filth and violence of a Third-world prison, he'd obviously come to Jesus. That would certainly explain the dramatic changes in him. But what about those numbers? Was Clay now involved in something illegal, trying to reclaim the wealth he'd lost when Nasty Dogs crashed?

The thought of it repulsed her.

Clay had secrets, and she wasn't eager to establish a life with somebody with a closetful of secrets. It was time to forget about Clay Rawlings.

Hannah switched planes in LA to continue the journey to Guatemala City. She was assigned another window seat. It was a comfortable flight through calm skies. But something immediately impacted her. She'd thought she'd spend most of her flight worrying, afraid of what she'd face on the streets of Guatemala, but she hadn't. Instead, she was relaxed, eagerly looking forward to landing and embarking on an adventure of trusting God. It was weird. She'd done some research. She knew the violence she'd face on the streets in Guatemala City. None of that was registering. She'd never considered herself a brave person, and yet she felt no apprehension. No fear. She *knew* that God was holding her hand. Weird.

Chapter Twenty-Eight

Hannah had been gone for a week. Clay hadn't recovered from the heartbreak, and Nigel knew it. So he stayed. He was there when Clay awoke night after night at two-thirty or three-thirty in the morning, unable to sleep, angry and blaming himself for the loss of Hannah. They'd sit and talk, or Nigel would read him scripture and pray with him. Nigel helped make his lunches for work, dropped him off at High-Q, and then picked him up again.

He was there and Clay appreciated every minute of it. He wasn't alone.

And then, late in the evening on day nine, a big change occurred. Clay stopped grieving the loss of Hannah. Instead, Nigel could hear him kneeling beside his bed quietly thanking God for having brought them together. He was thanking God for every minute he'd held her and enjoyed her smile. She was gone, and yet Clay declared his thankfulness for the few months they'd spent together as a couple. He acknowledged that he'd spent years pleading with God to restore their relationship, and He had. Clay was now openly praised Him for His goodness. He and Hannah's relationship hadn't lasted, but that wasn't God's fault.

Nigel sat on the floor outside his bedroom and listened. He smiled. *Okay then—*

The next morning Clay awoke and stumbled into the shower. He dressed and then moved towards the living room. The sleeping bag and pillow were gone from the couch. "Nigel—?"

Nothing.

"Nigel, are you here?"

No response.

Clay moved into the kitchen and there on the counter was a note. It was just a few words in Nigel's handwriting:

Clay,

You need to go to Guatemala City. And as you go, trust that God is with you.

Nigel.

Just before lunch an Air Canada jet lifted off from Vancouver International. Clay was aboard it. He stared out the little window and replayed the conversation with his boss when he'd asked for the time off. The parking lot of High-Q had still been dark, empty of other cars. His boss, Larry, had just arrived and was barely out of his Silver BMW when Clay approached him with the request for time off. Larry's response still struck him as surreal.

"Is this trip to chase after that girl you've been dating?"

"Yeah."

"Okay then. Good luck. Go."

"Larry, I have no idea when I'll be back—"

"Clay, if you liked her and lost her; don't let it end like that. Chase her to wherever she is. And don't come back until she's yours again."

He was still amazed. Who'd have guessed his boss was such a romantic. Or was this part of what Nigel had promised on the note? That God was with him.

Clay arrived to Guatemala City without a well formulated plan. Before leaving Vancouver he'd phoned the offices of Children from the Dark in the hopes they'd offer him a contact number within the city. Possibly there was a pastor or church leader who could help him find Hannah. He wasn't sure how badly Hannah had poisoned his reputation amongst her staff, but he prepared himself for an icy reception on the phone.

The icy reception never arrived. Instead, an intern named Val took his call and cheerfully gave him three phone numbers to try upon arrival. One was for the YWAM, *Youth with a Mission*, base where Hannah was staying. And then, before ending the call, Val encouraged him to not give up, but to keep pursuing Hannah until he won her back. She'd wished him good luck.

Clay was one of the last people off the plane, moving hesitantly. The airport was old, it stunk horribly, and badly in need of paint. He barely noticed any of it, his mind still churning as it had for most of the flight. *What was he going to say to Hannah when he saw her?* What if she wouldn't speak to him at all?

But he knew there were other, far worse, obstacles before he'd ever see Hannah. There was the phone call to what he guessed was a Spanish-speaking missionary base, and then the language difficulties of securing a taxi to get him to wherever Hannah was. His entire arsenal of Spanish was typical for somebody from Vancouver: taco, burrito, and Chihuahua. He had no clue about money or currencies, and carried only Canadian dollars. Could he get by with just a credit card? He cursed himself for being so poorly prepared.

In the end it didn't matter.

Clay exited security and there, waiting directly in front of him, stood a darkly tanned young man holding a cardboard sign with 'Rawlings' scrawled on it. He introduced himself simply as Dave. He and his wife, Shawna, were on staff with YWAM Guatemala City. He explained that Val had called, probably only minutes after Clay had talked with her, and the entire YWAM base had immediately began preparations for Clay's arrival.

Dave grabbed Clay's carry-on bag and led him to the parking garage where a very beat up Jeep Cherokee awaited. Anywhere in America, except the most redneck of outposts, and this truck would've been sitting on blocks with grass growing around it! They climbed in but Clay had serious doubts that it could actually run. After some excessive cranking the motor coughed into life. Trailing a lot of black smoke they pulled from the parking garage and made their way into the craziness of Guatemalan traffic. It was a zoo! Motorcyclists, mopeds, trucks and buses all competed for the narrowest edge of space, with no regard for traffic laws or safety. Traffic signals and stop signs were ignored, motorcyclists toyed with death as they careened wildly through traffic.

Dave didn't seem to notice. He weaved past colorful buses loaded down with boxes and livestock, cut off other cars, barely avoided several collisions, all while handling his own constant horn duties like a native. Through it all his left arm remained casually leaning out the window. With his right he steered, pounded the horn, and pointed out the local sights and color as they went careening past them.

Guatemala City was similar to many places Clay had seen in other parts of the world. Especially in Asia. Obscene wealth rubbed shoulders with crippling poverty. Spotless luxury sedans often sat only inches from starving beggars lying on pieces of cardboard. Ragged kids were everywhere.

Dave parked the Cherokee and they set out on foot, into a twisted puzzle of alleys that only got darker and more putrid as they pushed deeper into the city. Finding Hannah would prove impossible, Clay was sure of it. Until they came out into an empty space between two buildings, and there she was.

Hannah was surrounded by eight or nine Guatemalan youth, and although a translator stood beside her, she was making an attempt to give instructions to ten or twelve young people in Spanish.

In a flood of flawless Spanish, Dave addressed the group of young people. He nodded towards Hannah and then towards Clay. Neither of them would have recognized the Spanish word for 'sweethearts', but it wasn't hard to figure out what he'd said. There were smiles and exclamations of approval from the group of young people.

And then, Dave turned towards Clay and Hannah. "You've probably got a lot to talk about. C'mon, let's find you somewhere quiet—" With that, he was leading them out of the alleys.

Five blocks south he stopped. To call it an outdoor café would have been generous. It was a jumbled stack of plastic stools and tables that looked like they'd fallen off a truck heading for the dump. The tables hid from the late afternoon heat under faded red umbrellas that advertised a local beer. There weren't any other customers, the place was empty. Dave aimed them towards a table and Clay and Hannah sat. Dave disappeared somewhere inside and arrived back with a server. She looked to be nearing a hundred, her skin ridged and hardened like the shell of a walnut.

Dave ordered for them. "Dos platos de quince, por favor, y bebidas frias." There was no menu in evidence, but it didn't seem to matter.

The old woman responded with a flurry of Spanish and a wide smile.

Dave laughed. "Si, sabe bien que el churrasco es mi favorite, pero no me puedo quedar hoy. Cuida bien a mis amigos e yo regreare mas tarde."

She air-kissed Dave on the cheek and disappeared into the smoky little building. Dave pulled several bills from his wallet. He laid them on the table in front of Clay. "I'm leaving you enough money to keep this table as long as you want. Just keep ordering Coca-Cola and she'll be happy to look after you. Don't drink the water." With that, he made his exit.

And just like that, Clay was sitting in Guatemala City across a table from Hannah.

"What are you doing here, Clay?" Her tone held a measure of surprise, but it was served in a frosty glass of hostility. Her arms were crossed, her eyes narrowing.

"Hannah, those numbers on my wall aren't financial. Those second column numbers—" He leaned forward, his words rushing out, his eyes pleading. He'd rehearsed this moment a dozen times on the airplane. "The second column on the sheets in my bedroom. Those numbers record my worth, but they're not financial."

"I'm not an idiot, Clay. It was right there on your wall. Your current worth is six hundred thousand—*dollars.* The number is *financial.* I get it; you're chasing the lifestyle again. Trying to reclaim everything you lost when Nasty Dogs—"

"No. I swear. The second column isn't financial."

"Convince me. What else could a number like six-hundred thousand be?"

Clay breathed out. "It's my worth as a human being."

"What—?"

Clay waited an extra second before trying again. He'd had this same conversation when he first met Nigel. He knew what was running through her mind.

"That second column is registering my spiritual condition."

That stopped her. The arms uncrossed and she leaned forward. "What—?"

"Hannah, everything we do in life is being recorded. Regardless of what kind of life we live, it's all being recorded. Good or bad. It's being recorded.

The smallest details are being written down. Our entire life is a test."

"Okay—"

Time to throw four pounds of crazy onto the table. "So our spiritual condition registers as a number. And that number changes from minute to minute and hour to hour. It's constantly changing."

"So I'm supposed to believe that on your bedroom wall—?"

"In that second column, yes. Those are my numbers. I write them down to encourage myself I'm making progress. That I'm moving forward, like watching the speedometer of a car."

"No! No—! You are such a liar, Clay!" She slammed her fist onto the table, sending a shudder through the flimsy plastic . The venom was back in her eyes. "You come all this way! You make noises like you're sorry, and then you fabricate a lie a four-year-old could see through!" She pushed back her chair and bolted to her feet. "We're done here! Have a nice flight home."

He stood up, his knees rubbery. "Wait, Hannah. You know I wouldn't lie to you. I wouldn't."

"Oh yeah? Well, you're talking like an idiot." She glared at him across the table.

"And what if it's true?"

"It's not." Her fingers had curled into fists. "How could you possibly know anything about what's being recorded in heaven?"

"Can we—?" Clay motioned towards her chair. "Can we sit back down? It might take me a minute, but I can convince you. I promise. I can prove all of it."

She kept the scowl, but sat down again. Clay returned to his seat and let out a nervous sigh. He was about to do something he'd never done before. He unbuttoned the cuff of his shirt and extended his arm across the table.

"Take a close look at my watch."

She gave it a quick, uninterested glance. "It's one of those deep sea watches. Whatever." She shrugged.

"Take a closer look."

There was a long, icy hesitation before she leaned forward to look again. "Okay, what is this thing? It's—it's not a watch."

"Correct. It's not."

"What are these two numbers?"

"One of them is the minutes left in my life. It's on a countdown."

She threw a stiff glance towards him. "What do you mean a countdown?"

He hesitated. "Eternity is coming. For all of us. The countdown ensures I never lose sight of the coming end."

"So you're saying this watch knows when you're gonna die?"

"Yes."

She stared at him, like waiting for the punchline to a joke. An uncomfortable silence settled over the table when he didn't deliver the punchline. She returned her eyes to the watch.

"So this other number—?" Her skepticism wasn't at all camouflaged. He was lying.

"It's my current worth. My second column number."

"But it's changing so fast. Why is it scrolling upwards like this?"

Clay didn't look at her. "I keep pretty busy."

The watch passed six hundred and ninety thousand while she watched.

"You're lying! I don't believe any of this!" She shoved Clay's arm and the watch roughly back across the table. "That thing was probably made in somebody's basement somewhere! It could be calculating the gravitational pull of the moon, or the number of pet shops in Portland. Those numbers could be for *anything!*"

Her anger delivered a silence to the table, like dust settling after a gunfight. Into the empty silence their server, the elderly Guatemalan woman, arrived with their food on steaming plates. Thin, smoky cuts of charcoal-barbequed beef, thick corn tortillas, fire-blackened potatoes, and a deep serving of black refried beans, all topped with roasted green onion. If either Clay or Hannah had been in a different mood it'd have looked delicious. Neither had an appetite. Hannah was stiffly thanking their server in Spanish when Clay stopped her.

"Wait, just a second."

He yanked the watch off his wrist and pushed it across the table to Hannah. "Put it on. Put the watch on. Please—" Then with a smile, he reached out and gently took the wrist of the Guatemalan woman. He indicated he wanted her to remain with them for a second. She was confused, but nodded.

Clay looked across the table at Hannah. The watch was on her wrist. "Okay, what's your number?"

Hannah was staring at the watch. The numbers displayed on the watch were different. *What was this? How could passing the watch across a table completely change its numbers?* "It says 18,734."

"Okay. I want you to ask our server if you can pray for her. In Spanish. Right now." He smiled again at the old woman.

"What—?"

"This'll prove what I'm saying."

"How could it prove anything—?" Hannah looked across the empty cafe. And then she glanced again towards the watch.

"If you want to discover the truth, here's your chance."

"By praying for this lady? What does that have to do with this?""

"It's the only way for you to see the truth."

"C'mon Clay. The only way—?

"Sorry, but it is." Clay shrugged. He pulled a stool up for their server, and she hesitantly sat down.

"What—what would I pray? How do I know what—?"

"Ask *her* what she needs prayer for."

"Oh—yeah. I can do that." And so in her limited, broken Spanish, Hannah asked the woman about her life, and was there anything she could pray for?

The woman's eyes got big, and a single tear found her cheek. Her head lowered and her words came out slowly, sadly. She spoke for some long minutes, and whatever she said wasn't easy to talk about. Hannah wasn't sure about some of the words, and had to ask for easier terms several times, but she gradually gave Clay a play-by-play in English.

The *churrascero*, the café, made little money. The woman's husband was under-employed, his only work was as an *ayundante*, a caller on a local bus. He would stand in the doorway of the bus, calling out the approaching locations, and then collect the money from riders. It was a dangerous job mostly because the buses were controlled by street gangs, and he was threatened with a gun frequently. And then, though he was older and heavy, he was required to jump onto and off the still-moving bus throughout the day. The pay was a pittance, and he'd been badly injured several times. The woman stopped several times to wipe her eyes throughout the telling.

She paused at one point, the tears continuing. And then she talked about their son who'd gotten into the United States, and was working at a low-budget meat packing plant somewhere in Texas.

Any safety instructions were given in English, which he didn't speak, not that safety was a concern of the owners. The conditions were dangerous, hours brutal, and again, the pay was abysmal. She worried about him being so far from home. She'd heard the stories of other young men being lured away by more lucrative, less legal pursuits. She came to a quiet stop in the narrative.

Hannah had reached out and gripped the woman's hand, holding it as she'd spoken. Now she moved to embrace her. And then Hannah Taylor, a child of the Living God, prayed, in her limited Spanish, but with every ounce of love she held, for the woman.

It was long and emotional. The old woman's name was Maria. She remained after Hannah finished, riveted to her stool, asking questions until her husband appeared. He was happily introduced to Clay and Hannah, and then with much apologizing, he explained they needed to get back to work.

The elderly couple had been gone several long minutes when Clay turned to Hannah. "Okay, what's the number on the watch now?"

"What—?"

"Your number on the watch? It was 18,734 when you put it on. It should be 18,735 now."

Hannah looked down at her wrist.

It was 18,735.

"Wait. It's increased by one. But—why?"

"I don't know, maybe the gravitational pull on the moon was increased while we sat here. Or maybe somebody opened a new pet shop in Portland." He smiled. "Or maybe—maybe you just touched the heart of God."

Clay had barely begun to explain what the watch was registering when the Guatemalan couple arrived back to the table with an entirely new order of food. If it were possible, this order was bigger. Their thankfulness for what Hannah had shared with Maria wasn't hard to translate. They moved around the table in jittery little loops, amidst a constant stream of happy Spanish. And they were quite adamant that the entire meal was to be a gift to Hannah. After a lot of handshaking and hugs, and ensuring everything at the table was perfect, the elderly couple gathered up the original plates of food that had gone cold and returned to the kitchen.

Clay smiled at Hannah. "Check the number on the watch again."

She didn't look down. "It was 18,735."

"I'll bet it isn't anymore."

Hannah looked down at her wrist. "Whoa—but how?" She stared across at Clay.

"It went up by a digit, didn't it?" He smiled.

"It's at 18,736 now. But why did it increase again? We were just sitting here."

Clay smiled. He settled his napkin in his lap and took a first bite of barbecued beef. It was spectacular and he allowed himself to savor it. He knew somewhere Nigel was already celebrating the increases in Hannah's account. And now here she was, watching him, waiting for an explanation. Clay made her wait. From the look in her eyes, he could tell. Hannah knew he hadn't lied to her.

And with that, he and Hannah were back together again.

Chapter Twenty-Nine

The owners of the little restaurant returned to Clay and Hannah's table with a small basket of sugar-topped bread, and then two mugs of steaming, sweetened coffee. And then, just before six-thirty, they returned for a final time. They thanked Clay and Hannah, hugged them both, and told them to come back anytime. Dave arrived in the beat-up Cherokee, as if on cue, to escort them back to the YWAM base. On the drive, he cautioned them that Guatemala City was the eighth most dangerous city in the world, and risking a walk on its streets after dark was… in a word, foolish.

Dave showed them into a sitting room at the YWAM base. "No end to the coffee here in Guatemala." He smiled and pointed towards a coffee maker on a corner table, and then made his exit.

Clay poured them a couple of mugs and they sat together, knees touching, on a stiff green couch with cushions that should've been in a landfill. It was easily the least comfortable piece of furniture he'd ever sat on, but before he had time to comment, Hannah slipped her hand into his.

And Clay told her everything.

The mystery of Nigel's identity was discussed at length. There wasn't an easy answer of who he was and they both knew it. They then switched the conversation to the money. Clay gave her a brief, summarized listing of the investments he'd made.

"How do you do it? How do you give away big amounts of cash?" Hannah asked the question slowly. He wasn't sure if she thought it was heroic, or bald-faced nuts.

Several seconds passed before Clay answered. "I've been rescued. I never forget that. And because of it I want to live differently. I simply want to be a channel that God can depend on."

"A channel for financing the work of God's kingdom?"

"Yeah." Clay nodded.

"And so you've sacrificed everything for this—?"

He shook his head. "No. It's not a sacrifice. Not even close." He waited for their eyes to meet. "Until you've provided a source of clean water for a mother with children you don't know what joy is. Or what celebration means. You have no idea the celebrations I've enjoyed since starting this."

"You don't miss the money—?"

"What could I buy for a thousand bucks that would be more of a blessing to me than knowing an entire village awoke this morning to clean water? And their kids are going to be kept from sickness? There's nothing I could buy. Nothing."

He allowed his words to slow. "And once it's drilled, that well will remain there for generations. It'll remain there as a constant testimony to the love of the Christian God who cares about the people of that village. For me, that's a thousand bucks well invested."

"You make it sound like a no-brainer." She gave a hesitant laugh.

"It's simply a decision." Clay humbly shrugged. "In January, when it's cold and wet in Vancouver and you'd rather be vacationing in Cancun, you just pull out your checkbook. With a few strokes of a pen, seventy missionaries in the frigid mountains of Nepal each get a warm coat, a thick sweater, and a blanket. And then, now insulated against the cold, they're able to continue on, carrying the message of the Gospel to the next village."

"Seventy—?"

"Yeah. Seventy."

"Rather than a vacation in Cancun?"

"They're about the same price."

Hannah slowly nodded.

Clay continued. "Again, it's a decision. At some point you stop caring your furniture doesn't match and your clothes aren't designer. It doesn't matter anymore. You let go of what other people think of your life. You're living on a completely different track." Clay shrugged again. "People will consider you strange because of your choices. Or they'll think you're cheap. You've gotta be okay with that."

Hannah reached out and took his hand. "So your choice to have our first lunch date in a park at a picnic table—?"

Clay allowed a hesitant smile. "Earlier that morning I'd cut a check for six hundred Bibles and forty thousand tracts. Those Subway sandwiches were all I could afford right then."

Hannah was quiet for a long time.

"So, how much was accomplished that morning? With those Bibles and the tracts?"

"I don't know. I—I never know."

"Okay then—" She smiled, "What do you *hope* was accomplished? You must have hopes of something incredible happening. Something—huge."

He breathed out. "I do. Across India there are thousands of dusty little villages. The Gospel is making its way into those villages. A little church will be planted and they'll scrape together a few rupees to get a part-time pastor. Those pastors will be reaching out into their villages—"

"And they'll be using the tracts you're supplying?"

"Yeah, those little sheets will be being handed out everywhere. They'll find their way into the hands of Hindus and Muslims, often as a first introduction to the teachings of Jesus Christ. And then, for those who show interest, they'll be given a Bible. From there, God's Word will do what it does best."

"So that morning, as you wrote that check, you were hoping entire villages would be transformed?"

"That's always my hope."

A silence arrived as Hannah considered such a thing. And then the question that had plagued her all evening arrived to her mind. "Clay, why are my numbers so low compared to yours?"

Her expression told him she wanted to defend what she'd done with her life. She'd made good choices. She'd been reaching out to at-risk youth since high school. She'd spent a lot of time in the ugly places.

"Nigel taught me to pray."

A frown arrived to her face. "That's it? He taught you to… pray?"

Clay smiled. It was two-thirty in the morning and they'd finally arrived to the real conversation. Without saying anything he removed the watch and handed it to Hannah. She put it on and frowned at her numbers again.

Clay smiled. He'd once sat exactly where Hannah was now. He'd been skeptical about the abilities of prayer. He remembered Nigel's words to him at the Subway outlet in Horseshoe Bay: You won't be easily convinced. This'll demand something—unique.

Okay, one mind-blowing unique coming right up.

"It's easier to just show you." Clay smiled again at Hannah. "I think we'll use the prison system of Indonesia for this little demonstration…"

Chapter Thirty

An Air Canada 737 delivered Clay home from Guatemala. But his first weeks back in Vancouver were hard. He missed Hannah. He stayed later at work every night to keep his mind busy, and increased his early morning prayer. One Friday evening he got a call and agreed to a contract job that occupied several Saturdays. That helped keep his thoughts off her. With the extra cash he drilled another pair of water wells.

In his free moments, few as they were, he wrote long, windy emails to Hannah. He'd never thought of himself as a romantic writer, but he took a stab at it. The results seemed to be appreciated in Guatemala. So he wrote more often. And his emails got longer.

But their emails were more than just a lot of romantic babbling. Hannah was frequently overwhelmed by the poverty and pain she witnessed on the streets of Guatemala City, and that came through. She had good days and bad days, but it often seemed the bad days were winning. Every day she met kids who'd been used and exploited in the most heinous ways, and their hurt scraped across her heart like a rusted potato peeler. She cried a lot and didn't mind saying it.

Somewhere in all of this, Hannah Taylor let go of her own abilities. She fell to her knees in repentance and embraced a completely different strategy. If the dangerous streets of Guatemala City were to become a harvest field, she needed to learn to pray.

That sparked a whole new series of communication with Clay in Vancouver.

Meanwhile, a revival was raging across the slums of Asia. Millions of the poorest of the poor were coming to faith in Jesus Christ. Every couple of weeks Clay received another update from GraceUnfathomable about the unbelievable changes taking place across Asia.

The experts all agreed. The revival was being driven by prayer.

Chapter Thirty-One

Clay celebrated Christmas day, 1996, with Gary and Pam at the campsite. His parents weren't in town, having escaped to the sunshine and pampering of the Bahamas aboard a cruise ship. Clay knew they were struggling to understand his new priorities, especially his outspokenness about his faith, and so it wasn't surprising when they didn't offer him an invitation to join them.

In February of the New Year, Hannah used a word in an email for the first time. Marriage. Their relationship immediately shifted to another level and Clay missed her that much more.

Tax time arrived in April and he sent away his return. Eight weeks later he received a refund check for thirteen thousand dollars. That got turned into New Testaments to be handed out across northern India. 26,000 of them!

At the end of five months, Hannah left Central America. She left behind hundreds of young people who now considered her a trusted friend, and a spiritual mentor, all of whom she'd met and embraced on the dirty streets of Guatemala City. She'd learned to pray, and taught others to do the same. The results were evident everywhere.

She and Clay were married in August of 1997.

They paid for their own wedding when Hannah's mother angrily tried to insist on an opulent gala that would've outshone the coronation of a head of state. Their honeymoon was a week of budget motels on the Oregon coast. They were together and that was all that mattered.

But even as they watched the surf crash against the Oregon shores, they knew none of it would last. The minutes on the watch indicated Clay now had less than five years to live. And yet, somehow, for both Hannah and Clay, that was okay. They knew with certainty they were part of something orchestrated by the Lord of Glory.

Four years earlier, in 1993, the Pentium microprocessor had taken the computing world by storm. It certainly wasn't perfect, and poked along at a pedestrian pace of 66 Mhz, but had quickly found its way into prominence among the big computer makers. Intel followed up the next year with its bigger brother, the Pentium Pro. It had a clock speed of almost 150 Mhz, which was considered ripping fast, and every consumer wanted one. The MMX pushed that number to 200 Mhz. Again, millions of new computers were immediately sold. And then, while Hannah and Clay were on their honeymoon, the Pentium II processor was released, having made the volcanic jump to 266. Intel rocketed to $18 billion in sales and there was a whispered hope within the company that they could see speeds of 1 Ghz!

A Gulfstream IV, the fanciest of private jets, landed at the south terminal of Vancouver International. Onboard were three men. Two of them were senior vice presidents for Intel, important men with big egos and lots to accomplish. But they remained seated even after the aircraft taxied, and then came to a measured stop. A limo waited impatiently outside. Still, they remained seated, surrounded by the plush leather and filtered air of the Gulfstream.

"So we need this little company? In Canada?"

The third man was in no hurry with his answer. He spoke directly to both vice presidents. *Yes, you're going to need this company.*

"Bill, we're going to need this company."

Bill nodded. "I agree. We need it."

It was quiet for a few seconds until the third man spoke again. *Buying this little company is going to play a huge role in your success.*

"Bill, buying this little company is going to play a huge role in our success."

Bill nodded again. "I think you're right."

The third man again was in no hurry. *This is money well spent.*

Bill held a check for eighty million dollars. "Yes. This is money well spent."

At that, the two vice-presidents stood, without addressing the third man, and exited the aircraft. They got into the limo and headed south towards a business park in Richmond.

Nigel remained seated in the aircraft for a few extra minutes. He smiled. "Okay Clay, you've been faithful with little, now let's see you be faithful with much."

Hannah and Clay returned from the beaches of Oregon to discover High-Q Robotics had been bought by Intel, who were interested in its two massive floors of research and development. The race for computer speed was on, and they were throwing money at it like gasoline onto a fire.

On the Thursday after his honeymoon, Clay was called into Larry's office and asked to close the door.

"How does a hundred and twenty grand a year sound?" The question was delivered without any preamble, Larry barely looking up from his computer.

"Uh—it sounds… great." Clay remained standing, not sure if he should sit down. He reasoned such a large pay increase would probably arrive with an explanation.

"Okay. A hundred and twenty thousand it is. Keep up the good work." Larry gave the smallest nod of his head.

"Uh… thank you." The meeting was obviously over. *Okay, no explanation.*

The next two years passed rapidly. Clay and Hannah continued to live frugally, but knowing Clay wasn't going to survive, he insisted they purchase a home for Hannah. They bought a condo on a tree-lined street in East Vancouver, for eighty-two thousand dollars. The mortgage rate was good, but they often wondered if it'd been a good decision. *Would real estate in Vancouver hold its value?*

They avoided North America's growing love affair with tech gadgets that was propelling companies like Apple and Nokia onto the national stage. Neither carried a cell phone, and without a television they had little use for the cable packages that were growing in popularity. Expensive vacations and the stable of leisure toys that filled many people's garages were easily labeled unnecessary.

Clay's higher wages simply fueled their hope that more of India's Untouchables would discover freedom. That the poor would find salvation in Jesus. Their giving numbers grew until their income tax form showed contributions nearing fifty grand a year. Much of that was directed towards a variety of ministries that were helping the poor of the world, and also the reaching of runaway kids on the streets of Vancouver. The numbers on the watch continued to climb.

1,188,278…1,189,684…1,191,120…

But the watch had *two* numbers.

As the rest of the world prepared itself for the dramatic meltdown of Y2K, Clay and Hannah's countdown was far more personal. The number of minutes left in Clay's life had never disappeared at a static rate, but now as they spiraled down they grew far less predictable. Clay tried to keep himself in the nicer areas for prayer, but it wasn't the same. And so he returned morning after morning to the alleys, and under the bridges, and near the homeless camps of Vancouver. And he was soon down to eleven months.

Chapter Thirty-Two

Her real name was Benita Carlisle. On the streets they just called her Halo. Nobody that mattered knew why. She'd been in Vancouver less than a year, arriving in the cold weather migration as addicts moved west from frigid places like Calgary and Winnipeg. Halo had once been especially attractive. She was still tall and willowy, but like a vehicle having sideswiped a fencepost, heroin had badly marred her appearance. And she rarely smiled now.

Less than three years earlier she'd been valedictorian of her graduating class. On that evening she'd worn a dress she'd designed and sewn herself, and delivered a speech that had brought the entire audience of almost two thousand to its feet. The University of Waterloo awaited her arrival. At that moment, the world had stretched out before her with almost limitless possibilities.

Not so much now. It was three-thirty in the morning, another night of wandering in the torrential rain, trying to find a level of safety. Her three layers of sweatshirts, a canvas jacket, and torn jeans all smelled like a swamp. She was a cutter, and she could feel the threading of dried blood on her upper legs, the only expression of being alive still registering in her mind. She'd panhandled eight bucks earlier, but knew it wasn't enough, and she was getting jittery. Though it shamed her, she knew she'd have to sell, again, the only thing that sold easily on the streets.

Truth be told, she just wanted to die.

Clay slipped out of bed, trying hard to not awaken Hannah. She'd stayed late at one of the youth shelters until almost midnight and would probably want to be at the office again by nine. He fumbled into his jeans and a sweatshirt in the dark. The dresser clock said 4:02am.

"Morning—" It was just a faint mumble.

"I love you."

Something unintelligible arrived from her side of the bed. It might have been "I love you, too."

Clay went out to the kitchen, ate a bowl of granola, read a chapter of the New Testament, and got into his Gortex rain gear. The same routine he'd adhered to on so many other mornings. He stepped from his condo into the shadowy darkness of the early morning and fired up the Civic. The alleys of Vancouver and the prison system of China were waiting.

Life is made up of single moments, millions of them all strung together, and this was a single moment. Just not quite like the rest.

Halo chose to remain on Hastings, drifting slowly back and forth. At a different stage in her life, and in the right dress, she may have made the eighteen block journey to Robson or Davies Street. In those places she'd have auctioned herself off like a lady, and tried hard to convince anybody watching that she was someone's exotic princess. That she was somebody's pampered date.

That wasn't possible on East Hastings. Even in the pounding rain, islands of drunken humanity lay sprawled along the sidewalk, surrounded endlessly by piles of soggy trash and cast-off junk. Here Halo was just another one of the greasy cardboard figures the city wanted gone. Another piece of flotsam that blew along the street nobody cared about.

The stub of alley behind the Blue Boy Hotel isn't pleasant at four-thirty in the morning. Few lights empty their brightness into its shadows, so it's dark. And it's a dead end, so it doesn't attract through traffic of any kind. Instead, like a box canyon in a

Western movie, it seems only waiting for the arrival of violence.

Halo's jitters were increasing in intensity. She continued to roam the sidewalks without any action. The entire city drove past her. And deep inside, where nobody knew her anymore, she just wanted to cry.

Clay arrived to the alley behind the Blue Boy at four-thirty-eight in the morning. It was a Tuesday. The changing of the millennium would arrive in just a few days. He stepped from the rain into the slim shelter afforded by the entry to a heavily reinforced, rollup door. He pulled out his prayer list and was about to begin his morning when something happened— something quite unexpected.

His watch gave a muted ding.

The watch had never made any kind of noise before. And so Clay looked down.

One number was 1,302,781.

The other number, the minutes left of his life, was at zero.

Halo was beyond the knife edge of desperate before anybody slowed. Hundreds of vehicles, heading west into the city, continued to splash past her, anonymous and insulated from her pain. She was openly weeping now.

"Please, Lord…help me…" A prayer from childhood, buried words from long ago, escaped her before she could stop them. There was nothing else left.

Through her tears, Halo barely saw an aging pickup veer from the center lane, nearly sideswiping a taxi, its radials bouncing hard off the concrete of the curb as it came to a violent, breathless halt. From the passenger side, out flailed a hardscrabble middle-aged man gripping a bottle. He threw the bottle down, glass and foam spraying across the sheen of the wet sidewalk. He swore harshly. And then, stepping towards her, he pointed an unstable finger at Halo. "You—!" He swore again "You—" The profanity was flowing now. "You—you owe me a thousand dollars!"

Clay stared at the zero in disbelief. But right there, in the shadowy blackness behind one of the worst hotels in the Downtown Eastside, he could feel someone arrive to stand next to him.

Nigel.

Clay looked at him in the darkness. He'd never seen him look so serious, or more in control. Somehow he appeared far more regal, like the entire universe was awaiting his command.

He gave a tight smile. "Clay, it all comes down to this. Will you trust me—right here?"

Clay's mouth was dry, and it was hard to speak. "Am I going to die?"

"You are."

"So, this—this is the end?"

Nigel waited until Clay looked at him directly. "Far from it." He smiled again. "This is actually the beginning of everything."

"But why here? Why in this alley?"

Nigel paused, as though deciding how much to say. "Right here is where somebody else's story begins. It's a young girl. Even now, her parents and dozens of her high school friends are praying for her."

The alley remained empty, and so he shrugged. *Okay.*

Clay turned and embraced Nigel. "Thank you for everything."

"It's been my pleasure."

Halo and her drunken assailant arrived into the alley behind the Blue Boy with a lot of brutal profanity, and with him threatening her with a horrible death. He was dragging her by her hair, and she was screaming. A handgun appeared into the murky darkness, pressed to her temple, and time stuttered along like a phonograph played too slowly. Clay didn't have time to think. He was out of minutes anyway, and he knew where he was going.

The trigger felt nine pounds of pressure, and the alley was painted in Clay's blood.

Vancouver General Hospital is a world-class facility staffed by some of the brightest minds on the planet. The ambulance was three thousand watts of skull numbing siren, piloted by a guy named Chris who held the speed record between two isolated logging communities on the north Island. An entire team of doctors and nurses were waiting as Clay was pulled from the ambulance, and from that first moment every tactic of the most advanced medical unit in the world was thrown into action. No expense was spared.

It wouldn't be enough.

Clay Rawlings would survive the initial surgeries, but would remain in a coma.

Hannah remained at the hospital. But she'd seen the watch on the first morning they'd brought him in. It'd been with his clothes in a bag. And there, beside the big number, was the zero.

Clay would not recover.

Nigel often sat with her in the hospital. Somehow, his presence made it not hurt so much. He listened when she wanted to talk, and was always eager to pray with her. He encouraged her to find her strength through the coming days in scripture. To continue to trust in God's goodness.

And somehow, when he was around there was a peace that invaded the landscape she couldn't place. Hannah's world had completely crashed to the ground, and yet with Nigel beside her there remained a calm. As she'd once heard Clay describe it, the peace that arrived with Nigel was like a windblown prairie field a thousand miles across.

The hospital staff continued to assure her they were perfectly prepared for whatever the arrival of the new millennium, and Y2K, could throw at them, but Hannah barely heard any of it.

Clay's third night wasn't good. Hannah was emotionally wrung out, still trying to make sense of it all. Her words were barely audible. "The kingdom of heaven... is... like..." She started slowly. "The kingdom of heaven is like treasure hidden in a field. When a man found it, he hid it again, and then in his joy went and sold all he had and bought—"

"He bought the field." Nigel finished for her.

"And that's what Clay did, right? He discovered treasure in a field. He discovered Jesus. And in his joy, he sold everything he had, and bought the field."

Nigel nodded. "Yes, that's what he did."

There was a long pause and then Hannah wiped a tear from her cheek. "After Clay goes, will I see you again?"

Nigel smiled. "I've always been with you Hannah."

"But will I *see* you? Will you be visible?"

He patted her knee like her own grandfather had done. "I'm always visible. You can see me in every person who chooses to walk in faith, and to stand firm when the bowels of hell spews its worst at them. That's my strength living within them. Those kids you work with who find a new life of purity and goodness after years on the streets are a visible image of me working through them. And listen to the world news. The poor of India are discovering salvation in Jesus Christ in record numbers. The same goes for China. That's all me. I will always be visible to those with eyes to see me."

The next night Hannah checked the bag of clothes, searching for the watch. It was gone. In its place was a single card with a quotation from Hebrews 12:

> 'Therefore, since we are surrounded by such a great crowd of witnesses, let us throw off everything that hinders and the sin that so easily entangles, and run with perseverance the race marked outfor us.'

In his own handwriting, Nigel had added a note: *Later this evening Clay will be joining that great cloud of witnesses.*

Chapter Thirty-Three

It was an ancient panel van, painted in the bright reds and yellows common across northern India. The paint job was done years earlier, accomplished with leftover house paint that hadn't suffered the dust of the roads easily. A missing passenger door replaced with a piece of shredded tarpaulin certainly wasn't helping its physical beauty.

Inside were five young Indian men, baking in the midday heat. The two in the rear were seated on wooden benches that gave little insulation from the jarring ride. With lumps of rag they shielded their noses and mouths from the dust that clouded into the cab. The folds in their clothes collected the dust like a filter. If they noticed, or cared, it wasn't obvious. They'd been on dustier roads, and in worse vehicles.

Their cargo was precious and they all knew it. Their journey would be worth it, regardless of what they had to suffer.

The driver, Jarpal, gave a shout as they approached the first evidence of a village. The excitement inside the van was immediate and palpable. To anybody seeing the village it wouldn't have looked like much to get excited about, but it was their destination. The outlying huts weren't much more than a leaning collection of sticks wrapped in stained canvas and plastic. Rusted tin pressed into service as roofing. Just beyond the huts a fence of piled rocks corralled in a couple of scrawny goats. A cow was tethered under a shade tree, watching them as the van slowed and crawled past the meager huts.

The ground anywhere near the animals was trampled flat. Dusty and barren. In every direction was the same hardscrabble landscape that had surrounded them for much of the journey.

Half a mile further along, the village seemed to officially begin. As they passed the ramshackle dwellings the van grew colorful streamers of running, jostling children. The driver slowed to a walking pace and they crept through the streets, the crowds of tattered children growing.

Jarpal pulled the van into a large, empty lot and shut off the ignition. His team didn't wait. They jumped from the van to interact with the appreciative audience of children. They were strangers in a place that didn't see many strangers. And they seemed genuinely interested in the kids, which was equally rare.

But far more memorable was their announcement they'd arrived to show a movie. A full-color film to which everyone could invite their family and as many friends as they could find. And it'd be free for everyone.

The younger kids quickly embraced such an idea, but several of the older boys, in a display of teenage bravado, scoffed at such an outlandish claim. Why would these people have journeyed to their little non-descript village to show a movie?

The nay-sayers were quickly silenced when Jarpal opened the back of the van and lifted out a heavy box of colorful fliers depicting the highlights of the film. He pulled out several copies and handed them to the boys. But to remove the box, Jarpal had pulled back the dusty canvas that had covered the van's cargo. And that movement had revealed far greater treasures.

The crowd of children exhaled in collective amazement. For there in the back of the beat-up panel van was something that confirmed everything the team had claimed. It was a newer Honda generator. And the Sony logo of a video projector held in a protective case. This same projector and generator had once journeyed from village to village on the carry racks of several bicycles.

The darkness of the night only made the screening of the Indian-made Jesus film more intimate. Entire families, many who'd never seen a movie before, were lost into the story of a Savior who'd left heaven to live among them. They sat open-mouthed as He walked on water, and cast out demons. They were astounded as He chose lepers, bad people, and children over the religious leaders. And yet it was to these self-proclaimed, broken people that He offered eternal life.

Four hundred faces pressed upward towards the screen, soaking in the story of Jesus. They covered the gentle slope of the rock-strewn field, tightly pressed together, the crowds reaching back as far as a steep hillside far in the rear. And there, seated in their usual place of subservience, separated from the higher castes, were the residents of the worst slum of the village.

The Untouchables.

They sat on the fallen concrete and jagged slabs of what looked to be entire floors of a collapsed building. It had obviously plunged down the mountainside with great violence to its final resting place, now half-buried into the earth. In the darkness above them, Jarpal could see the shadowy silhouette of what was left of its bent framework, spires of unfinished rebar reaching upward like grotesque fingers into the night sky.

These despised people, excluded from polite Indian society and treated worse than the mongrel dogs that roamed the edges of the village, were riveted to what was transpiring on the screen. Like air was being offered to drowning victims.

Many of them were missing limbs and leaned forward on crutches. Or were seated in rudimentary wheelchairs.

Jarpal watched them. And inside he celebrated. He knew his team were simply the front men as the entire Christian community across the globe had joined together to bring the message of the Gospel to this little village.

The little village of Shiliguri.

Nigel leaned against the panel van and smiled. The five young Indian men had answered questions until midnight, and then led hundreds of people in a prayer of repentance. It was dark, but few seemed to care. The poorest among them, the Untouchables, had been the most receptive, with every last one of them embracing the salvation offered in the film. Hundreds of new believers could be seen huddled into little groups scattered across the field. Many were weeping in joy at having discovered forgiveness for their sins in the person of Jesus Christ.

But against the backdrop of the collapsed remains of a building that had once housed an audio assembly facility for a company called Nasty Dogs was a young man. He was dancing.

Nigel wasn't at all surprised. Clay had died six hours earlier.

Epilogue

Halo had fled from behind the Blue Boy Hotel as fast her legs would carry her. She'd run as far as she could, her lungs on the verge of bursting, Clay's blood still covering her jacket. After two separate attempts to clean the blood off, she'd tossed the jacket. There was still a psycho with a gun hunting her, she was sure of it. She needed to keep moving. She ran up the stairs two at a time at a SkyTrain station, headed east on the Expo line, and watched every rider for any elevated threat level. She stayed on through Burnaby and New West, right until the last stop.

Surrey.

If she was going to disappear, this was the place to do it. No crackhead with a gun could track her this far, and then find her amongst all the people of Surrey. She'd just have to stay vigilante, and watch her back, and she'd be fine. Nobody could find her here.

That worked for a week. On the eighth night she was panhandling on 104 Avenue and had made almost twenty-two bucks. She was being careful, her hoodie pulled low over her eyes, and she was mostly hidden into the shadows. And suddenly a weathered pickup truck cruised past her for the second time within about eight minutes. Her mouth was immediately dry, her thoughts aflame. *Damn.* She couldn't be sure it was the same truck, but she wasn't taking any chances!

Within seconds she was running, across the Safeway parking lot, across City Parkway, pushing and dodging the crowds and vehicles, into the SkyTrain station, up the stairs, and onto a westbound train. She rode it to Commercial, the busiest station of the entire route. There she mingled with the crowds until an east bound bus appeared. She waited until the driver was pulling away before she made a running leap to board, forcing open the doors. She sat in the rear, her knees pulled to her chest, watching every person who boarded. Her heart was pounding. *Will I ever be safe again?*

Halo exited at a random stop, and found an all-night coffee shop. She sat in a corner booth where she could watch both the entrance and everything outside in the darkness. A tired girl approached her with a menu, but she waved her away with a request for coffee and a cinnamon bun. The waitress retraced her steps to the kitchen.

Halo was shivering.

"Your coffee and cinnamon bun, Benita."

Benita—? Halo spun around to confront the person who'd used her real name, her hands already clasped into fists.

It wasn't the waitress.

"How do know my name?" She spat it out.

A smile. "We know everything about you."

"Who are you?"

"Mind if I sit down?" Nigel, dressed in a black button-down shirt and black jeans, set two coffees and a pair of cinnamon buns onto the table. He slid in across from Halo. "Losing yourself into a city, making yourself completely invisible, is difficult, so don't be hard on yourself. That running jump onto a moving bus was a masterful stroke. You'd be hard to pursue, but—" He shrugged as though the rest were self-explanatory.

At any other time Halo would have bolted. She'd have thrown the coffee in his face and ran. *Why was this so different?* Instead of fear she was wrapped into a feeling of safety she hadn't felt since she was a child. It arrived with a surety that if anyone could protect her, from almost anything, this man could.

Halo could feel her fists unclench. "Who—who are you?"

"I'm Nigel Lockheed. I'm your investment broker."

Halo just stared at him. "Uh—Mr. Lockheed, I think there's been a mistake made here. You have no idea who I am, and if you did, you'd know I'm completely broke. My drug habit has completely garbaged my life. I got nothing."

"Call me Nigel. And oh, you're a lot worse off than you think you are, Benita." Another of his wide smiles. "Far, far worse." He leaned back. "But like I said, we know *everything* about you."

"I've never met you before. How could you know—?"

Nigel held up a hand to cut her off. "Benita, we want to work with you. All of us at Thirteen44 Global Investments want to work with you. We want to give you a life you can't even imagine sitting here."

"Thirteen44 Global—?

"We're an investment firm with a rather unique skill set." Nigel reached into his pocket and pulled out the watch. He laid it gently on the table. "We'd like to give you a gift, in good faith, as a demonstration of our abilities."

She smirked. "You're giving me an expensive diver's watch?"

"You might want to look at it more closely." He gave another of his disarming smiles. "Go ahead, put it on."

She looked at Nigel to see if he was serious. *Yeah sure, buddy. Easiest eighty bucks I'll ever fence.* She slid it on. It was a perfect fit.

"It's yours to keep. I don't think you'll want to pawn it."

Halo stared at the watch. It wasn't telling the time. Instead it displayed two numbers. "Okay, so what do these numbers mean?"

"Those are *your* numbers."

Halo looked harder at the two numbers. Neither meant anything to her. The first was in the negatives. About nine thousand, two hundred. The second number was a lot bigger. 31,126,421. It was slowly counting down. "*My* numbers—?"

"Everybody has numbers. These are yours."

"The first number is negative. Why?"

The bubbly smile disappeared for a moment, a grandfatherly concern pulling at the lines of Nigel's face. "Benita, that first number is what you're worth."

"But it's negative." Benita blinked.

"Yes." Nigel smiled at her. "Yes, Benita, it is."

Author's Note

Okay, so who is Nigel? When I first started thinking about this story, I was intrigued with the idea of making the Holy Spirit of God visible to a main character. So I created a flawed character, Clay Rawlings, and I simply let the Spirit work, *visibly,* in his life. Nigel Lockheed is the Spirit of God working in the life of a man who, before meeting Him, wanted nothing more than to kill himself.

They always told us in writing class, write what you know.

Acknowledgments

Thank you Francis Chan, both for the life you've lived among the poor and for the rope illustration which I included in the story.

I'd like to thank the Surrey Biker's Church for their powerful, Christ-like example, which I've attempted to recreate in some detail during Clay's salvation story. And of course, a big thank you to Rob Prepchuk for introducing me to them.

I'd like to thank my kids, Shawn, Darrin, and Shannon, who once allowed me to move them into a borrowed travel trailer in a municipal campsite for several months to pay for the building of a church in northern India. And yes, our friends thought we were homeless.

Christian Freedom International was a huge help in verifying details of the persecution in Indonesia during the 90's.

A big thanks to the girl at Esperanza Bible Camp who sat with me on the dock until two-thirty in the morning, trying unsuccessfully to explain the Gospel of Christ to me. I don't remember your name, but I *was* listening.

Thank you to Dan Nicholson who was my pastor during the 1990's. If any of my life has looked even vaguely similar to Clay Rawlings', it was his fault.

A huge thank you to my daughter, Shawn, as she journeyed me onto the streets and into a cafe in Guatemala City. For a translation of what Dave and the server talk about in that café, you'll have to ask her.

But my greatest thanks go to my wife, Dawn, who continues to trust God with her life, and finances, and allows me to live a life of adventure.

To contact me with questions or comments:
jon.climie@gmail.com